Men of Dunwich

MEN OF DUNWICH

THE STORY OF A VANISHED TOWN

Rowland Parker

Holt, Rinehart and Winston
New York

Library of Congress Cataloging in Publication Data
Parker, Rowland
Men of Dunwich.
Bibliography: p.
Includes index.
1. Dunwich, Eng.—History. 2. Dunwich, Eng.—
Social life and customs. I. Title.
DA690.D86P37 1979   942.6′46   78-14167
ISBN 0-03-046801-9

First published in the United States of America in 1979
by Holt, Rinehart and Winston, 383 Madison Avenue,
New York, New York 10017.

Printed in the United States of America

1 3 5 7 9 10 8 6 4 2

Contents

Contents (contd.)

Maps and Illustrations

Acknowledgments

My editor says I ought to make Acknowledgments. He is quite right, as usual. An author, once the last sheet has been rolled off the typewriter with a flourish of satisfaction, likes to imagine that it was all his own work. But of course it cannot be. Even before the printing stage is reached, many people help in the making of a book; some of them unwittingly. All the more reason why their contribution should be acknowledged. My contacts in the research and writing of this story have been with books and places rather than with people, and it is difficult to sound sincere when one cannot actually name those whom one wishes to thank. I do nevertheless sincerely thank those nineteenth-century scholars – they must number scores – who deciphered, transcribed, indexed and, in many cases, translated the medieval documents which constitute the bulk of my material for this book. I did pay one visit to the Public Record Office, just to get the sight and feel of one of those enormous rolls of parchment covered with cramped handwriting which seven centuries of time and use have not quite obliterated. In the space of two hours I succeeded in almost deciphering and translating just *one* entry, a mere dozen lines or so, in the Patent Rolls. That was after spending two hours in getting there, and a further hour in obtaining the roll and locating the entry. If I had had to do *all* the work of searching, deciphering, etc. myself, this book would never have been written, for I should have been blind, if not dead, before my research was even half completed. So, to all you unknown scholars long since dead, my heartfelt thanks; and I hope that you did not ruin your eyesight in that arduous task.

Thanks, too, to the staff of the Cambridge University Library, whose unfailing courtesy and co-operation made my many visits to that treasure-house of learning a positive pleasure.

A special 'thank you' to the charming young lady in the office of the Danish Tourist Board in London for producing the very book I needed for information which not even a trip to the Faroes would have provided.

I trust that living authors whose books are listed in the Bibliography will accept the thanks implicit in the inclusion of their works, for I have mentioned only those which I have actually used. They are not asked to share the blame for any errors which may be detected in my text. Those, at least, are all my own work.

Preface

'Dunwich is a magic place,' a professional historian said to me recently, echoing my own opinion and that of many others. More than sixty years ago W. A. Dutt in his *Highways and Byways of East Anglia* wrote:

> Like the tales of the lost Atlantis and the mythical land of Lyonesse, the story of Dunwich seizes upon the imagination; though when one sees how little remains of what may once have been the chief city of East Anglia it is difficult to believe that Dunwich, too, was not a phantom city of a land of dreams.

In 1754 Thomas Gardner, a native of Southwold and secretary to the Board of Commissioners charged with the reconstruction of the harbour of that town, published his *Historical Account of Dunwich, etc.* Prized today as much for its rarity as for its content, the book is a veritable well of information on which I have drawn to the fullest extent. In his Preface, Gardner tells of his curiosity being excited by the sixteenth-century annalist John Stowe, who, on the testimony of the oldest inhabitants of the neighbourhood, referred to Dunwich 'in antient Time' as 'a City surrounded with a Stone-Wall, and brazen Gates,' having 'fifty-two churches, chapels, religious houses and hospitals, a King's Palace, a Bishop's Seat, a Mayor's Mansion and a Mint, as many Top-Ships as Churches, etc. and not fewer wind-mills.'

That would be enough to excite anyone's curiosity, and provides a fair indication that, even four hundred years ago, Dunwich was already a place of legend. Many writers since then have traced an outline history of the vanished town; others have used it as the setting of a fictional story, an inspiration of prose or verse; and today the television or film camera crews are never absent for long from this haunting stretch of coast.

The quality of magic is easier to feel than to define, and

9

almost impossible to explain, but its association with legend is inevitable. Indeed the 'fame' of Dunwich today rests largely on the legend that church bells can be heard ringing beneath the sea when the water is very rough. I have never heard them, or met anyone who has. No one, I believe, takes the legend very seriously, but it makes a good talking point. It also serves to emphasise the lack of real knowledge about the vanished town, and points the need to try to get at the truth which, one feels, would be more entertaining than legend in this case.

The popularity of Dunwich is real enough, as is testified by the thousands of summer visitors and the fact that the limited accommodation is in great demand, both by visitors and by residents in retirement. The first-time visitor, having perhaps heard of Dunwich as a town that has vanished, might well approach it with mingled curiosity and apprehension. To go to a place which does not exist is a move hardly calculated to inspire confidence, and the narrow roads which lead there, whether through dense forest or across a stretch of desolate heath, only serve to heighten the sensation that one is getting near to nowhere.

Having arrived, the visitor who had expected to find a small seaside resort similar to Aldeburgh or Southwold will be mystified still further; perhaps disappointed; or perhaps enchanted – it depends on mood and temperament, and on the weather. The 'attractions' of a modern resort are here almost wholly lacking; no promenade, no shops, no bingo, boating or amusements; no beach to speak of, and the would-be bather needs more courage than I possess, except on a really hot summer's day. True, there is a pub, a cafe where one can get all one needs from a cafe, and a couple of huts where one can buy fish which only an hour before were swimming. There is the sea, and the air is even fresher than the fish. Attractions enough these days for many people; but hardly enough, surely, to account for a car-park filled to generous capacity on most fine days throughout July and August.

Inclement weather and total lack of protection against it may drive the visitor to explore the 'village' in search of visible links with the past. Such links are few, and some would say they hardly justify the fifteen minutes walking time which their discovery entails. Five of those minutes suffice – unless the Museum happens to be open – to walk the length of the street lined on one side with a dozen or so nineteenth-century houses interspersed with a few more modern ones, as far as the church. Here, surely, is something ancient. But no; it was built in 1830. Alongside however is a ruined building which undoubtedly bears the stamp of another age, another world, and which raises more questions than the notice-board answers. Similarly that isolated buttress standing in a corner of the churchyard; obviously part of a medieval church; but where is the rest of the church?

Strolling uphill past a farm and along the sunken lane, the visitor might wonder where the rest of the village is. Turning sharply at the top he enters another narrow lane, flanked on one side by a massive wall of flint and stone half-hidden by bushes of elder and ivy, and there, suddenly, is a medieval gateway arch, its rugged edge outlined against the sky. Two gateways, one barred by fence and nettles, the other by a ramshackle gate above which appears incongruously a pony's head. The road falls steeply; pantiled roofs show through the trees, and one is back where one started. That, plus a few more houses, a country club and a caravan site hidden among the trees to the south, is Dunwich today.

That, apart from those three ancient relics, is not the Dunwich of my story. To 'find' my Dunwich you should turn sharp right at the bottom of that steep shady lane and head towards the sea by either of two narrow sandy paths. In a minute or two you will find yourself on the top of a cliff some fifty feet above the shingle beach, the breeze fanning your face – or a gale tearing at your hair, as the case may be – the sibilant song of the surf in your ear, and a sense of space that only the contemplation of sea and sky can give.

Stand there – preferably alone, for spells work best in solitude – and give your imagination free rein. Looking seawards, let your gaze move slowly through an arc of radius about a mile until it rests on shingle once again. There, beneath that arc of water, lies the Dunwich of my story. The uninspired eye sees only water. If the tide were suddenly to recede to an unprecedented distance one would see mainly mud and sand, with here and there a seaweed-covered chunk of masonry. Better that it remains hidden, for thus the mind's eye penetrates more easily the magic barrier, moves back in time six centuries or more to see beneath the rippling waves a town of streets and houses, a hive of human activity. Then come the questions flooding in. What was the town like in the heyday of its fame? What sort of people walked those streets which man will never walk again? How did they react to the disappearance of their town? How, when and why did it all happen?

This book is an attempt to answer those questions, to tell the story of the town – and, more particularly of the 'men of Dunwich' – throughout the Middle Ages and up to the time when it and they were no more. Archaeological evidence in support of the story is inevitably slight; I have made the most of what little there is. By contrast, the documentary evidence is amazingly plentiful. That fact in itself constitutes evidence of the one-time importance of the place. The Bibliography at the end of the book gives some idea of the variety of sources; it gives no idea of their extent. To mention only one source, there are no less than one hundred and eighty-four entries in the *Calendar of Patent Rolls* relating to Dunwich, some brief, some very lengthy and detailed. I have used them all, and quoted from some. I have not given precise references for my quotations and statements and I apologise for the omission to those readers who consider it to be a serious one. Many readers, I think, will share my view that reference numbers and foot-notes tend to distract from the course of the narrative; make it more difficult to read. They would have given the book too much of the appearance of a normal history-book.

It is not meant to be a 'history-book.' It is meant to be a 'story,' something more than a relation and interpretation of facts. I wanted to carry the reader with me, if I could, across the intervening gap of centuries; to penetrate, as it were, that square mile of turbulent cloudy water out there; to get a glimpse, if only momentarily, of some of those vanished 'men of Dunwich'; meet them on their own ground and get the 'feel' of them and their lives. One cannot do that by sticking rigidly to facts. I have at times given free rein to my imagination – I have at all times, I hope, used some imagination – but the reader will not be deceived, for such passages are clearly marked.

I have aimed at truth. Not the *whole* truth. That will never be known. If it ever existed, it now lies somewhere out there at the bottom of the sea, or mingles with the insubstantial breezes that caress the cliff-top grass. But something like the truth. I can vouch for the fact that *all* the events in this story did actually happen, that *all* the people mentioned in it did exist, and nearly all did do what I have said they did. My interpretations may well be wrong. If they are, I will patiently listen to a demonstration of my errors; and, if *proved* wrong, retract them. Like Thomas Gardner I flatter myself that 'the studious in the ancient State of Things will favourably interpret any Ambiguities contained herein.'

Rowland Parker

Cottage on the Green
Foxton
November 1977

1 Romans Were Here

Deny the historian, or the story-teller, the right to speculate, and either you encourage him to serve up a series of unrelated facts, often dull and indigestible, or you drive him to take refuge in a silence broken only by the frustrating observation that 'nothing is known.' That is particularly true of the Dunwich which must have been there in the first four centuries A.D. Contemporary documentary evidence is nil; later documentary evidence extremely thin. Archaeological clues are as rare as the bits of amber which, it is said, can sometimes be picked up on the beach from among the millions of pebbles which they so closely resemble. As it happens, that is where most of the clues have been found; odd bits of pottery, a few coins of the second and third centuries, an enamelled brooch (which could be Saxon); a few sherds of pottery recovered not long ago from the infilling of the medieval rampart-ditch. The excavation prior to that was all done by the waves; little of the evidence was seen; still less recorded.

A Roman naval base or military station, or a combination of the two, at Dunwich is a tempting hypothesis, despite the lack of military bits and pieces which Roman soldiers always seem to have thrown around. Roman roads in this part of East Anglia are notoriously difficult to trace, or to distinguish from later medieval roads and earlier pre-historic tracks, but three roads generally accepted to be Roman – one from Coddenham, one from Caistor-by-Norwich, and one in between – look as though they could have led to Dunwich. Some say they did. The place on which those roads converged was almost certainly what the Antonine Itinerary, a road-book of the fourth century, called *Sitomagus*, thirty-two Roman miles from *Venta Icenorum* (Caistor-by-Norwich). Was *Sitomagus* the Roman Dunwich? The name, like nearly all Roman place-names, offers no sure topographical meaning, not even in its

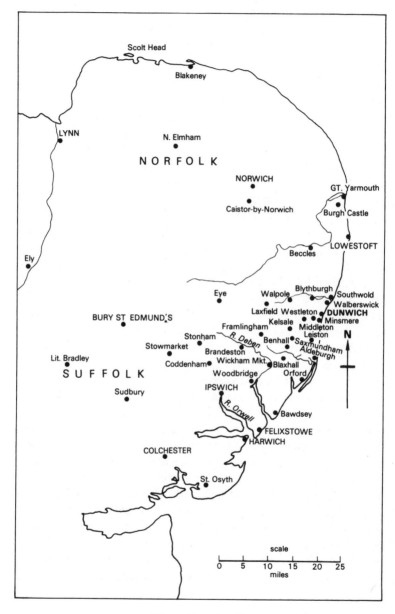

Fig 1 East Anglia

dubious later form of *Sinomagus*. I favour its location at Hacheston, near Wickham Market, where recent excavation has revealed the existence of a Romano-British town of sorts; it, too, is thirty-two Roman miles from *Venta Icenorum*.

Did a Roman road go on from there to Dunwich? Did it need to? We know of no Roman road leading to Burgh Castle (*Gariannonum*) near Yarmouth, or to Walton Castle near Felixstowe; yet at both of those places were located important – and, in the case of Burgh Castle, still impressive – Roman Forts of the Saxon Shore. Was there a similar fort at Dunwich? It was suitably situated mid-way between the other two, and did possess, later at any rate, a good sheltered harbour. Did Roman galleys row where later medieval galleys rowed?

Gardner, writing in 1754 about the effects of the devastating storm of 1740, supplies a few tantalising details which compel speculation. Here is part of what he wrote:

Part |of |the| Old Key, built with Stone, lay bare – The Sea raged with such Fury, that *Cock* and *Hen Hills* (which the preceding Summer were upwards of forty Feet high, and in Winter partly washed away) this Year, had their Heads levelled with their Bases, and the Ground about them so rent and torn, that the Foundation of *St Francis's Chapel* (which was laid between the said Hills) was discovered; where, besides the ruins of the Walls, were five round Stones near of a bigness; the Dimensions of one (I took) were four Feet the Diameter, and near two the thickness. There was likewise a Circle of large Stumps of Piles, about twenty-four Feet Circumference – Also a Stone Coffin, wherein were human Bones covered with Tiles – At the same Time, and near the Chapel, the Pipes of an Aqueduct were found, some of lead, others of gray Earth, like that of some Urns—

That was on a site which, for as long as anyone remembered, had been covered with four or five feet of made earth, bearing crops of grass and turnips. The layer of 'ouze' (clay) beneath it bore 'impressions of the Spade' in several places. Gardner goes on:

In the year 1740, as the Men of Dunwich were digging a Trench, near their *Old Fort,* across the Beach, to make a Water-gang – they happened on a Stone Wall, cemented exceeding strong, which was part of their *Old Key*; and near that, on a Well; both which I saw as they were working. At which Time several Pieces of old Coins and other Curiosities were found—

Most of the 'curiosities' which he illustrates are clearly medieval; but he mentions in a footnote the emperor Constantinus 'whose Coins and Medals have been so frequently met with, where this was found.'

So – a solidly-built stone wall, tiles in association with a burial (or re-burial?); an aqueduct; a lot of Roman coins whose whereabouts is now unknown – it does seem to add up to the strong possibility of a Roman establishment of some importance. What to make of those five round stones, four feet in diameter and two feet thick, I am not at all sure. No medieval millstone, to my knowledge, was ever like that; but some Roman millstones were, especially those used on a horizontal axis for oil-extraction or stone crushing. As for that eight-foot diameter circle of piles, the base of a mill seems the obvious explanation. But that was no fit site for a mill, surely? Unless it was a tidal mill, like the one on the Deben at Woodbridge; which was not circular. Could it have been a watertower? Or a beacon-tower? Not, surely, with two forty-foot-high natural mounds nearby. But were they natural; or were they Roman burial-mounds, like those at Bartlow in Essex? Or was that circle of piles the inner sanctum of a temple dating from long before Roman times, a miniature version of the one at Arminghall near Norwich? Nothing could be more normal than that the Chapel of St Francis should be built on the site of pagan worship.

The Romans — some Romans — were at Dunwich. That much is certain. The rest is speculation.

2 Saxon Shore

Litus Saxonicum – Shore of the Saxons. Was it the shore which the Saxons attacked, shore which the Saxons defended, or shore which the Saxons held? All three in turn, in that order, I would say. As early as the third century, piratical raiders from across the North Sea had begun to visit this coast, so admirably suited to their particular form of commerce. A brisk day and half a night's sailing; half an hour of strenuous rowing up tidal river; silent approach to sleeping villa or village; a few minutes of bloody pandemonium; then away to the boat with the carcasses of several pigs and sheep, a couple of trembling slaves, and any other loot they could find; down the river once more and out on the open sea, pulling hard in the direction of the rising sun, to cease rowing when the offshore wind bellied out the sail.

The Forts were intended to put a stop to that sort of thing – perhaps. Some recent writers maintain that they were for the defence of Britannia against Roman invaders. There is good reason to believe that, before the end of the Roman occupation, some at least of the Forts were being manned by Saxons, one-time pirates turned mercenaries, whose task it was to keep Picts and Scots and suchlike barbarians at bay. It is quite certain that, within a relatively short time after the Romans had departed, the shores of East Anglia saw a large-scale and prolonged incursion from the opposite shores of visitors who had no intention of going back, unless it were to fetch their kinsfolk to help in the work of settling. One of the strangest things about English history is the extent of our ignorance about this, the most significant happening in our history. Gardner sums it up in a gem of an understatement: 'History is pretty silent concerning the pristine Condition of Dunwich.' Then he spoils it by bringing in the Iceni in the same paragraph as Sigebehrt.

The plain truth is that nothing whatever is known about the history of Dunwich throughout the fifth and sixth centuries, and part of the seventh. Except that it was there. The sea and the shore and the rivers were there. And since the sea and the shore and the rivers are in a sense the main characters in my story – the only ones who were in it at the start and still in at the end – it seems fitting that their role should be explained now. The speculation which that inevitably involves is speculation based on reasoned deduction, a knowledge of what happened later, and observation of what is happening now on this and other sections of the coast.

Leading actor in the drama is of course the sea, that mighty mass of tireless time-mocking energy for which a million years are but another yesterday; remorselessly seeking ever to destroy that which it had patiently created. That it should seem to have singled out for special attention the Suffolk coast denotes no particular malice on its part; merely a geographical accident. The whole of the Suffolk coast, like most of Norfolk and much of Essex coasts, consists of sand and gravel lying on top of clay, in places to a thickness of sixty feet or more; easily eroded by even a normal tide, disastrously vulnerable to the sea in a violent rage. In places, particularly in the area north and south of Dunwich, a strip of land as much as three miles wide has disappeared within historical time. Where has it gone?

Much of it is still there, spread out in long undulating swathes on the sea-bed. Local fishermen tell of a 'bank,' about a mile wide, stretching for five miles south from off Southwold; that is where they catch their cod in winter. Coastal charts are constantly having to be revised. This stretch of coast has caused more wrecks than any other in the British Isles since records were first kept. Much of the eroded material has been pushed on to the beaches, forming a temporary barrier against further erosion. There is movement all the time; nothing here is stable; things will not be the same a hundred years from now. The general direction of movement here is from north to south (east to west on the North Norfolk coast, but do not bank on it always being so). Some of the pebbles which torture your feet as you go in to bathe at Dunwich were once part of a cliff two miles north-east of Southwold.

Rivers as unpretentious as those charmingly meandering Suffolk streams could hardly, one would think, have much say in the conflict being waged between sea and land at the end of their leisurely journey. Nor do they. In every case outflowing fresh water yields before in-flowing salt water, and it is the latter which has given rise to 'sea-ports' situated many miles from any coast; though far less so now than in Saxon and medieval times. But even a river merely twenty miles in length including tributaries, such as the River Blyth, carries at certain seasons a sufficient volume of water to make a breach in an unstable barrier of sand and gravel, and at all times enough solid material in suspension to form a bit of new-created land, given time, and the necessity of depositing it somewhere. It may be 'only mud' to look at now. Give it time. One day it will be land.

It would be too much of a conjectural exercise to try to work out the time-table of events in the conflict between sea and river which resulted eventually in the establishment of Dunwich as a port. But we can safely deduce the broad outline of the situation which had been reached by, say, the year 500 A.D. There was a sort of headland jutting out eastwards north of Southwold; another south of Dunwich. In between was a bay into which the Blyth and Dunwich Rivers, and a nameless stream midway between, discharged their waters, and dumped their mud. Then the sea gradually eroded both headlands, pushing the debris of the northern one across the mouth of the bay, that of the southern one across the mouth of the Minsmere river. So that, if Roman ships had found safe anchorage here, Saxon ships found even safer, and good landing ground to loot. The adjoining map (Fig 2) will make it clearer than can words.

At the risk of appearing to stress the obvious, let me remind you that the map is static. The situation which it portrays was not. The point of sand and shingle, marked A, was gradually extending southwards and curving westwards all the time. The headland B was for ever being eroded. The point marked C was behaving in the same way as A. The shaded areas along the rivers are marsh, liable to be salt-water inlets or mud-flats according to season and the state of the tides. (Just as some of them are today, especially at Blythburgh.) Dunwich would have been an ideal base for Roman ships. Blythburgh would have been a better one for Saxon ships. Southwold in the sixth century would have been a small hamlet, if it existed at all. Walberswick's situation was so precarious that it became, and remained, merely an offshoot of Blythburgh. The 'port' of Minsmere disappeared before it had any real chance of developing.

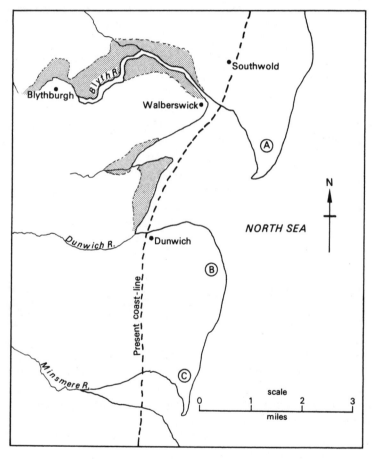

Fig 2 The Coast c.500

3 Unfortunate Felix

Dunwich eventually finds its place on the map, metaphorically speaking, in or about the year 630 A.D., when it was called *Dommoc*. Or something similar. Bede was the first person to write the name, about one hundred and thirty years later. He presumably wrote what he heard, then someone – several people in fact – copied what he wrote. They rang the changes on *Donmoc, Dumoc, Domoc, Domnoc, Donuuoc*. Looking at this ancient writing, one can easily see how that could happen. King Alfred embellished it to *Domnoc-ceaster* (the camp, or fortress, of Dunwich); which might have been speculation on his part, or he could have known something definite about that possible Roman fort which we do not know. In the end the writers settled in the main for *Dunwyc* or *Donewic*, a good Saxon-sounding name, but one still leaving scope for speculation as to what it meant.

There must have been something special about the place, something to raise it in status above Gyppeswyc, for instance. It may or may not have been the 'Town having then the Precedency of all others in that Kingdom (of East Anglia)' as Gardner asserts, but it can hardly have been a mere fishing-village or pirates' nest, otherwise King Sigebehrt would hardly have chosen it as the place in which to install Felix, sent over from Burgundy, as the first Bishop of East Anglia. Bede, unfortunately, is rather deficient in topographical exactitude. All he wrote was:

> He [Felix] received the seat of his bishopric in the city of Dommoc [*in civitate Dommoc*] and when he had ruled over the kingdom as bishop for seventeen years he ended his life there in peace.

Brief, but definite; yet it has recently been argued that Felix's *Dommoc* was in fact Walton, the Roman fort near Felixstowe. It must be admitted that there is no concrete evidence to support the belief, generally held, that the earliest church in Dunwich was that of St Felix; or that Sigebehrt had his 'palace' at Dunwich. If he did, his 'palace' would have borne a striking resemblance to a barn of later times. Moreover, there must, one supposes, be some good reason for Felixstowe being called what it is. However, in the light of subsequent developments, the case for Felix at Dunwich is pretty strong, even when stripped of the embellishments of sixteenth-century historians and chroniclers. This bishopric was definitely there in 673 A.D.; possibly having been moved from Felixstowe (on account of marine erosion?); the list of bishops until 870 is recorded; and the 'schools' said to have been founded by Felix (at both Dunwich *and* Felixstowe) were still in existence at Dunwich more than four centuries later.

As for King Sigebehrt himself, he took Christianity seriously enough, it is said, to resign his crown and adopt the life of a monk in the company of St Fursey at Burgh Castle. His kinsman Egric was so harassed by the Mercians that the East Anglian warriors insisted on Sigebehrt returning to the fray. Armed with only a white wand, the monk-king was, not surprisingly, slain by the Mercian King Penda in 642. His successor was apparently King Anna, about whom little is known other than that he had coins minted bearing his name. Gardner says: 'I have seen three Brass Coins of the same Stamp found at Dunwich, one of them with ANNA legible.' No coin has ever been found bearing unmistakable evidence of having been minted at Dunwich.

The bishopric of Dunwich came to an end in 870, when it was transferred to North Elmham, where there had already been established a bishop's seat in 673; later it was transferred to Thetford and eventually settled on Norwich. Stability was not a feature of early bishoprics. Felix may have lived in peace. His bones were not to be allowed to rest in that state. They were moved first to Soham in Cambridgeshire; possibly because their resting-place at Dunwich was in danger from the encroaching sea; probably because possession of saintly bones was a source of profit, being credited with miraculous powers for which pilgrims were prepared to pay. Or it could have been that Felix's resting-place was threatened with sacrilegious sacking at the hands of marauding Danes. They did in fact sack the monastery at Soham, whereupon the

sacred and profitable bones were moved once more, this time
to Ramsey Abbey. By then they must have been dusty, if not
dust.

We know absolutely nothing about Danes in Dunwich. We
might had done, if the Anglo-Saxon Chronicle had been com-
piled by Essex men instead of Wessex men. One version of it
tells us that Bishop Aelfun died at Sudbury in 799 and was
buried at Dunwich; so there was obviously an ancient church
there. And that, together with the names of three more
bishops (somewhat uncertain) is the only mention of the place
for a couple of centuries. History, as Gardner says, is 'pretty
silent.'

4 Dunewic — 1060

We are still on the fringe of speculation in the mid-eleventh
century, but two retrospective glances from dates further
ahead provide some insight into a situation which would
otherwise be wholly conjectural. The first insight is provided
by those clauses of Domesday Book (1086) written in the past
tense, or which would have been in the past tense if they had
had any verbs.

They reveal that *Dunewic* in 1060 or thereabouts was a
small town. Like most small towns at that date it was a
'manor,' the lord of which was Edric de Laxfield. The inhabitants consisted of a hundred and twenty burgess families,
owing customary services and allegiance to their lord, but
free to indulge in the activities of fishing and, possibly, a
limited amount of trading on their own account. There were
twelve peasant families tied to the lord's demesne and tilling
an area of land, for him and for themselves, amounting to
about two hundred acres. There was only one church. This,
together with the town, the land and all else taxable, was
reckoned to have an annual value of £10. It hardly looks like

the assessment of a 'city.' The record states specifically, perhaps significantly, that, in the time of King Edward, 'there was no *cambitor* there, but in Blideburh.' A *cambitor* was a money-changer, assayer or coiner. That is a clear enough indication that there was not a mint in Dunwich in 1060; though it might imply that there had once been a mint there, as some scholars have assumed. There is no mention of a market, or a mill; which does not necessarily mean that neither existed.

The other glimpse of the situation at approximately this date is provided by my interpretation of the charter of Blythburgh Priory dated 1294. Like all such documents, it states what has been the case for a very long time and seeks to ensure that such shall always be the case, 'for ever,' along with all the advantages accumulated meanwhile. It confirms a charter of Richard I, which confirms a charter of Henry II, which enumerates benefactions and endowments over a period of about two centuries. The date of the foundation is not attested with any certainty; Dugdale and other authorities on monastic history are at variance on this point. Most agree that the priory was *not* founded by Henry II. I am pretty sure that it was founded very much earlier. The question would be of little interest or significance but for the fact that it involves Dunwich men and Dunwich land.

The first benefactors listed, in a list that totals nearly a hundred, are thirty-two men and women of Dunwich, holding land '*in Donewyc.*' They include Brictrih, Godwin Oxefoot, Huntman, Arnold the Priest, Safuli, Ulf the Rich, Walter Leadenpenny, Ulf Canun, Snotyng the Rich, Alwin Bunt, Adwin Kenewald, Godeseald, Dice, Lenene Tod, Godenard, Thiedri, Brithmar son of Gotha, etc. Saxons, all of them; not a Norman amongst them; possibly a couple of Danes. That list of donors must, I think, have been written before the Norman Conquest, then copied again and again before 1294. Had those lands been given away after, say, 1070, they would not have been given to Blythburgh Priory, but to the Priory of Eye. They would not have been given by the men of Dunwich, but by the lord of Dunwich. They – the lands, that is –

would not have been *in* Dunwich. That first section of the charter ends with the stipulation that the said lands should be quit of all land service and secular dues on payment of twelve pence per year, as they used to be *ante extensionem factam in Donewyco* – before the extension made in Dunwich. And that is the bit that interests me.

What extension? Why? The answers are, I think, to be found, and clarified, by reference to the map on p. 22 and comparison between it and the adjacent map (Fig 3, p. 28). Six hundred years or so have slipped by since the situation illustrated in the first map. That shingle point has become an elongated shingle spit which has crept steadily south and west until it stretches almost across the bay, and is getting so close to Dunwich that it could reasonably be considered part of the town. The men of Dunwich, reasonably or not, have claimed it as theirs. The marshes at the mouths and along the course of the rivers have consolidated to form good grazing land. As always when new land is created, there have been long and perhaps bitter disputes as to its ownership. The men of Dunwich having established their claim to the shingle spit – unfit for cultivation, but probably of some use as grazing – have had to make concessions with regard to the river-marshes, which the men of Blythburgh and Walberswick (which was one manor) have vigorously claimed, and the men of Westleton (which was two manors, one having the name of *Ernetune* or *Ernetherne*) have also claimed. The compromise agreed upon was evidently that the men of Dunwich gave some of their land to the Priory of Blythburgh, thus profiting their souls at the expense of their pockets. The documentary evidence, so tantalisingly brief, makes it appear as though it might all have happened in a short time. Actually it was more likely to have been the outcome of a hundred years or so of wrangling, to say nothing of a great amount of effort expended on embanking and draining by the men of all three vills concerned.

There is a hill, now wholly overgrown with trees, rising to the south of St James's Church at Dunwich, well outside the bounds of the medieval town. It is called Leet Hill. It never gets a mention in the annals of the town, though it still appears on all the maps. It was on this hill, I am convinced, that men assembled month by month to thrash out the problems created by the extension of their territory, as well as attending to the normal business of manor, hundred and shire. Two results of long-lasting significance arose from decisions arrived at then.

First, the boundaries of Dunwich, Blythburgh, Walberswick and Westleton, in so far as they were contiguous, were

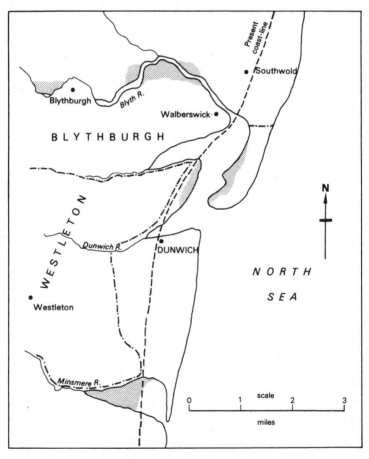

Fig 3 The Coast c.1060

settled for what, it was confidently hoped, was 'for ever'; although the men of those four vills must have known that nothing was 'for ever' on their eastern flank, except the sea which had made it, and could change it at will. The boundaries which I have marked on the map (Fig 3) are, obviously, speculative.

Secondly, when the men of Dunwich came to realize, as they undoubtedly did in time, that they had made a bad bargain; that their gain was eventually to be converted into a loss, they developed an animosity towards their neighbours which was to persist for a very long time, reaching eventually the pitch of hatred. To the initial land-greed which sparked it off there was later added another greed – or the desire to satisfy a natural hunger – which dominated much of Dunwich life. This conflict between Dunwich and her neighbours is one of the major themes of my story.

5 Frenchmen

The other clauses in the Domesday survey of *Dunewic,* those relating to the situation as it was 'now,' that is in 1086, tell in their cryptic way of drastic changes over the previous quarter of a century; emphasising that the Norman Conquest meant more to Dunwich than it did to many other places. Before dealing with the manorial re-shuffle, it may be of interest to note one administrative detail. Whether it was an innovation or the continuing of an established custom, I do not know, but it suggests that Dunwich was playing second fiddle to Blythburgh in one respect at least:

The king has this custom in Dunewic, that two or three men shall go to the hundred (court) if they are correctly summoned. If they do not do this, they shall pay a fine of two 'ores.' If a thief is taken there (Dunwich) he shall be charged there, but capital sentence shall be awarded in Bliebure, and his goods be forfeited to the lord of Dunwich.

Just another bone of contention. No one seems to have been unduly concerned as to what happened to criminals; except the criminals. But what happened to their possessions was a matter of real importance.

Possession, they say, is nine points of the law. It was ten points of the law in those days. The Prior of Ely has acquired the Westleton manor of *Ernethune*; about 200 acres of land; twenty peasants to work it; a little bit of wood and meadow (reclaimed marsh?); half a church (i.e. half the revenues of the church of Westleton); one horse, eight oxen, twenty-eight sheep, eight pigs, sixteen goats, and – this is the oddity – eighty townsmen 'in Dunewic belong to this manor and they dwell upon fourteen acres.' It need not surprise us to find, at this date, men being inventoried along with oxen and goats. They had to be, for purposes of accounting, which is what Domesday was all about. 'Belonging to' probably meant no more than rendering certain services, like carting and ferrying, when required; paying rents and court-dues; and pleading law-suits in the Prior's court. The financial benefit to the Prior cannot have amounted to much, for the whole manor – land, church, ploughs, peasants, sheep, pigs, burgesses and all – was only valued, annually, at £5. To be precise, £4 and 8000 herrings. As a matter of interest, that same manor was leased two hundred and fifty years later for 'one clove gillyflower annually,' when the acreage of land had been considerably reduced. What intrigues me is how the arrangement came about in the first place. Was it part of the complicated agreement arising out of the territorial disputes earlier in the century? Or was there a hamlet to the south of Dunwich which later disappeared? Or did it refer to part of the hamlet of Dingle? Whichever it was, one Gilbert Blundus was renting the 'manor' from the Prior in 1086.

Earl Roger Bigod has acquired the manor of *Blidebure* (there is no mention of Walberswick, but it was part of the same manor); about 600 acres of land; forty-seven villeins and bordars (peasants); wood for forty swine; six acres of meadow, and a market. Within his manor, but exclusive of the £23 value at which it was assessed, was a body of seven freemen holding a further 400 acres, sixteen peasants along with themselves to work the land; and wood for thirty swine. This, it seems to me, was most likely Walberswick. Within the 'vill,' but not within the manor, was a church. This could only be the Priory of Blythburgh, particularly as it 'owned' two other churches, two hundred acres of land (much of which it had acquired from Dunwich), wood for twenty swine, and thirteen peasants. The rents of all this were valued at fifty shillings and 3000 herrings.

I am sorry if all this sounds tedious or irrelevant. My only reason for mentioning it is to draw attention to the complicated system of land-tenure and rights, in itself a source of contention, and to the situation in which Dunwich was placed. The town was entirely surrounded on the landward side by powerful neighbours who had certain claims on Dunwich, a circumstance which was to have emotionally-charged repercussions in the centuries to come.

On the seaward side, along a frontage now extending to nearly six miles, Dunwich had an even more powerful neighbour. The sea. One of the first grim facts we learn from the Domesday survey is that, whereas there used to be two carucates of land (roughly two hundred acres), now there was only one. *Mare abstulit alia* – 'the sea removed the other.' This, of course, refers to land under cultivation, not to the area of the town. The sea had removed about the same amount of usable land on the one side as the rivers had created on the other. The descendants of those men who had been so generous, albeit compulsorily, to Blythburgh Priory were doubtless already bitterly complaining about the injustice of life. This is the first marine encroachment of which we have definite record. It must have occurred about 1070.

There were yet other changes in the fortunes of Dunwich. The manor has been acquired by Robert Malet, lord of Eye, then a very extensive 'honour,' almost an earldom. He evidently did not rate Dunwich very highly, but found it a useful asset with which to insure his soul against damnation, and gain a little favour with a few of the people who mattered. To the Priory of Eye, which he founded, he granted all the tithes of Dunwich, including those of the market which had just been established, the tolls of a three-day fair to be held at the Feast of St Leonard, the 'schools' (why plural?) and all the churches which then existed or might subsequently exist in Dunwich. There had been only one; presumably that founded by Felix. The Prior of Eye, understandably, saw to it that two more churches were promptly built. (One must surely have been St Leonard's.) The value of all three in 1086 was £4–7–0 a year. Roger Bigod had claimed two small parcels of land in the town and attached them to two of his numerous manors. Three other land-holders had done the same thing; legally, of course; though what constituted legality at that time would keep lawyers arguing for years now, as it did then. So, even if the sea had not claimed a fair slice of Dunwich, there were plenty of claimants for what was left, the value of which had now risen to over £50 in cash and 60,000 herrings. We shall find herrings being used as 'currency' for a great many years to come. They were actually used for making payments, though they tended to be commuted to cash payment later.

The population, too, had changed quite markedly in the space of twenty years. The number of burgess families now stood at 226 (306 if those eighty belonging to the Prior of Ely are to be included, as presumably they are). This was a fantastic increase, difficult to match elsewhere. Only *two* peasants are listed. The term 'manor' applied to Dunwich clearly no longer has any validity; or at least it means here something totally different from what it means at Blythburgh, for instance. The survey lists 178 'poor men'; again an unusual feature. If it meant 178 poor families, as it almost certainly did, then well over a third of the Dunwich population were poor; they held no land; they were of no taxable value. Was that yet another indication of the sea's incursion? It was certainly a social problem of great significance. Dunwich was never free of this problem. We shall meet it often in the course of our story.

Finally, and most significant of all, there were *24 franci homines.* I thought at first, as did Gardner and others, that they were 'free men.' It is quite clear from a perusal of contemporary documentary records relating to the neighbourhood, and from subsequent records of Dunwich, that they were Frenchmen. In addition to the thousands of land-hungry knights who had come over with Duke William of Normandy in 1066 and later, a considerable number of French families had migrated to settle in the conquered kingdom. They were all of the merchant class, men of substance to start with, bent on increasing that substance, assisted by a favourable attitude on the part of the government, i.e. the king. Their names — Valeins, De la Falaise, FitzRichard, FitzJohn, FitzWilliam, FitzRobert, FitzRoger, etc.— loom large in the story of Dunwich. Some of them will even be found inscribed in the pages of the history of England. It was they, perhaps more than any other group of people, who were to make Dunwich what it became within the next century. It was already what we might call a 'development area.' Within a couple of generations it would be a mercantile town and port of some renown. It might have been so yet – consider Felixstowe – if that eastern neighbour had not been so turbulent and persistent.

The sea struck another blow in 1091, if William of Malmesbury got his dates right. He does not mention Dunwich. No one does in the period 1087–1173; history is still 'pretty silent.' But he tells of a south-easterly gale which 'destroyed six hundred houses in London.' That, or something like that, being the case, the Suffolk coast would have taken a hammering, and a bit more of Robert Malet's manor would have disappeared.

This is perhaps the appropriate place to mention 'Dunwich Forest,' for I shall not have another opportunity to do so. There is a 'Dunwich Forest' in existence today; of a totally different nature, in a different place, and serving a wholly different purpose from the one I am talking about. That was a natural forest bordering the sea to the south-east of the town; probably about a square mile in extent; big enough for King William to designate it as a royal hunting-ground. Gardner mentions the existence of several documents, since lost, referring to the forest, and goes on to say that:

> In the Year 1739 – the raging seas – uncovered the Roots of a great Number of Trees once growing there, which – in all likelyhood was the Forest.

In all likelihood he was right. And in all likelihood the forest had almost disappeared by the time that William Rufus was chasing after game.

6 King's Town

Reading the chroniclers of the Middle Ages, or indeed reading some modern history-books dealing with the realm as a whole, one gets the impression that nothing much happened in the England of the eleventh and twelfth centuries apart from kings, bishops and barons fighting each other all over the place. One suspects that the impression is false. There must have been a lot of people in England and France who had better things to do. Moreover, the closer one looks into the matter, the more evident it becomes that a lot of this 'fighting' was not really fighting as we understand it. It had nothing whatever to do with patriotism, or religious beliefs, or principles such as liberty, justice, unity and the like. It did not even have the primary objective of killing enemies; which, I suppose, is a point in its favour. It was really a game, a combination of sport and gambling. The stakes were often high; they could range in magnitude from kingdoms and principalities, through dukedoms, earldoms, counties and lordships down to single castles and manors. The play was rough. Not entirely without rules. There was a tricky rule about allegiance; not at all the same thing as loyalty. But one of the most widely observed rules was that you only observed the rules when circumstances made it necessary, prudent or profitable to do so. The most respected principle was that, if it was both profitable and possible to take a certain course of action, then it was right; and if it was not right, it could be made right by payment, usually with someone else's money. The casualties, considering the amount of play, were surprisingly few among the players. The bulk of them occurred amongst those who were not taking part, but who had the misfortune to be living in the path of those who were.

Dunwich was fortunately placed in this respect. It could not very well be caught between two opposing armies, or find itself in the path of an army going somewhere. The three thousand or so good people of Dunwich were thus able to get on with the business of life – buying, selling, fishing, getting and begetting – oblivious of the fact that their overlord, Robert Malet, had backed a loser. King William II died in 1099 as a result of a carelessly – or carefully? – aimed arrow in the New Forest. Henry, his younger brother, promptly secured the throne of England. Some barons considered that the English throne should by rights have gone to Robert Duke of Normandy, the elder brother. That is to say, some barons, Robert Malet among them, considered that there was more to gain by supporting the claim of Robert than by supporting that of Henry. There was no actual fighting. What might have been a battle at Winchester was won by Henry's timely deployment of three thousand marks, and Robert went back to Normandy.

Robert Malet soon followed him, banished from the realm and stripped of his English possessions, namely the 'Honour' of Eye, which the king took into his own hands; in accordance with the rules of the game. Dunwich, from that time on, early in 1101, became the king's town. That sounds rather fine; patriotic even. In fact the difference it made to the men of Dunwich was negligible, as far as day-to-day life was concerned. They paid their services and dues as before, avoiding paying taxes when they could; they were subject to all the administrative machinery of shire and hundred, and Leet Hill continued in use as before. The rulers of the town were royally-appointed officials from outside, no different from the steward and bailiff of Robert Malet. Yet there was one respect in which it mattered, both to them and to the king. On the king's part, he could count on the allegiance of the Dunwich men when the next phase of the war-game broke out. For their part, the men of Dunwich were relieved of the responsibility of making a choice of sides, and knew what to expect if they did make a choice and it proved to be the wrong one. To give them their due, they did observe the rules throughout the whole of the twelfth century.

They were lucky in another respect also. There was no castle at Dunwich to act as a bait to rebellious barons or as an excuse for depredation and pillage under the guise of protection. As the century wore on however, and the town grew steadily richer, it seems evident that the lack of any protection must have caused grave concern to the burgesses. The Fitz-Johns, Valeins, FitzRogers and the rest would have slept more soundly of nights if there had been a solid stone wall round the town; or a stout palisade. Why did they not build one?

Well, for one thing, they could only have done so with the permission of the king. He would have granted it, I am sure. In fact, he did. The delay in providing the town with adequate defences was almost certainly due to reluctance on the part of the burgesses to foot the bill. They thought, no doubt, that since it was the king's town, he ought to pay. He thought that, since it would be for their protection, they should pay. In the end they did; not for a wall, but for the next best thing, a ditch and rampart.

Precise information about this defensive ditch is, understandably, difficult to obtain. Less than thirty yards of it, or the site of it, remain. This was excavated seven years ago and this much ascertained: the ditch was forty feet wide and fifteen feet deep, revetted with timber on the inner face; it is not known how wide or high the rampart stood, but its size and profile must have corresponded roughly with that of the ditch in reverse; timber buildings had been demolished to make room for the rampart. A disconcerting discrepancy arises from a study of the pottery found under the rampart. The archaeologists say that it dates from the late twelfth and thirteenth centuries; therefore the rampart was constructed at some time early in the thirteenth century. But documentary evidence indicates that the rampart was there in the third quarter of the twelfth. Which is right? I favour the documentary evidence. Pottery dating is notoriously difficult.

Originally the rampart – called Pales Dyke, from the palisade of upright posts which surmounted it – would have extended for about $1\frac{1}{4}$ miles along the west and south sides of the town, and four gates gave access through it: Bridge, Middle, Gilden and South Gates. (The name 'Gilden' probably accounts for the absurd notion, propagated by Stowe, that the gates were of brass. It was actually a shorter and later form of 'Gylderhall Gate,' the gate which led to the Guild Hall.) The probable date of its construction I would put at around 1142, when the alarm and confusion of King Stephen's reign were at their height; certainly not later than 1160. My reason for thinking so is that the Pipe Rolls (a detailed account of the king's receipts and expenditures) are complete and continuous from 1169 on, and they contain no hint of expenditure on the defences of Dunwich. (Yes, I know I have just said that the burgesses paid for it; but they would have squeezed *some* concession from the king, if it was only the cost of the nails. And it would have been recorded.) The Rolls do contain a detailed account of the repairs to the castle of Eye in 1173 at a cost of £20–18–4. And they contain ample evidence that the burgesses of Dunwich were having difficulty in paying the dues expected of them. It took them seven years, for example, to pay an 'aid' of £58 for the marrying of the king's son. One should perhaps not read too much into that. The burgesses of Dunwich, as far as I can ascertain, were never wholly free of debt throughout a period of over two hundred years.

It does seem reasonable to suppose, though, that the vast expenditure involved in the construction of the Pales Dyke and the gates would have crippled the town's finances for many years. I feel sure, knowing what I do of the attitude of those burgesses later, that the bulk of that expenditure came from the common chest. A certain amount of voluntary labour might have been supplied; horses and carts and tools were probably loaned free of charge for limited periods; but as for the handing over of money, that was a different matter.

Those same Pipe Rolls provide a few hints of the growth of the town towards the end of the twelfth century. Twenty ships were sent on behalf of the king from Dunwich to Sandwich in 1173 'for the safe keeping of the sea,' and earned the Dunwich mariners and merchants £27–10–0. This is the first recorded instance of what was to become a regular feature, **though never a very lucrative source of income.** An assize of the itinerant justices was held regularly, that is every two years or so, at Dunwich. That *was* a major source of income for the king; one session could earn him as much as £200. That very amount, in a single fine, was incurred by the Dunwich burgesses who foolishly got involved in a law-suit, which they lost. It took them, as it took everyone else, many years to learn that 'justice' was something which had to be paid for, and paid dearly. When they did learn, the 'law-game' became as popular a pastime for them as the war-game was for their social superiors. The rules were stricter, but there was one ploy which nearly always worked: if one played badly, and lost, one stalled on the payment of the fine. Sooner or later the king would die, and with any luck the fine would be forgotten.

7 Their Finest Hour

The war-game was waged with even more vigour than usual in 1173 on a field extending from the north-west of France to the Scottish border. The preliminary moves in the game were, as so often, marriages and 'settlements,' which invariably unsettled somebody. King Henry II of England had four sons: Henry aged eighteen, Richard aged fifteen, Geoffrey and the infant John. The two elder boys wanted more than their father had given them. Their mother, Queen Eleanor, wanting a change from troubadours and tournaments, encouraged them in their unfilial aspirations, and the game began. Eleanor, masquerading in male attire, was captured before the rebellion had really got under way. King Louis of France took on the role of chief trouble-maker, his object being to place young Henry on the throne of England – for which he was already designated, and had in fact been 'crowned' – in the place of his less amenable father. The Count of Flanders was enlisted as an ally, won over by the promise of the castles of Kent and £1000 a year. The barons of Normandy, Poitou, Brittany and England made their choice, as usual with little co-ordination of thought or action.

Castles were besieged and some of them were captured. Villages were burnt. The countryside here and there was plundered. 'That,' said the Count of Flanders, 'was the way to start a war.' And he should know. Things went badly for the rebels, and peace nearly broke out, but King Louis kept the game going. England was invaded from the Continent by Robert Earl of Leicester at the head of a Flemish army. They landed in the Orwell on Sept. 29th and marched upon – of all places – Dunwich. The Suffolk countryside was not unduly ravaged, as far as we know, apart from a forced collection of cash, but rustic ears were outraged by the sound of a taunting refrain, according to Matthew Paris:

Hoppe hoppe, Wilekin, hoppe, Wilekin,
                             Hop along Billy-boy, hop Billy-boy,
England is min ant tin.   England belongs to you and me.

And what happened when they got to Dunwich? Let Jordan Fantosme tell the story. He was there. Or, if not actually there himself, he was in close contact with those who were. Fantosme was one of the clerks of the Bishop of Winchester. He wrote up the whole affair in a long poem written soon after the events which he describes. He made mistakes, as modern reporters do. The copyists who copied his manuscript (two copies have survived, one at Durham, one at Lincoln, both dating from the thirteenth century) also made mistakes. The poem was intended to be read aloud to an assembly of high-born company familiar with the technique of the war-game.

It is informative and entertaining, to us as it was to them. I quote here only the relevant verses:

l.818

Do you know what news we have heard?
The Earl of Leicester has shown himself a bad bailiff to us all.
He landed in Orwell, no doubt about it,
And has fleeced the land as though it were his.
From there to Dunwich he collected money by force.

842

From there to Dunwich all is at his command.
Many a Flemish knight follows him this day,
Which later gave the King of England joy.
Earl Hugh Bigod has sent his messengers
And announced to the men of Dunwich that he is their friend.
Let them side with the earl if they would have games and mirth,
Or those now living will lose their heads.

To which the loyal men of Dunwich replied that they would sell their lives dearly rather than play a traitor's game. The rebel army appeared before the gates. A spirited exchange of compliments took place across the rampart and ditch.

857

The Earl of Leicester was prepared to beseige them,
And swore his usual oath that
If the burgesses and worthies did not surrender to him
Not a man would escape death or injury.
And those who were to the fore answered:
Cursed be the man who has a pennyworth of fear for you!
The good lawful king is still alive,
Who will very soon bring your enterprise to nothing.
As long as we can live and stand on our feet
We shall not surrender the town for fear of an attack.

The Earl of Leicester began to get angry,
And caused gallows to be erected to frighten them.
Then he bids sergeants and squires to arm in haste.
He resolves to make every effort to attack the town in
    strength.
That day you would have seen burgesses, right valiant
    knights
Sally forth to the ramparts; each man knows his task;
Some to draw bows, others to hurl spears.
The strong help the weak to rest frequently.
Within the town there was not wife or girl
Who did not carry a stone to the palisade for throwing.
Thus did the people of Dunwich defend themselves,
As these verses tell which are written here.
And so stout-hearted were both great and small
That Earl Robert withdrew completely discomfited;
He felt no love for the people of Dunwich.

On the following morning at daybreak the rebel army withdrew. Fantosme says they went to Norwich, and that he was
not there. Actually they went to Bury St Edmunds, near
where, at Fornham, they were routed by Humphrey de Bohun
assisted by the local peasantry armed with forks and flails. The
Earl of Leicester and his wife were captured and sent to cool
off in the dungeons of Falaise. Hugh Bigod secured a temporary truce and forgiveness on condition that he sent home
the Flemish mercenaries who, says Fantosme, 'were mostly
weavers' and were only there for the loot. In the following
spring the war-game started up again. King Henry returned
from Anjou to find that another force of Flemings had landed
in Suffolk and had captured Norwich. Within a year or so,
however, it was all settled, for the time being. A few castles
were destroyed; most of the rebels were pardoned, except
Queen Eleanor; most of the Flemings went home, though a
number stayed on and settled in East Anglia. Life in Dunwich returned to normal, which meant that it was no more
peaceful there than in many other towns.

We need not believe every word that Fantosme wrote. The

noble sentiments which he attributes to the men of Dunwich probably reflect his own diplomacy and artistry. The whole affair, considered carefully, assumes a farcical air. That, in my view, enhances Fantosme's credibility. The war-game was a farce. Nevertheless, there would have been little for the Dunwich people to laugh at if their town had not been protected by that deep ditch and palisaded rampart.

The records of the rest of that century tell of no further epic events; just the normal sequence of business and judicial transactions; payment of fines and tallage, eventually; recovery of fines unjustly imposed; payment of the fee-farm rent, which appears to have been fixed for the first time by Richard I at £108 a year, plus £12 in alms to the Prior of Eye; and so on. The odd entry here and there however reveals the existence of a story of which one would like to know more details.

Like that of the Dunewic family, for instance. It was inevitable that a number of families should take their family-name from that of the town. I had thought of trying to do a potted family history; but they turn up in so many widely-separated places, and there are so many of them, that they cannot all belong to one family. The only 'Dunewics' I shall write about are those who actually belonged to Dunwich.

Robert de Dunewic in 1177 incurred a fine of five marks (£3–6–8) for some offence unspecified; infringement of export regulations, very probably. In 1181 he had still not paid the fine, and the reason is clearly stated: *sed nihil habet* – he has nothing. A year later Robert was in Sussex, still owing five marks. Meanwhile his son William was in trouble. He had forfeited all his houses in Dunwich, worth in rents a total of 6s. 10d. which the Bishop of Ely dutifully collected and paid in to the Exchequer annually for the next six years. The reason for the forfeiture? *Jordanus falsonarius vicit in duello* – Jordan the counterfeiter overcame him in judicial combat. This was a different kind of war-game; in fact a combination of war-game and law-game. Trial by combat. William had apparently elected to solve his father's financial problems by pitting his martial skill against the wrong-doer; or against a man who was employed to represent 'right.' (The choice of a counterfeiter for the role seems a bit odd; but then, it was an odd practice.) William lost; not his life, though the contest might have gone that far; only his property. Sixteen years later, in 1197, William was again before the justices, and fined half a mark for a 'false claim.' He was not very good at this law-game. He paid two shillings of the fine three years later, and never did pay the outstanding 4s. 8d. (So he was not too bad at it.) At the same court his brother Reginald was fined one mark for 'wine sold contrary to assize.' A year later Ode de Dunewic was fined 20s. in Kent, and the following year Albert de Dunewic was fined one mark at Dunwich. I think that maybe old Robert had a wife in several ports.

Then there was that case in 1193, when the burgesses of Dunwich owed forty marks *pro murdro* – for murder. Had they callously tortured some poor widow to death because she could not pay her rent? No, all it means is that a body had been found, and that no one knew who was the murderer, or indeed whether it was in fact a case of murder. This was a novel twist of the law-game introduced by the Normans, and intended as a means of protecting them against those treacherous English. If a murder had been committed and the culprit could not be discovered, it was assumed that the victim was a Norman unless his 'Englishry' could be proved, and a fine was imposed on the whole community amongst which the body was found. The law persisted until well on into the thirteenth century, in theory. In practice the extortionate fines were rarely paid.

In 1193 King Richard I carried the war-game too far; or played it badly. On his way back home from a crusade he was shipwrecked and had the misfortune to fall into the hands of the Duke of Austria, who hated him, and was handed over to the German Emperor, who kept him. The honour of transporting the chancellor, William Longchamp, Bishop of Ely, and a huge sum of money to ransom the captive king was bestowed on the men of Dunwich, Ipswich and Orford. The interesting thing is that payment for the men and ships was made immediately. Since those ships were carrying perhaps as much as 100,000 marks, it would have been tactless, imprudent even, to have delayed payment of £29–6s.–8d. for the transport. It would have been pleasing to record that King Richard, on his return to England, landed at Dunwich. In fact he landed at Sandwich.

8 Age of Faith

Words painstakingly copied in their thousands on enduring parchment often richly embellished; stones skilfully fashioned to form breathtakingly beautiful cathedrals and abbeys, or more crudely but not less lovingly laid to form the humbler parish churches which outlived by many centuries the lowly homes of those who built them; these are the testimony on which is based the traditional description of the Middle Ages as 'the Age of Faith.' How true are those words? What really did inspire the fashioning and laying of those stones? How one-sided is that label? Fascinating questions to me. I wish I knew the answers.

I wish I knew more of the facts concerning the manifestations of spiritual activity in Dunwich. They are, for obvious reasons, more difficult to collect or deduce here than elsewhere. The legendary 'fifty-two Churches, Chapels, Religious Houses and Hospitals' of the later chroniclers writing about medieval Dunwich is clearly nonsense; only worth mentioning as an instance showing how a legend, once fabricated, can persist despite all reason and a considerable body of evidence to refute it. The situation as regards the churches and religious houses existing in the year 1200 is fairly clear. Here it is, along with some of the evidence:

St Leonard's church stood on the east side of the town. It had been built, or impropriated, by the Prior of Eye by 1086, and gave its name to the fair.

St Martin's church was also on the east side of the town; also impropriated by the Prior of Eye, probably soon after 1086; like the above, it is mentioned in the Bishop's Register.

St Nicholas's church stood at the south end of the town. It was a very large parish with lots of open space. In 1201 Christiana Swetyng, widow, successfully claimed from the parson of St Peter's 'four acres of land and appurtenances lying outside the door of the church of St Nicholas at Dunwich, on the west side,' and paid one mark of silver for it. A hundred and forty years later the land was still called 'Swetyngs land.' The church disappeared in about 1355, but it took the sea a further three centuries to swallow the graveyard.

St John's church, standing in the centre, just east of the market-place, was the largest and most impressive of the churches, and continued until about 1540 when it was demolished by the parishioners to prevent the sea from getting it. I am inclined to think that it may have stood on the site of Felix's original church, rebuilt several times since his day. Its size and position lend support to this view, as does also an interesting discovery made at its demolition, as described by Gardner, quoting Stowe:

—in the Chancel was a large Grave-Stone, which when raised discovered a Stone Coffin, wherein lay the Corpse of a Man, which fell to Dust when stirred; upon his Legs were a Pair of Boots picked like Crakows; and on his Breast stood two Chalices of coarse Metal. He was thought to have been a Bishop of Dunwich.

Whether he was a bishop or not, he gave some indication of the antiquity of this church.

St Peter's church stood at the north end of the town, near the harbour, and a good twenty feet above the tides. It was stripped of lead, timber and bells in 1702.

All Saints church. It is not certain that this existed in 1200. The Rev. A. Suckling (*History and Antiquities of Suffolk,* 1846) says it was built about 1350, then re-built c.1527. But there was definitely a parish of All Saints in 1270; not very large, on the western edge of the town. It seems probable that the church could have been built in the early thirteenth century to replace one lost earlier on a different site.

Two other churches had existed, those of *St Michael* and *St Bartholomew*. The only mention of them is in the Register of Eye for the year 1331, when the Prior petitioned the Bishop of Norwich for permission to impropriate the church of Laxfield to compensate for revenue lost by the encroachment of the sea. Gardner could find no other mention of these churches. Nor can I. It is clear that they had gone some time before 1331, and they may not have been there in 1200. One of them, I believe, was the third church mentioned in 1086. As for *St Felix's* church, there is no evidence for it; a church built *by* Bishop Felix, yes, but its dedication is unknown. On reflection, a church built *by* Felix could not be dedicated *to* him.

So then, there were probably not more than six parish churches at any one time. There were in addition three chapels. That of *St Francis* stood at the north end of the town, between Cock and Hen Hills; its foundations were uncovered in 1740. *St Anthony's* chapel disappeared too early for any thing but the name to be known. *St Catherine's* was in St John's parish, and seems to have been a guild chapel. It is unlikely that more than one of the three existed in 1200.

Of the religious houses, Grey Friars and Black Friars came into existence in the mid-thirteenth century. A small Benedictine monastery, a 'cell' of the Priory of Eye, certainly existed at Dunwich in 1200, probably housing no more than two or three monks who had charge of the 'school'; it had disappeared before 1300. The Temple was founded in 1185 and is well documented for several centuries (more about the Temple later). Then there were the hospitals, each equipped with a church or chapel as an important part of its premises. That of *Maison Dieu* (*Domus Dei* or 'God's House'), dedicated to the Holy Trinity, the site of which can still be identified close to what was the inner harbour (and is now a car-park), was probably founded shortly before 1200. The Leper (or Lazar) Hospital of *St James* calls for fuller mention, to be given shortly.

That list falls a long way short of the fabled fifty-two. It falls a long way short of establishing medieval Dunwich as the abode of exceptional piety, or indicating that faith was more abundant here than elsewhere throughout 'silly Suffolk'; which, they say, is a corruption of *selig* (i.e. 'blessed') Suffolk. Those seventeen churches undoubtedly met a spiritual need as places where all, high and low, could be baptised, married and ultimately buried. For many they provided the only means known to them of ensuring entry into Paradise when the present life of woes was done; for others the assurance that life in the next world would be as pleasant as it was in this, with the added bonus of leaving behind them a good reputation. For a few they presented a means of escaping summary justice, temporarily at least; we hear of 'sanctuary' most frequently when it was violated.

The analytic faculty needed to distinguish faith from superstition and both from materialism, real or disguised, is beyond my powers. Non-spiritual considerations force themselve's on one's notice. Almost every time one of those churches earned a mention in the records it was in connection with money – tithes, impropriations, endowments, assessments, claims, etc. It became apparent in 1086 and becomes increasingly apparent that, for some people, a church was primarily a source of revenue; as was a court of justice. The material evidence of that fact is slight. At Dunwich it consists of a number of trinkets, medallions, leaden 'lacrymatories' to contain tears of repentance or sacred 'Relicks,' etc. They probably have as much to do with real faith and piety as do the contents of many 'souvenir' shops found today in the vicinity of cathedrals and shrines. The documentary evidence is almost as slight, for commercialism of faith was not something to be placed on record.

That said, let it be acknowledged that these churches would never have been built and maintained if large numbers of people had not believed that it was right to give their money and goods for such a purpose. We cannot know to what extent their actions were influenced by feelings of true charity and brotherly love; only hope that life and thought was not really

as brutally harsh as most of the documentary evidence would
lead us to believe. We cannot know what those men and
women of Dunwich thought and felt as, one after the other,
their churches disappeared by the agency of a force beyond
their control.

In most villages and towns it is possible to sit or stand in
silence within the walls of an ancient church and contemplate
– a salutary exercise – the human experience, the faith and
hope and folly which those walls enshrine. One can look at
wood and stone, and – if nineteenth-century restoration and
limewash have not too completely hidden it – read the story
of successive rebuilding and alteration to conform with changing fashion. At Dunwich no such place exists, but there is a
spot where one may stand, before a massive iron grille –
guarding the tomb of the Barne family – and contemplate
beneath the sky the remains of what eight hundred years ago,
was an impressive building and which even now, despite rank
weeds and creeping ivy, bears striking testimony to a faith
once held to be unassailable. These are the ruins of what was
once the church of the Leper Hospital of St James, commonly
known as 'the Leper's Chapel.' No nineteenth-century restoration here. If the adjacent church of St James, built in 1830
by Miles Barne, had been made somewhat bigger, there would
have been no Leper Chapel to be seen. But recent salvage
operations by the Ministry of Works have preserved, for a
long time, I hope, this interesting relic. Visitors might wonder
why, for a two-minute inspection suffices to see all there is to
see.

That is, the solidly built stone walls of a round-ended apse
pierced by a round-headed window and lined with an arcade
of twelve recessed spaces which once held *'sedilia'* (seats). Even
the most cursory glance tells two things; that this was a building which cost a lot of money, and that it was built in the
twelfth century. The precise date cannot be known; my guess
is c.1150. Gardner supplies a drawing of the building as it
was in 1750, from which it is evident that the whole church
was built in one style, and was of one date. What remains is
about one quarter of what was standing then, and perhaps

about one sixth of the original building, which must have been the largest and finest building in Dunwich. Not actually *in* Dunwich; it was, like all leper establishments, built well outside the town, for lepers and ordinary human beings did not mix. One reason for the date which I suggest is that the Hospital was built on the lower slope of Leet Hill, which went out of use as a public assembly-place, I believe, when the Pales Dyke was constructed. It is unlikely that a public meeting-place and a leper establishment would have existed side by side.

Few people in this country today know much about leprosy, though it is still a major scourge in some parts of the world. The disease is caused by a bacillus very similar to that which causes tuberculosis, affecting mainly the skin, eyes, nose and throat; a disease not normally fatal in itself, but resulting in a condition which renders the sufferer an easy prey to other

Fig 4 Leper's Chapel

49

killing diseases. We do not like to think of such diseases originating in our own country, so readily accept the suggestion that it was introduced into Britain by the Romans. The Crusades cannot be implicated, for there were several hundred 'lazar-houses' already established in Britain before the eleventh century, and a great many more in France. The incidence of the disease may well have increased here after the Norman Conquest, but not because of it. The lazar-houses, or 'hospitals' as they came to be called, were not for the treatment and cure of lepers – there was no cure, though numerous remedies were tried – so much as for their isolation. Such was the loathing and fear inspired by the disease that the sufferers were excommunicated and deprived of normal human rights. Many lepers were only saved from being brutally done to death by the fear which their proximity evoked. It was therefore truly a work of 'charity' to provide some of them, albeit a small minority, with a haven of refuge where they could exist until God chose to terminate their existence.

Very little is known about leper-hospitals in general, and about this particular one 'neither History nor antient Records give any Light.' (Gardner again.) There does exist however one document from which I will quote at some length – craving your indulgence – as an example of the manner in which such institutions were endowed. It is a charter which can be dated to the reign of King John, and clearly refers to a house already established. The 'H. de Cressie' mentioned in it was born c.1150, was the husband of Margery de Cressy (about whom more later) and died c.1205, shortly before this document was written. Here it is, much abbreviated, but still longish:

> Be it known to all those faithful to Christ that I, Walter de Ribof, for the sake of God and moved by Piety have given – to the church of St James and the House of Lepers of Donewic and to the Chaplain Hubert, who shall minister in that Chapel for life, and to all Chaplains who succeed him – for the soul of H. de Cressie, and for the salvation of my Soul, and for the salvation of the Souls of my predeceased Friends, my Successors and Heirs—

Then follows a detailed account of the land given; all in

Brandeston; forty acres and a house; thirteen other small parcels of land; fascinating stuff for anyone writing a history of Brandeston. It goes on:

and in addition one coomb of wheat each year at Michaelmas, and two loaves from each baking at my house, and from each brewing one sester (two gallons?) of ale, and the tithes of my mills. All the above – along with an annual pension of five shillings and a coomb of wheat annually to the Leprous Brethren – in order that the said Hubert and his successors shall for ever minister as is needful to *one* leprous brother of Donwic, and likewise to *one* leper whom I or my heirs shall place in the said chapel we will provide the necessities; moreover, the Leprous Brethren of Donewic shall retain half of the offerings which the leper of my choice may bring with him, and the other half shall belong to the chapel – The Chaplain shall swear to the mother church of Brandeston that he will not be the cause – whereby the said church shall be the loser in tithes, revenue or in any of its rights. But those workers who are fit to take the holy sacrament and do their oblations shall on feast days go to the mother church. When they die they shall be buried in the graveyard of the mother church. For the small tithes and oblations – I have given to the chapel of – the church of Brandeston two pieces of meadow—

That document was witnessed by fourteen named witnesses, including a prior, an archdeacon, two priests, 'and many others.' You will have noted that, even in a charitable act of this nature, one could not get away from money. The church at Brandeston had to be compensated for the loss of tithes and offerings. All that elaborate arrangement was for the sake of *one leper* to be placed in care, and *one* leprous monk already there. We have no means of knowing how many leprous monks were in residence (if the *sedilia* are any guide, it was twelve); nor how many lepers could be accommodated. The church could have held a couple of hundred, but that is certainly no safe guide. The annual value of Walter de Ribof's gift would be about £3 (the equivalent of about £700 today). The cost of feeding, clothing and lodging two lepers would, I imagine, be well under half that amount. That explains how such a grand church could be built. It was fortunate that it was built when it was. A hundred years later the Age of Faith was fast giving way to the Age of Plunder, and the Hospital of St James was granted a licence to beg in order to stave off poverty.

9 Free Town

September 29th, 1198, must have been a day-to-be-remembered for Hubert de Turtose and Reginald FitzRobert, burgesses of Dunwich. Laden with sacks of silver marks and florins, they staggered into the office-for-the-time-being of the king's treasurer-for-that-district and triumphantly proceeded to pay off the debts which the men of Dunwich had accumulated towards the king over the past five years. For the year 1194 they owed £40 6s 8d. and 12,000 herrings. They did not, you may be sure, dump twelve thousand herrings on the table. They paid £54. Thus anyone who so wishes many work out the price of herrings, having first deducted £6 for a half-year's tithes payable to the monks of Eye, plus 6s 8d. and a further 12,000 herrings to the monks of Ely. Then they handed over £120 6s. 8d. and 24,000 herrings, or the cash equivalent, to clear the debt for 1195. Likewise for 1196, 1197 and the current year of 1198. £540 in all. *Quieti sunt,* wrote the treasurer's clerk on their account. They are quit. Dunwich was out of debt! For the first time ever, since their town had become the king's town!

Not, alas, for very long! Within a few days, perhaps that very same day, they learnt the staggering news that the men of Dunwich had been fined the enormous sum of one thousand and forty marks (£692 13s 4d.) for 'exporting corn to the king's enemies in Flanders.' There are many moments in the history of Dunwich of which I would dearly like to have been an eye-witness, or an eavesdropper of the comments then made. This is one. I would gladly exchange a thousand lines of Chaucer, or half of Fantosme with twenty pages of Froissart thrown in for good measure, just for a verbatim report of what those burgesses said when they heard that news. How else could they have paid off their debts to the king but by exporting corn? Where else could they have exported corn but to Flanders? They must have bitterly resented their own honest endeavours; resolved that in future they would use more caution, more guile. The following year they paid in only £20, and let the monks of Eye and Ely whistle for their herrings and their tithes – 'constituted alms,' they called it. Constituted fiddlesticks – or words to that effect! Actually, just for the record – and it is the record of the Pipe Rolls which reveals this – the men of Dunwich never did pay that fine of 1040 marks. It remained on the books for twelve years, and was then diplomatically forgotten. It may be of interest to know, for purposes of comparison, that at the same time as Dunwich was fined for exporting corn so also were Lynn (1000 m.), Ipswich (200 m.), Yarmouth (200 m.), Beccles (40 m.), and Orford (15 m.). Lynn paid half the fine immediately; the rest of the fines remained unpaid.

Was there a subtle plan in the minds of the burgesses of Dunwich when they made that heroic effort to get out of the king's debt? I think so. Civic consciousness was in the air. Towns all over the country wanted a measure of independence and self-government. It was not right that they should be treated as though they were no more than outsize villages, with the sheriff interfering in their affairs at every turn. London had its charter of liberties, so why not Dunwich? Why not, indeed!

They got it. Their first charter was signed on June 29th, 1199, and witnessed by Eustace Bishop of Ely and Hubert Walter, Archbishop of Canterbury and Chancellor, at Roches d'Orival, a castle overlooking the Seine near Rouen. King John, after a hasty visit to be crowned king of England, had returned to secure his duchy of Normandy, and was ready to sign anything which would secure him a little more badly needed money. It was a hastily drawn up document, but it did at least state specifically that 'the borough of Dunwic is a Free

Borough,' with all that that implied. It did not imply – and no one in Dunwich, I am sure, thought that it would imply – that Dunwich would henceforth pay no rent. The rent continued to be exactly what it had been. What is more, the men of Dunwich promptly paid the next instalment when it fell due. How much they had to pay the Chancellor and the Bishop of Ely for placing that strip of parchment in front of the king we shall never know; but the official fee for having their charter was three hundred marks (£200), ten *chasceurs* and five gerfalcons.

Chasceurs were 'hunters,' i.e. horses for hunting. Seven years later the word had been altered in the Rolls to *osturos* or *austurcos,* i.e. goshawks, a kind of falcon. The difference was immaterial, for they were never paid. The men of Dunwich paid one hundred marks right away. The livestock and the remaining two hundred marks were debited to them in the accounts of the town with the Exchequer for the next sixteen years, then conveniently forgotten. The men of Dunwich were learning fast.

In the following year, 1200, they noticed a serious deficiency in the sketchy terms of their charter; it made no mention of 'wreck' or 'lagan' ('wreck' was the right to claim ships and goods washed up on a specific stretch of coast; 'lagan' the right to claim goods found in the sea; more about that later). This was rectified, at a cost to the men of Dunwich of a further 200 marks and 500 eels; which price – need I say it? – they never paid. In 1205 they incurred a further debt of 100,000 herrings 'that they may go safe and sound with their ships.' In that same year they were charged with yet a further 500 marks 'payable within the year' for having their fee-farm rent reduced 'for ever,' so that henceforth they were to pay a rent of £80 and one mark and 24,000 herrings. They did not pay the extra fee, and the Exchequer clerk did not make the necessary adjustment in their account, despite a subsidiary confirmation of their charter in 1206. I have no wish to weary you with the endless tale of unpaid debts. It goes on and on. In 1211 they were in debt to a total of £1235 10s. 0d., to say nothing of eels, herrings and hawks. They got some relief in the end by the much wished-for death of King John.

One of the points in mentioning these financial details is that one should not attach too much weight to them as an indication of the importance, actual or relative, of a particular place at a particular time. In 1204, for instance, a special tax of a *quindena mercatorum* – a fifteenth of the merchants – brought in, nominally, only £5 4s. 9d. from Dunwich (and, as far as I can judge, it *was* paid!) whereas Orford was assessed at £11 7s. 0d., Lynn at £651, Lincoln at £656, Yarmouth at £4 15s. 6d. and Norwich at £6 19s. 10d. There are oddities and discrepancies which we shall never sort out; definitions different from ours; ways of accounting for which we can not account. Let us leave it and try instead to form an assessment of what the men of Dunwich got in the way of 'liberties,' paid for or otherwise.

The clearest statement comes in the confirmation charter of 1209, signed at Dunlas. Bishops were getting scarce, owing to the papal interdict on England and the impending excommunication of King John, but those of Worcester and Salisbury, as well as the Archbishop of Dublin, were there as witnesses. Leaving out the frills, here is the substance of the charter (I am quoting from the translation given by Gardner):

We have granted and – confirmed to the honest men and our burgesses of Dunwich – for their faithful service, a free Borough and—

1. A Guild of Merchants, with a House and other customs, liberties and freedoms to the said Guild belonging—

2. It shall be lawful for them to take *Nanna* for their debtors (i.e. the right to take goods by distraint for non-payment) and their sureties for all debts due to them—

3. They shall plead in no other place, nor be summoned to plead outside their town, but shall have law and justice ministered to them in their borough—

4. They shall not make any *battel* (trial by combat?) within or without their town, neither for land, nor robbery nor felony or any other thing except only for the death of a man who is a foreigner—

5. If any – of the said town shall happen to be sued – for any felony – they shall purge and clear themselves by the oath of twenty-four free and lawful men—

6. If any other man's villein or bondman shall come and dwell within the town, and shall hold land in it, and be in the aforesaid Guild and House – for the space of one whole year and a day, he shall not after be taken thence, but shall remain and continue a freeman in the said town.

7. Also we have granted to our said burgesses – *Soc and Sac,* and *Toll and Tame* and *Infangenthef* (Saxon words, already obsolete, relating to judicial rights) and that they and their men, with their chattels and ships and all their goods – shall be discharged and quit from murage (wall-building) lastage (duty on certain cargoes, e.g. herrings) passage (toll on river-crossing) pontage (bridge toll) stallage (market toll) and of and from leve (levy of money) and Danegelt (tax for defence against the Danes) and from Gaywite (forfeiture of goods on failure to pay rent or services) and – all other customs, taxes and exactions by and through all our power and jurisdictions as well within our Realm of England as in all other our lands.

This is a high-sounding clause, a wonderful bit of 'legalese' utterly without any real or practical value. Some of the terms were by now obsolete, e.g. Danegeld; others contradicted the laws of the land; others clashed with the rest of this charter, and all of them clashed with the charters granted to other towns at about the same time. It was a colossal confidence-trick, and caused endless trouble in the years to come, because some at least of the men of Dunwich really believed that the charter meant what it said.

8. They may freely marry their daughters wheresoever they may, can or will, without the licence of anyone (except the Church!). And none shall have the power or authority to marry them except it be with their own good will, neither in the life-time of their parents nor after their death.

This clause makes the Dunwich charter a 'historic' document in more senses than one. It is the only instance known, of this date, granting such explicit freedom. There must have been, among the womenfolk of Dunwich, a powerful element of women's libbers!

9. No one shall have the ward or custody of their sons, daughters or heirs, nor of their lands or goods, except only their own parents or friends, or those to whom they shall assign ward and custody thereof. And that none of their sons or heirs shall be compelled to marry a wife except of his own will.

So there was a pretty strong youth movement in the town also!

10. And their widows in their donations and bestowings shall be at their own will and discretion.

The over-sixties, too, had their say. Why shouldn't an old lady leave all her money to the monks if she wanted to? (Was it their say, or had the Prior of Eye done some lobbying?)

11. Our burgesses may freely give or sell or buy whatsoever they have – to any person – and thereof appoint heir whomsoever they shall think fit.

12. Those liberties we have granted – to be had and holden – for ever, well and in peace, freely and quietly, peaceably, fully and honourably with other liberties and free customs and good uses which in their town they have accustomed—.

Bravo! Now that *was* a charter of liberties! Apart from the meaningless Clause seven, it was as fair a charter as one could wish for. No doubt you will have noticed that it says nothing about 'wreck' and 'lagan'; nothing about any modifications which the sea might make in the territory and circumstances of those burgesses of Dunwich. Father Neptune was not present at the signing. There had already, in 1202, been a dispute about 'common pasture,' when the three sons of Robert Malet (no relation to the original lord of Eye, as far as I know, though they could have been descended from him) had paid £1 for a fair hearing in court. It said nothing about the rights of Dunwich clashing with those of Blythburgh and Walberswick, or Southwold. In other words, it barely touched upon those aspects of the situation which were to ensure that to live 'freely and quietly, peaceably, fully and honourably' was soon to become almost impossible in this free borough.

Nevertheless, it was a document to be proud of. The new Guildhall was a building to be proud of. The new seal of the burgesses (Fig 5) was a minor work of art in its way, and of considerable historical interest, in that it is as accurate a picture of a ship of that date as one will find anywhere. The leading merchants of the town lost no time in acquiring seals of their own as badges of their status (Figs 6 and 7).

Another omission from the charter is any reference – other than the compurgation by twenty-four lawful men in Clause five – to the way in which the affairs of the town should be managed. The earlier one had stated that 'twelve lawful men of the town should represent them all,' and that, if they were to be fined, it should be by 'six honest men of the town.' A later confirmation of Henry III states that the bailiffs of the town may answer for all their debts and that 'the burgesses of themselves may choose and make a Coroner.' The charter of Henry V goes into great detail on the subject of civic administration. But by that time there was precious little left to be administered. How was the town governed in the heyday of its fame and prosperity?

We know that from 1215 onwards there was a mayor and four bailiffs elected annually. Gardner gives the complete list of their names. I would hesitate to cast doubt on its accuracy, but there are so many discrepancies between his list and the numerous references to named bailiffs in the official State records that one must admit a certain degree of confusion. There were obviously more than five men running the complex affairs of a populous and thriving maritime town; customs officers, secretaries, assessors, defence officers, treasurers, overseers of this, that and the other; a small army of them, any one of whom might be considered by higher authority as a 'bailiff.' The mayor seems to have been very much a figure-head; always an ex-bailiff, evidently a man getting on in years, sometimes holding office for several years in succession; he rarely figures in the many frays, civil and uncivil, which punctuate the history of the town. I should think that his chief function was to greet and entertain the many visiting dignitaries and officials.

We shall see presently how the burgesses and bailiffs chose to interpret the terms of their charter. How they and the citizens reacted in the first instance to their newly acquired

Fig. 5

Fig. 6

Fig. 7

Fig 5 Seal of the Burgesses, *Figs 6 and 7* Merchants' Seals

status is difficult to determine. When Ipswich got its charter of liberties, at about the same time as Dunwich, there was junketing and ceremonial for a whole week. I cannot imagine that Dunwich lagged behind its humbler neighbour in that respect, and would wager that the newly appointed dignitaries were, not just for one week but for many weeks afterwards, frequently found in a posture far from dignified.

10 Faithful Service

Evidently the king, in granting the charter to his subjects of Dunwich, and to those of other towns, was well aware that it was a convenient way of extracting money from them. He added a further hundred marks to their account a year later, merely 'that the charter might be kept.' But, for all that, the reason given in the charter itself for the granting of it was no idle phrase. They had indeed rendered him 'faithful service,' and continued to do so, despite all the financial embarrassments. Or perhaps because of the financial embarrassments. Difficult to decide. What is clear is that the king would have been powerless without the co-operation of the merchants and their ships; also that, whatever he had of them in the way of shipping and the use of it, he paid for. He became even more dependent upon them when the loss of Normandy in 1203 robbed him of ports on the other side of the Channel and rendered the English ports more vulnerable to attack. It was at this time that the burgesses of the Cinque Ports and London were given the title of 'barons'; an honour never bestowed on Dunwich or Yarmouth, though they, alone of east coast ports, were subject to the laws governing the Cinque Ports. The seemingly sudden rise of both ports in importance must have been due in some measure to this change in the political situation.

Much of the service rendered was in the form of normal

trading, supplying the king's household and army with food-stuffs and commodities. For example, in 1203 the king re-mitted to the men of Dunwich £26 19s. 4d. which he owed them 'for a shipload of corn received at Rouen.' An interest-ing detail here is that the original payment was made in Angevin currency, which the Exchequer clerk entered in the roll as *C et (XIX^c) (VII li et) XIXs. Andegauensibus*; and no doubt he understood it. Ordinary merchant ships were hired whenever an army had to be carried overseas, which was frequently. More than a hundred vessels were needed to trans-port King Richard on his crusade, and in 1211 King John paid 48 m. (£32) 'for 30 ships hired to go from Dunwich to Ireland.' In the same year he paid £5 6s. 8d. for 'four ships from Dunwich to Lynn for carrying corn'; which indicates some inconsistency in the hiring rate.

The real significance of Dunwich, however, is revealed in these entries:

1206. In expenses of Richard de Seignes & others, for the galleys, 10 marks. In expenses of the galleys, £26 5s. od. by royal brief.

1209. And receive for repairing three galleys and taking them to Portsmouth, £57.

1214. And in the purchase of masts, booms, yards, straps, sprits, hair-cloth, pikes and ropes for the royal galleys, £41 4s. 1d. by royal brief, at the oversight of Nicholas FitzRobert of Dunwich.
And by letters patent of William de Wrotham who re-ceived all the above for arming the galleys. And in the carriage of all the above to the sea, and in addition for hair-cloths (*hairis*) 23s. by the same brief. And he has £47 14s. 4d. left in hand now.

From that it is evident that Dunwich was a major ship-building and ship-repairing port; which accounts to some ex-tent for its lowly position in the commercial scale. It was well situated for such a role, with a good land-locked harbour and a plentiful supply of timber within easy distance; similar to Portsmouth, whose growth dates from this time.

I had always imagined the galley to have been propelled solely by oars. There is no mention of oars in the list of supplies

– *mali, lovi, vergae, reini, sperti* – unless I have mis-translated one of those words (or someone mis-read one of them; *reini* for *remi*). I am not sure whether the 'hair cloths' were what the sailors wore, or what the sails were made of. But it is clear that these vessels – there were at that time fifty of them, the nearest thing to a Royal Navy for some time to come yet – were meant to be sailed as well as rowed. Forty years later a galley of fifty-six oars (*remos*) was built at Dunwich, and at the same time a barge (*bargia*) of twenty-eight oars. Throughout this period the term 'galliot' is in use. There was evidently some confusion about the precise meaning of many nautical terms. However, Dunwich men would have known exactly what was what.

They would have known, too, how to use them, whether in the king's service or their own. There is something eminently satisfying to the mind's eye in the picture of a huge galley surging majestically through the blue waters of the Mediterranean to the rhythmical sweep of a hundred synchronised blades – until one thinks of the three hundred sweating slaves unseen below the deck. I have not encountered any evidence to suggest that 'slaves' – as distinct from criminals condemned to this service – were employed in English galleys at this date. Men were mostly hired for the task, and paid a standard rate of 6d. a day – double normal service pay. But picture, if you can, the feelings and physical hardship of those fifty-six men of Dunwich as their clumsy craft butted through the grey waters of the turbulent North Sea or battled with the tide-race through the Straits.

Faithful service indeed! But northern waters were no place for galleys and northern men were mariners, not mules.

11 War Games

It was to be expected that, sooner or later, the chief victims of the war-game, the lower orders, should invent modifications of the rules which would facilitate their own participation with profit. That phase of the game which began in May, 1215 followed a fairly orthodox course. The barons were divided into two roughly equal factions, one for the king, one against. The insurgents seized London. King John returned to England, and went so far on the road to reconciliation as to accede to just demands and sign the *Magna Carta* on June 13th. The rebels revealed themselves in their true colours and ignored it. What they really wanted was to get rid of King John; to this end they allied themselves with Louis, son of King Philip Augustus of France, offering him the crown of England. Civil war, the inevitable ultimate stage of the game, broke out. King John introduced a foreign mercenary army and proceeded to attack his own towns and castles. The rebels, in the main, sat tight in London. In December King John marched north as far as Berwick, then returned through Lincolnshire and the eastern counties, ending up at Colchester in the early spring of 1216.

If he ever was at Dunwich – tradition says he was – it would be about March 1216, and his presence there must have put a considerable strain on the loyalty of his good and faithful subjects. For an army of foreign mercenaries was accustomed, and expected, to live off the land through which it passed, and the chroniclers of the time report terrible ravaging and plundering, violent lawlessness of a kind not seen in England since the last dreadful phase in the reign of Stephen. If not actually afflicted by the presence of the king and his Flemish soldiers, towns were compelled to pay exorbitant sums of money to be spared such unwelcome visitations. Not surprisingly, those very chroniclers on whom we have to rely for accounts of what it all meant to the ordinary people were themselves often confused as to the sequence of events. In May, 1216, the French Prince Louis joined the insurgent barons in London. While the king was away in the south-west, another army of a kind visited the eastern counties, and it is to this that Matthew Paris (*Historia Anglorum*) was evidently referring when he wrote:

At the same time a certain section of the barons, who had remained in London, rode out and invaded the region of Cambridge, looting it, and captured the castle and took away with them in fetters twenty soldiers found there. Proceeding thence through the counties of Norfolk and Suffolk, they took the fortresses and plundered the inhabitants, the people being wretchedly ground as it were between two millstones turning in opposite directions, namely that of the barons and that of the king's adherents. They also compelled the towns of Yarmouth, Dunwich and Ipswich to pay heavy ransom. In this they unfortunately provoked God to anger, as subsequent events lead one to infer, in that people became ever more troublesome to people, servant against servant, subject against master, low-born against noble, laymen against the religious.

Twice in the space of a few months, then, Dunwich was involved in this war-game. Their Pales Dyke probably saved them from the worst effects of looting, and they may have escaped with a sum of money handed over for 'protection' on each occasion. They might even have got away with a very small exaction, using a combination of threats, promises and guile. Several episodes, which only appear in the records after the death of King John and the return to a semblance of law and order, reveal that the men of Dunwich were learning to play the game in their own way.

In Sept. 1216 the Justiciar, acting for the young King Henry, wrote to his chamberlain:

> We order you to release at once 7 sacks of wool, 3 lasts and 15 'dickers' (150) of hides which the men of Dunwich took of the merchandise of Stephen de Croy and are held at Scarborough, as we have already ordered. You should also distrain on the galliots that they restore the goods at once, and let us hear no further complaint about it.

This was followed by another letter to Geoffrey de Neville, chamberlain, Robert Wodecock and Laurence de Dunewic, 'keepers of the galleys and ships which are at Scardeburg,' ordering restoration of the stolen goods. Then, a year later, a more threatening order concerning 'goods which your mariners of Dunwich took from Stephen de Croy and his associates, subjects of the king of France.' 'We shall distrain on your lands,' said the Justiciar, 'if you do not return the goods, or the price thereof.' The men of the galleys had apparently been making good use of their time whilst on royal service.

A letter, written in Jan. 1217, arrived at Westminster from the King of France:

> Our burgesses of Rouen have complained to us that, during the period of our truce (there was a truce between King Philip Augustus and King John, but that did not prevent Prince Louis from invading England!) many things were taken from them in England, although they did not take part in the war of our dearest faithful son Louis, wherefor we beseech you to cause to be restored to our burgesses at once their goods, lawful proof being given. Otherwise, understand that we shall in no wise tolerate that they lose their goods.

The letter was passed on to the 'bailiffs and good men of Dunwich' with a covering letter ordering most strictly 'as you value yourselves and all that you possess' that they should restore to Roger FitzMichael of Rouen his missing goods, 'which Robert Wodecoc and Vincenius de Dunewic took from him.' All very legal and diplomatic; but those sacks of wool and lasts of hides – and who knows what else? – were not handed back to their rightful owners, ever. A new twist had been given to the war-game.

'Letters of protection' were granted to the burgesses of Dunwich. It was the correct thing for such 'protection' to be applied for, paid for, and granted. Safe-conducts were granted to individual merchants also, but unless the port of departure and the destination were in safe hands, and no privateers were encountered en route, the safe conduct was not worth the parchment it was written on. There was no guarantee of security even in the dealings between two English ports. In 1219 the barons of the Cinque Ports raided Yarmouth and wrecked the herring-fair, despite the efforts of the guardians, one of whom was Nicholas de Dunewic. A group of London merchants claimed a debt incurred by the whole town of Dunwich, the amount of which appeared to change with each successive court-hearing, of which there were no less than eleven. The Dunwich men – and they were the leading

citizens, FitzRichard, FitzRalph, FitzRobert and the like –
at one stage tried to evade settlement by invoking their
charter and their declared right not to be summoned outside
their own town. The London merchants retorted that their
own charter was earlier than that of Dunwich, and anyway
the Dunwich charter was invalid because it was made 'in time
of war.' The case was finally closed in 1229, ten years after it
started, and the London men settled for £30. The original
debt had been £166 plus or minus a few thousand herrings.
Let it not be thought from that, however, that the men of
Dunwich were a lot of rogues. The difference between the
debt incurred and the debt paid was undoubtedly accounted
for by legal expenses. The Dunwich men did not gain anything; the London men certainly lost a lot. The law-game was
expensive. To be sure – well, nearly sure – of emerging with
a profit, you had to know how to combine successfully legality
with illegality.

This the men of Dunwich were learning quite fast how to
do, as another episode illustrates. It began in 1216. There
had been nothing but pillaging, extortion, violence and
threats of violence for months. The Dunwich men – Fitz-
Richard, FitzHerbert, FitzWilliam, in collusion with some
English like Godfrey Mod, Umfrey Mowe and Arnulf Hase –
evidently thought that it was high time they hit back at somebody. The obvious target was Lady Margery de Cressy, lady
of the manor of Blythburgh and Walberswick. Not just because she was an elderly, unprotected widow, nor because
two of her sons were in rebellion against the king; though
those two facts might possibly have influenced the decision of
the Dunwich stalwarts. Lady Margery, to Dunwich eyes,
represented Blythburgh and Walberswick, and those two
places represented a threat to Dunwich simply by being there.
There had been hatred towards them for longer than anyone
could remember. Now was the moment to give expression to
it.

They sallied forth to Walberswick and set fire to about a
dozen houses. Next they went to the manor-house and burnt
the old lady's chapel and all the ornaments in it. Then they

did something which I think you will find it hard to believe:
*'they dragged a certain image of St John by its neck as far as
Dunwich.'* My first reaction on reading that was to laugh at
the sheer absurdity of it. A party of grown-up men putting a
rope round the neck of a stone image (it might have been of
wood) and dragging it behind them for five miles along a
sandy road! On sober reflection, though, it is rather shocking.
Not the sacrilegious aspect of it; there is ample evidence, of
which this is just another example, that the superstitious
veneration of relics and images in the Middle Ages was by
no means universal, and that there was as much cynical mockery as there was pious adoration. Those Dunwich men were
probably drunk. What they did may have been to them 'a bit
of fun'; in which case I would have expected them to throw
the image into the river. They may have considered it as loot,
and set it up in their own church; or intended to; I cannot
believe that the parson would have accepted it. But there was
more to it than a stupid prank. The destruction of a chapel
and the deliberate desecration of an image had little to do
with the real issues of the dispute. It can only be considered
as an act of wanton malice, intended to hurt a pious old lady,
which it undoubtedly did.

She sued them, of course; claiming fifty marks from each
of the twelve named culprits. Unfortunately for her – though
I cannot see that she had any alternative – she sued them in
an ecclesiastical court (*curia Christianitatis*). The upshot of
that was that, after seven years of stalling, they sued *her* in
the king's court for suing them in the other court. Dame
Margery did not appear in person; she was old and infirm,
and had no wish to confront those heathen swine. Her
attorney defended, and lost. She was forbidden to take the
matter further, and ordered to have the culprits absolved!
She was also fined for a 'false claim,' but pardoned by counsel
of the king. That was in 1223. She sued again, in the king's
court this time, and the charge was brought against the
bailiffs of Dunwich that they 'vexed her contrary to the
liberties which she had by royal charter.' Thus revealing the
real cause of the whole affair. Her charter and that granted

to Dunwich both granted liberties which each party considered detrimental to his own interests. The bailiffs refused to answer the charge at Norwich; and at Woodstock; and at Westminster. Fair enough; their charter said they should not be summoned outside their own town. They were summoned yet again, with 'surer' pledges in the persons of William FitzRalph, Godfrey FitzAde, Adam FitzSimon and Robert FitzAlan. The pledges defaulted. The sheriff was ordered to arrest the bailiffs. (What about that charter?)

Joscelin FitzRichard and Laurence FitzRobert, bailiffs (but not according to Gardner's list), turned up at the next session, armed with the charter. Having displayed it, or defiantly brandished it, they returned to Dunwich. For there, and nowhere else, said they, would they answer to a charge. The king's justices sat at Dunwich in 1228, and 'agreement' was reached at last. The burgesses, represented by Robert Fitz-Reginald and Robert Clark (and *they* were not bailiffs, either), conceded that the men of Blythburgh and Walberswick should have in their towns as many fishing-boats and as many ships as they used to have, so long as they paid for each fishing-boat of twelve oars or more, to the said burgesses, five shillings per year; and for each boat of eleven oars (I know, but that is what it *said*) or less, they paid no toll; and no other tolls than that. Dame Margery, for herself and her heirs, agreed that she would not entice any of the townsmen of Dunwich to go and live in her towns of Blythburgh and Walberswick, unless the king gave special permission. (It sounds almost as silly as dragging saints by the neck!)

The old lady was not finished yet. I say 'old lady'; I do not know how old she was; but I know that her daughter was married in 1198; her husband died in c.1205; she had a son Roger who was married before 1201 and captured at Lincoln, on the wrong side, in 1217; another son Robert who was a fully-fledged knight in 1206; yet another son, the eldest, about whom more later. She must have been at least seventy by the time the above 'agreement' was made. She insisted on her charter being viewed by the justices, and a hearing was fixed for a fortnight after Easter, 1229. Had Dame Margery, or her attorney, attended that court, the justices would have learnt that she could rightly claim 'wreck' on the stretch of 'coast' between Eye Cliff and the port of Dunwich; and *that* would have started the argument all over again, as will be explained presently. They would have learnt that she could maintain a ferry-service across the Blyth River, charging one half-penny for every man and horse using it; and that she controlled the bridges at Blythburgh and Walberswick, charging one penny toll for every laden cart shod with iron, and one halfpenny for each cart not shod with iron, passing over either bridge, her tenants being responsible for the repair of Walberswick bridge. They would not have read in her charter one word about the tolls payable to Dunwich in respect of ships and boats passing through the haven-mouth.

They did not learn any of that. Dame Margery did not appear, nor send her attorney, to present her charter. She did not appear at the adjourned hearing fixed for the morrow of Ascension, 1230. She had been summoned to a court whose judgements were not enrolled in any documents we know of; where rights of wreck and tolls and customs counted for naught; but where, for aught we know, insults to saints were ultimately avenged.

12 Time and Tide

It may seem strange that the burgesses of Dunwich should have been able, or should have tried, to dictate to the men of Blythburgh and Walberswick what ships they should have and what tolls they should pay. Strange also that Margery de Cressy should be accused of 'enticing' away the citizens of Dunwich to go and live in her 'towns.' And my assertion that her claim to right of 'wreck of the sea' would only have caused further argument calls for explanation.

The accompanying map (Fig 8) makes for clarity and

economy of words. It is of necessity somewhat speculative. I cannot guarantee that shapes, distances and dimensions are wholly accurate; but events and known circumstances make it certain that the situation was approximately as I have shown it.

The southward-moving shingle spit – which from now on will be referred to as King's Holme – had almost reached the town of Dunwich. Only a narrow strip of tidal water, perhaps

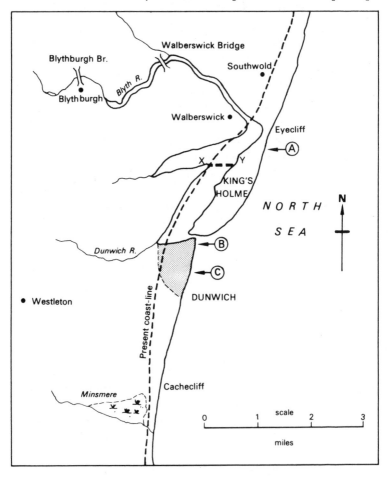

Fig 8 The Coast c.1225

no more than eighty feet wide at high tide, and half that width at low tide, separated the town from the northern bank. Evidence comes later – nearly all the evidence comes later than the events in this story – to show that the maintenance of this narrow channel was a major problem for Dunwich *and* her neighbours. Through this 'haven-mouth' every ship loading and unloading at Dunwich must pass to reach the open sea or return from it; every ship of Blythburgh, Walberswick and Southwold also. It was perfectly easy, therefore, for Dunwich to control the movement of shipping and demand tolls and customs. If agreement on an amicable basis, equitable from the Dunwich point of view, had not been reached in 1228, it could have been enforced by a catapult-crew on the town bank, with a pile of large stones at the ready, or by stout posts on each bank with chains slung between them. The Walberswick fishermen no doubt cursed, but paid. The Dunwich men earned more hatred than cash. And I wonder how many twelve-oared boats were converted to ten-oar boats after 1228?

As for 'wreck of the sea' pertaining to the manor of Blythburgh, it had meant something when first granted, three or four centuries earlier; when there was in fact a stretch of coast several miles long on which wrecks might have been cast ashore between the mouth of Dunwich river and the northern shore of the Blyth estuary, as far as Eyecliff. (That cliff does not exist today; it would have been located about $1\frac{1}{2}$ miles south-east of where Southwold front is now.) By the early thirteenth century there was no longer any danger – any hope, from the Blythburgh point of view – of a wreck on that stretch of coast. The Blyth estuary was completely protected from storms by King's Holme. The tides crept quietly up the sinuous five-mile inlet, then quietly down again, helped by the river to scour the channel. The lords of Blythburgh nevertheless continued to claim their right of wreck; it was still officially credited to Margery de Cressy several years after her death. Her successors tried to give it meaning by interpreting 'from Eyecliff to the port of Dunwich' as the seaward edge of King's Holme, but the men of Dunwich saw to it that such claims came to nothing.

Dunwich, then, had acquired a safe land-locked harbour two miles long and half a mile wide with a good deep channel down the middle; anchorage and wharfage for a hundred ships, or more if need be. There was no port to equal it between Lynn and London, and few better in the whole kingdom – for the time being. This situation is reflected in the amount of 'tallage' (an arbitrary tax imposed at irregular intervals, mainly on towns) assessed in 1218. The figure for Norwich was £100, Yarmouth £40, Ipswich £20, Orford £10, and for Dunwich £66 13s. 4d. One need not dwell too long on their significance, for those taxes were never paid. They were remitted, after being on the books for twelve years, 'because of help given to the king with ships' and 'because of poverty.' The first reason could not have been valid in the case of Norwich; the second was an excuse rather than a reason in the case of Dunwich. There was however a good reason why the Dunwich burgesses withheld payment, apart from the fact that the tax was wholly unjustified; and it links up with Margery de Cressy's enticing away of their townsmen.

Margery was not to blame. The Dunwich burgesses were more at fault than she was. But the main culprit was the sea. King's Holme had made Dunwich harbour; it gave no protection whatever to Dunwich town. At the point marked C on the map the tides continued to pound and grind against the eastern side of the town, which was not a cliff, but a gently-sloping spur not very much above sea-level at its edges. Common sense and a rudimentary notion of planning, to say nothing of centuries of experience, ought to have prohibited settlement on that area. That is perhaps an unfair observation to make. People had lived on that land, owned it, used it, for centuries; it was natural that they should cling to it; there was no known authority – no human authority – that could rightly move them. But the town was expanding as regards population. The Pales Dyke and its implied protection barred expansion westward on to higher ground. Those who occupied the lower ground were, in the main, the poorer classes. They must have become accustomed to having their homes flooded by an exceptionally high tide, until a succession of more-than-exceptionally high tides proved too much for them.

They could have been re-housed and re-settled within the bounds of the town – or without the bounds of the town, as they were in fact, very much later – on higher ground. There was still plenty of vacant space; enough, at any rate, for two more monasteries to be founded; but not enough land-owners, apparently, willing to give up a few spare acres for re-housing the homeless poor. So they left. And some of them evidently went to live at Blythburgh and Walberswick, 'enticed away' by Margery de Cressy. Some of the Dunwich men saw their departure as desertion to the enemy. I wonder whether the houses burnt in 1216 were the houses of those who had 'deserted'?

Whether out of compassion for the poor who remained, or out of concern for the safety of their own property, the burgesses realized that something must be done about this periodic flooding, which was getting worse. The problem was by no means peculiar to Dunwich, and by no means limited to a particular period. The monastic chronicles and cartularies reveal that all through the twelfth and thirteenth centuries, and right round the coasts of Yorkshire, Lincolnshire, Norfolk, Suffolk and Essex, the tides were causing havoc. The only known defensive measure then – and I know of no other now – was to build a 'sea-wall' ('bank,' 'dyke': the name varied according to locality; many of them still survive; none of them are really 'Roman'). To build a sea-wall was a mammoth task, involving much labour at great cost. Even when a man's wage was a penny a day, it meant so many hundreds of men for so many hundreds of days that there had to be financial gain visible at the end of the operation – or at least the avoidance of financial loss – for it to be undertaken.

The burgesses of Dunwich, true to form, first tried to alleviate the financial shock by sending a petition to the king in 1222 for aid in 'enclosing' their town, i.e. building a sea-wall. The king's advisers kept their purse-strings tight and politely pushed the problem back into Suffolk, sending a letter to all 'the earls, barons, knights and all free tenants' in that county, couched in these terms:

> Our honest and faithful men of Dunwich have informed us that the tide of the sea has occupied, and occupies from day to day, a great part of our town of Dunwich and the adjacent land, whereby great loss will result to us and to you unless preventive measures are quickly taken. Therefore we beseech you most earnestly, for love of us and for this our petition, that you render to those honest men speedy aid in this enclosing and embanking, to our honour and commodity as well as yours, that you may have honour and advantage thereby, and we may have reason to reward you with tokens of our goodwill.

But fine words, they say, butter no parsnips. They certainly build no sea-walls. I have no direct evidence that the barons and burgesses in the rest of Suffolk refused to help – except that Margery de Cressy's refusal can be taken for granted. Nor have I any evidence that any of them so much as contributed one man or one penny to help. It is a safe assumption, I think, that the men of Dunwich tackled the job themselves, at their own costs, and built a sea-wall along the whole of the eastern edge of the town, linking up with the Pales Dyke rampart to the south, and probably running partly along the south side of the haven. The wall could only have been built of sand and shingle, with a facing of clay, and revetted on the seaward side with timber posts driven into the underlying 'ouze'; or, more likely, with bundles of sticks ('faggots,' or 'kidds' as they were called in Lincolnshire) laid end-on to the tide. The cost of the undertaking would fully justify, in Dunwich eyes, refusal to pay the tallage of £66 odd. The sea-wall probably staved off disaster for a generation or so, and was thus not a complete waste of time and money; though I wonder if there were any farsighted enough to realize that, sooner or later, the sea would make a mockery of their efforts.

The future held other problems, which must have been foreseeable to many men in the Dunwich of 1225. Take another look at the map on p. 70. Two points, A and B are clearly marked. I think you will have no difficulty in guessing what is going to happen at A, opposite the Blyth River, or at B, the haven-mouth. The only question is – how long?

13 Hidden Deeds

There is a fascination about historical research which is unparalleled, I believe, in any kind of research except perhaps that of the criminal investigator. The scientist, for example, moves forward chronologically in straight lines from one discovery to the next. The historical researcher after truth has to move back and forth, covering the ground again and again, but leaving gaps which he, or someone else, hopes to fill one day. The clue needed to fill a gap may turn up a hundred years away from the gap to which it relates; it may never be discovered at all; it may have been deliberately concealed, or destroyed – and that in itself is a clue.

I was not happy with the conclusion of the Cressy affair. There was, I felt, a gap in my knowledge of it. Justice had not been done, or seen to be done. Dunwich had won an unfair advantage over Blythburgh, Walberswick and Southwold; so unfair that I could not understand how the lords of those places should have accepted the situation without putting up more of a fight. It was only when I had completed my story to the point at which I originally intended to stop, then decided to continue it a bit further, that I discovered the vital clue. The lords of Blythburgh and Southwold *did* put up a fight. *And* they won! Dunwich was *not* given, by law, such an unfair advantage as I thought. Dunwich men *did*, later, deliberately conceal a truth which it would have been to their disadvantage to reveal. They may, for all I know, have destroyed the document containing the truth; they certainly never produced it when it ought to have been produced. Had they done so, much strife and bloodshed might have been averted. The story of Dunwich would not have been very much altered in outline; but the men of Dunwich might have emerged in a more favourable light. The vital document came to light in the year 1409 – one hundred and seventy years after it had been written, and several months after I had finished, as I thought, my story.

I mentioned earlier the eldest son of Sir Hugh and Lady

Margery de Cressy. Little is known about him, as is so often the case with those who behaved sensibly and lived peaceably. Gardner knew that a Sir Hugh de Cressy was an itinerant justice for Suffolk and Norfolk, and thought that he might have been Lady Margery's husband. He was in fact her son. He was succeeded as lord of Blythburgh by his son Stephen, who was succeeded by yet another Hugh in 1263. Immediately after the death of his mother, Sir Hugh formed an alliance with Gilbert de Clare, Earl of Gloucester and Hertford, head of one of the most influential families in the land, and lord of the manor of Southwold. Both men, Earl Gilbert in particular, were too busy with affairs of State and county to attend personally at hearings of law-suits (except those at which they presided), but they appointed attorneys, men experienced in the law, to attend for them, and kept those attorneys on their toes. For two whole years they hammered away at this vexatious Blythburgh-Dunwich affair. Writ after writ was issued; summons after summons; 'a day fixed for the morrow of Midsummer,' 'a day was fixed for after Michaelmas,' 'a day was fixed for the term of St Hilary.' The Dunwich men 'could not answer without the king,' etc. etc. etc.

At last those elusive burgesses of Dunwich were pinned down. In the autumn of 1231 the mayor of Dunwich, Roger Forsell, the bailiffs – Henry Clark, John Bridgeman, John de la Falaise and Robert de Leche – other leading burgesses, their attorney, the attorneys of Sir Hugh and Earl Gilbert (who had just died) met at Westleton in the presence of the justices, and the whole matter was thrashed out. Nothing was said about burning houses and strangling saints. Here, in full, is the statement of their findings (the italics are mine):

The earl holds his town of Southwold as parcel of the earldom of Gloucester, and Hugh Cressy the elder [so this Hugh had a son called Hugh] holds Blythburgh of the king in chief by service of one knight's fee, as granted by Henry II to William de Norwich, and they [i.e. Blythburgh and Southwold] are *merchant towns* from time immemorial. There is a harbour, and has been since time out of mind, dividing the town of Dunwich on the south and the town of Walberswick, which is a hamlet of the town of Blythburgh, on the north; *and it forks* on the land of the town of Westleton towards the west. *From the entrance of the harbour as far as that fork* and so back to the town of Dunwich, the harbour is *part of the town of Dunwich*, by what authority they know not. All merchants, foreign and others, wishing to put in with ships and boats and anchor in the harbour, i.e. from the entrance as far as the said fork and back from there towards Dunwich (on the other side), must pay 4d. for each anchor fixed in the harbour or in the land of the town; and 4d. to Hugh de Cressy for each anchor fixed in the north of the harbour or elsewhere on the land and soil of Walberswick, and need pay no other anchorage fee.

From the fork of the harbour to Blythburgh is, and always has **been, a** *general hithe* of Hugh, of the manor of Blythburgh, and **on it the burgesses and men of Dunwich** should not make attachments or distraints upon **merchants or goods or ships**, because the hithe is within the town **and soil of Blythburgh**, and *not within the port and liberty of the town of Dunwich*. From the time of the Conquest all merchants, foreign and others, used to come to the said port and hithe and to the said towns of Southwold, Blythburgh and Dunwich with ships and boats, and unload and sell various merchandise and victuals, and then load them again and return, *until the burgesses and men of Dunwich maliciously hindered them from coming to the said towns of Southwold and Blythburgh.*

And the mayor and burgesses showed no evidence, except the charter of King John, granting certain liberties within their town, *which does not give them power to do so.*

Those findings were confirmed by royal writ of March 4th. 16 Hen. III (1232), and judgement was given in favour of Earl Gilbert and Sir Hugh.

That must be one of the most simple, straightforward and lucid legal documents ever written. To make it even clearer, let me refer you to the map on p. 70. I have inserted a line marked X – Y across the middle of the harbour. South of that line the harbour belonged to Dunwich. North of it was the domain of Blythburgh and Walberswick, in which the men of Dunwich had no rights whatsoever.

It must have been a severe blow for Dunwich pride, and a slight blow at Dunwich pockets. Though nothing to worry about, really – so long as the harbour mouth remained where it was! But what if the harbour mouth should move to somewhere else? As the more farsighted men of Dunwich may have already foreseen. Then there *would* be trouble.

Now, I want you to read the next twenty-five chapters bearing in mind that:

(a) I did not know that that document of 1232 existed when I wrote them.

(b) **The burgesses of Dunwich** *did* know that it existed.

(c) **The men of Blythburgh, Walberswick and Southwold** knew that it existed, *but could not find* it when it was most needed.

14 Boom Town

The second quarter of the thirteenth century was undoubtedly the heyday of Dunwich. In those twenty-five years, despite the interference to commerce caused by wars and rumours of wars, and by rivalry between one port and another, trade was steadily on the increase; more and more ships were built; longer and more frequent voyages undertaken; Dunwich merchants got richer and richer. Their plea of 'poverty' to the tax-man simply meant that they had become more experienced in the art of evasion. Pressed for an honest explanation, they would, I think, have said: 'We have better ways of spending our money.' Covering this period of twenty-five years are more than sixty entries relating to Dunwich in the various official records: Patent Rolls, Close Rolls, Curia Regis Rolls, Feet of Fines, Pipe Rolls, etc. If I quoted them all in full in chronological order it would give a good idea of the complexitiy of growth of a thriving port in the Middle Ages. It might also, I fear, prove rather indigestible, so I will summarise and briefly comment.

Since we are dealing mainly with maritime commerce, it

would have been fitting to begin with a detailed description of the port and harbour installations. Such details do not often figure in the records, yet there is one remarkably revealing case in the *Curia Regis* Roll of 1228. It concerns a dispute between the men of Yarmouth and Roger FitzOsbert, lord of the manor of Lothingland, very similar to that between Dunwich and the lords of Blythburgh. The Yarmouth men, paying a fee-farm rent of £55 and having, as they said, 'only the four winds and the sea,' accused FitzOsbert of setting up a port on the other side of the river and enticing merchants and ships away from them. They say that 'he causes ships to be unloaded there *cum molis ascere et ferro;*' which means either that he had made a wharf, using piles of steel and iron, or that he had erected a sort of crane or winding-gear, partly of iron. 'Steel' at that date for either purpose seems most surprising. *Molis* ought to mean 'mill-stones,' though it hardly makes sense; it must be 'mole' or jetty or wharf. (And yet – it could be a clue to those stones uncovered at Dunwich in 1740.)

They say also that he set up a weigh-beam or weigh-bridge (*tronum*) 'where goods are weighed all day'; erected shops which were always kept open; held a market there at the time of Yarmouth fair and all other times; forcibly prevented ships from going to Yarmouth; and charged a toll of only 4d. per ship, whereas Yarmouth charged 8d. His defence was that Yarmouth harbour was 'public and free like all other ports, such as Dunwich and elsewhere; ships entering were free to anchor where they chose.' Moreover, half the water of Yarmouth belonged to Lothingland anyway. (The similarity with the Dunwich situation is quite remarkable. I wonder if the same sort of thing happened at Aldeburgh, Orford and elsewhere?) FitzOsbert was fined for undercharging on tolls; Yarmouth fined for making a false claim; and the weigh-bridge had to be dismantled.

Presumably, then, all one needed to establish a 'port' was access to the sea, a wharf or jetty of sorts, gear for unloading and weighing, and a market for the goods. We can be sure that Dunwich was more elaborately equipped than that. There would be numerous wharves and quays, each with the necessary gear for loading and unloading; ship-building yards and slip-ways; sail-yards, rope-walks, warehouses, fish-curing sheds, etc.; in fact all the features of a sea-port of yesteryear – together with all the sounds and smells and fascinating sights accompanying the same. The bailiffs and merchants were constantly engaged in improving and expanding their facilities. In 1233 the king remitted £67 10s. which was owing for rent, and a further £10 promised to him, to help the Dunwich men 'in the strengthening and improvement of their town.' That probably included repairs to the sea-wall, and certainly included work done on the harbour mouth.

If evidence relating to the port is scarce, that relating to the ships is even scarcer. We know what the ships carried, where they went, who owned many of them, and roughly what they cost to build or hire. For an idea of what they actually looked like we have to rely upon the not-too-reliable impressions of contemporary artists, or much later artists (some of whom, one suspects, had never looked very closely at a ship). They usually portray vessels of an estimated displacement of between thirty and sixty tons; broad in the beam; considerably higher fore and aft than amidships, with a single mast surmounted by a 'main-top' — a sort of bath-tub affair used as a look-out post – and steered by means of a large 'oar' fastened on the starboard side ('steer side'). They must in fact have been very much more elaborately fitted out than those simplistic drawings suggest.

There were two galleys stationed at Dunwich, in the charge of Robert Frese and Reginald Cock. The whole galley-fleet in 1235 seems to have numbered eighteen (Southampton 1, Thames 2, Ireland 6, Bristol 2, Winchelsea 2, Romney 3), only a third of what it had been thirty years before. Galleys were being phased out – only one more was to be built at Dunwich – and replaced by larger merchant ships, the carrying capacity of which was usually indicated as so many casks or tuns (*dolia*) of wine. Eighty casks was the largest number at this date; later it increased to 120. These ships were built by private individuals, owned and managed by them, and hired by the king when necessary for purposes of State.

The king endeavoured to maintain control of the ports, and succeeded to a limited extent. In theory he could call on the service of ships and men as of right. In practice he often had to ask nicely for it, and always had to pay for it in some form or other. In 1229 it 'well pleased the king' that the men of Dunwich should provide him with '40 good ships of their port, well equipped with all kinds of armament, good steersmen and mariners' to be sent to Portsmouth by Michaelmas. When told that he would only get thirty ships, he accepted the reduction, but told them to get those thirty ships ready in time 'that the king may thereby be pleased and commend those men.' He ought indeed to have been pleased, for Dunwich supplied one eighth of the fleet which sailed from Portsmouth in May, 1230, carrying a few hundred knights and their horses, about four thousand soldiers, and the king's entourage to Poitou. Another round of the war-game had started. Most of the players were back home within six weeks.

In 1235 the good men of Dunwich were asked to fit out a good ship 'manned by at least 40 good men,' with provisions for forty days, *at their own cost,* to go 'with the first favourable wind' to Winchelsea. By some odd chance, there was no favourable wind. At the same time, March 1235, the sheriff of Norfolk and Suffolk was ordered to 'go in person to the port of Dunwich and other ports in his bailiwick if necessary' to procure ten ships for the transshipment of the king's sister **Isabelle from the Orwell for her marriage with the Emperor Frederick; and the mission was successfully accomplished. A Dunwich ship went on royal service to Denmark in 1240. In 1242 King Henry was determined once more on a warlike** venture, and demanded of the bailiffs of Dunwich 'five ships armed with *balistarii* (crossbow-men) as many as possible, and five boats' to be sent to Dover. The king did make the crossing; the expedition, as usual, was a failure. It seems doubtful whether the Dunwich men responded to his call, for later that year the sheriff was once more ordered to go in person to Dunwich to order all ships found there capable of carrying '80 casks or more' to 'go with the next wind' to Portsmouth to transport the king and his army to Gascony after Michael-mas.

In 1245 the theatre of war shifted to North Wales and Ire-land, and we know for certain that Dunwich ships were in-volved:

> 1245 (Pat. Roll) Mandate to justiciar of Ireland to pay Geoffrey de Dunewic 30 marks for the freight of his ship called *La Damaysel* in coming to the king from Ireland to Gannok (Deganwy) and back to Ireland, and for his losses in the long keeping of his ship at Gannock.

> 1246 (Close Roll) To the mayor and honest men of Dunwich. This is to inform you that, of the £103 1s. 10d. which you owe us, we have assigned to John FitzWilliam, Andrew FitzAugustine and Gerard FitzRobert £60 for the damages which they incurred with three of their ships wrecked near Gannock in our service. Pay to them, on the oversight of honest men, each his due share.

There was little profit or pleasure for the king, and no profit at all for Dunwich men in his service. Fortunately they had other fish to fry. Literally, for the prime commodity of Dunwich commerce at this date – at any date, for that matter – was herrings. In 1225, when restrictions on the movements of ships were tightened, Dunwich men had 'licence to go freely where they will with ships laden with herrings for trade.' In 1235 two Dunwich ships with cargoes of herrings, masters Richard of Walberswick and Augustine Ball, were wrongly arrested at Portsmouth. Eleven ships were arrested at Hamble by the Southampton bailiffs, not because of licence restrictions, but because the Dunwich men refused to pay customs duty, asserting that their charter exempted them from tolls and dues in every other port. This was too much of an affront for the Southampton bailiffs. They produced their own charter 'which was made before that of the men of Dunwich,' and won their case. Taking herrings to Southampton then must have been something like taking coals to Newcastle now. One contemplates with awe the apparent richness of the her-ring harvest, if the men of Dunwich and Yarmouth, having satisfied the demand for home consumption and met their obligations to supply herrings in thousands every year to the monks of Ely, could still send boatloads of the fish to ports hundreds of miles away.

As with all important commodities, the marketing of herrings evolved its own peculiar set of weights and measures. A 'hundred' of herrings was six score (120); six hundreds constituted a 'cade'; ten thousand made a 'last' (or load). They were dried, smoked or salted before being transported long distances in wicker cages lined with straw; but fresh herrings – varied occasionally by sprats or 'sperlings' – would seem to have been the staple diet of a fair proportion of the Dunwich population. Competition for the market was a constant source of conflict between Dunwich and Yarmouth, and elaborate regulations governing the landing and sale of the fish were in force all round the coast.

The other main exports of Dunwich were corn, wool and hides. Wool was reckoned in 'sacks' weighing 364 lbs.; corn in sacks of varying weight according to the type of grain, though it was usually shipped in 'quarters,' of which five made a ton. Wool-fells (skin still attached) were shipped in bales of 300, which must have weighed about a quarter of a ton; hides were bought, sold and taxed by the 'last' which seems also to have numbered 300; though I think it must have been a specific weight, for some hides could be three times the weight of others. It is obvious from those weights that a port had to be equipped with cranes and derricks for the handling of such bulky cargoes; equally obvious that a ship so laden stood little chance of survival when swamped by heavy seas. That is no doubt why the export trade of Dunwich and other English ports was very largely coastal at this time; the longest voyages made out of sight of land were the crossing of the Channel and the narrower part of the North Sea. Even the Gascony run, a round trip of sixteen hundred miles, would often be made with land in sight all the way. I shall have more to say about navigation later, but, being on the fringe of the topic, this is perhaps the place to say that there *was* in use a sort of mariner's compass at this time. The man who makes the earliest reference to it was Alexander Neckham in

his *De Naturis Rerum* written about 1210. He had obviously
seen one, and as obviously did not understand how it worked:

> 'Likewise sailors traversing the sea, when they cannot see the
> sun clearly in cloudy weather, or when the world is obscured by
> black darkness, and they do not know in what direction the
> prow is pointing. place a needle over a magnet, which spins
> round until, when stationary, it points to the north shore.'

He evidently thought that the purpose of having one of those
things was to avoid a north shore, whence all evil came.

It would be impossible to list all the imports of Dunwich.
I can quote a few which got specific mention: alum (from
Spain), corn, ashes, pitch (Hamburg), flax, bowstaves, wax
(Prussia), and occasional references to armour and weapons.
Some of the pottery found at Dunwich had been imported
from Germany. The 'ashes,' incidentally, were for making
soap. Much of the wool exported to Flanders came back
again in the form of cloth. The two chief imports seem to have
been wine and salt, both from Gascony. In 1224 Reiner Fitz-
Robert, merchant of Dunwich had a safe-conduct 'in coming
to La Rochelle and other ports of Poitou with his merchandise, to buy wine and salt and other goods.' In 1242 the con-
stable of Dover was ordered to restore at once to their owners
'three ships of Dunwich laden with salt which the men of
Sandwich arrested and plundered at sea.' In 1243 the king,
at Bordeaux, granted licence for 'the master of a ship called
La Blome of Dunwich to cross and put in either at Boston or
Lynn, unless he sell the wine in the said ship in some other
port before he reaches there.'

That indicates that a number, perhaps the majority, of the
Dunwich merchants were actively engaged in the carrying
trade, and that many commodities carried in Dunwich vessels
were destined for ports all over north-western Europe. I had
assumed that the financial risk – and it was a very considerable risk – was one which the merchants and ship-owners bore
entirely on their own shoulders, or pockets. One interesting
entry occurs in the Curia Regis Roll of 1233 to show that this
was not so. Richard FitzAlexander successfully claimed from
another merchant, Dionys Fitz Ralph and his wife Basilia:

'six marks for a certain horse which he sold them; six marks which he paid to Robert de Cressy for a certain pledge; *six marks which he invested for them as a share in a certain ship;* and two marks which they owe him for the breakage of a certain ship, whereby he suffered loss to the extent of a hundred shillings.' Evidently, then, merchants invested their money in other merchants' ventures. Whether the non-mercantile element of the population was also encouraged, or permitted by the rules of the Guild, to have a flutter, I cannot say. A gamble was always a difficult thing to resist, but few gambles can have been more risky than to send a ship-load of goods on a voyage of several hundred miles, especially in winter. When one did win, the prize was worth winning, but not dazzling. There is absolutely no comparison between these ventures of the Dunwich merchants and the glamorous – often over-glamourized – adventures of the merchants in the sixteenth century who sailed across the oceans in search of gold and silver.

These Dunwich men were comfortably well-off, but the work which earned them their substance was a humdrum, ordinary, work-a-day task, routine for the most part. The king and his advisers frequently behaved as though they thought the merchants were 'made of money.' Some merchants, in inland towns rather than in the ports, were very wealthy. Some merchants, even in Dunwich, were no doubt greedy, ruthless and arrogant, like many of the barons. Such evidence as there is however points to the existence in Dunwich at this date of a body of men as interested in the welfare (not social welfare as we understand it, mind you) of the town as in their own; recognising, of course, that the two were complementary. Law-suits, on which we have to rely so largely for information – and which can present a distorted picture of the state of affairs – are mainly concerned with the 'rights and liberties of Dunwich.' There was, or appears to have been at this time, a relative scarcity of violent and outrageous crime.

One would hardly rate as even mild 'crime' the action of certain un-named men of Dunwich in 1242. The current situation in the war-game had rendered legitimate, for the moment, the seizure of goods contained in French ships in English ports. The rules of the game allocated a major share of the spoils to the king. Several ships from Rouen were relieved of their cargoes, which were classified as *res guerrinas,* spoils of war. Many of them had mysteriously disappeared when the sheriff came to make an inventory of them. What was left of the goods, rather less than the king's due share, were offered for sale. The Archbishop of York, acting as regent while the king was away in Poitou, was very angry when he discovered, later, that the king's wool had been bought for 6s. 8d. less per sack, and the king's hides for 13s. 4d. less per last than the current market prices (which were £3 for a sack of wool and £10 13s. 4d. for a last of hides). But business was business, as the archbishop should have known; he was actually staying in Dunwich at the time. Perhaps he was annoyed that he had not done some buying on his own account. Unfortunately, this tendency for seized goods to disappear was to develop into something really serious, as will be shown later.

I have said very little about individuals, beyond mentioning some of the names which have cropped up in connection with topics, for the simple reason that I know little. I wish I knew more, especially about this:

> 1237 (Close Roll). Edmund de Dunewic pledged life and limb that he would *fight a duel with five men,* as he promised in the presence of **Reginald Kaln, Richard Haselden, William Dernford and Hamo de Bockhampton,** or *more if they could persuade more.*

What sort of a man was he who dared challenge all comers at once? *And* in the presence of four justices of the peace! I know he came of a family famed for its men of action – you remember the Dunewics of a previous chapter? Dunwich men in general were doers rather than talkers, but here was one of them really talking big. Had he spent too long in Dublin, or was it the Gascon wine talking?

15 Time and Tide Again

Referring back to the map on p. 70, you may remember a dark hint that something was bound to happen at the points marked A and B. Well, it did. I think it happened first at point B, though the happening at point A must have followed very closely on the other; they could indeed have been simultaneous. The time must have been the winter or early spring of 1250, for on April 25th of that year the Close Roll has this entry:

> The king remits to the good men of Dunwich 20 marks which they owe him for tallage, and 10 marks which they had promised, and £47 10s. of their fee-farm rent due at Michaelmas this year, as an aid towards *the moving and re-making of the harbour* of his said town. Order to the barons of the Exchequer to give quittance.

What had happened was that the southward movement of the point of King's Holme had been accelerated by an unusually high tide coinciding with a strong north-easterly gale, completely blocking the haven-mouth. It is more than likely that such an eventuality had been foreseen, and plans made in advance to deal with it. There was no point in trying to re-open the blocked channel; its alignment was such that it would inevitably get blocked again. Instead, a new channel was cut, in firmer ground, on a different alignment and slightly nearer to the town centre. It would be lined with a revetment of stout timbers on both sides, and very probably protected by a projecting groin on the north side.

That was one half of the problem. The same wind and tide had broken through the narrow neck of the isthmus at the northern end of King's Holme (point A) opposite the Blyth River, which, with perhaps a slight delay while the waters were building up inside the harbour, had then swept through the breach and created a new haven-mouth. Surely the Dunwich men could have used the new harbour entrance instead of making another one alongside their former haven? Yes, they could. But that would have meant Dunwich using a haven controlled by Walberswick. They could hardly hope to impose tolls on Walberswick ships using their own port, and the lord of Blythburgh – still in the hands of the de Cressy family – was not likely to neglect the opportunity of imposing tolls on Dunwich ships; he could not claim the land, but he could, and did, claim the water. So the breach had to be stopped. It was, as soon as the new haven-mouth was ready. Again quoting from the Close Rolls, of Jan. 30th 1253:

> Re the obstruction of a certain port at Dunwich. The king, for the repair of his port and for the *stopping-up of a certain port north of Dunwich,* gives to his men of that town as aid the fee-farm rent for the term Easter to Michaelmas next. Order to the barons of the Exchequer that the men of Dunwich be quit for that term.

I have no idea what the two operations cost in labour and materials; it must have been hundreds of pounds, the equivalent of scores of thousands today. The task was one of urgency evidently tackled with the necessary expedition. Gardner quotes a document, which I cannot trace, stating that the new cut was made through the ground of William Helmeth. Peter Helmeth, his son, was bailiff in 1251, and it would appear that there was some gerrymandering going on, for 'William Helmeth exacted for every ship passing there four pence, and as much for anchorage, without licence from the king'. The mere fact that it was recorded indicates that someone complained, and 1 have no doubt that old William's attempt to establish ownership of the new haven-mouth was very soon scotched. I can understand him trying it on – after all, it was his land – but it is odd that he should have been able to get away with such blatant extortion even for a few weeks.

One feature not mentioned anywhere is that the new cut must have breached the sea-wall, which would not have mattered very much because it would have been useless by this time in any case. Another is that the disaster, if one may call it a disaster, with the threat of more to come, must have resulted in a number of inhabitants leaving the town. Some, in fact, must have been displaced by the siting of the new cut. They would almost certainly have been the poorer families, whose removal would have presented no problem. Some exodus is confirmed by an entry in the Fine Rolls of Oct.

1274, when the temporary Keeper of the Town was ordered 'to assess and let to the best advantage to trusty men *all empty sites* in the town, and to certify to the king the names of the tenants'. My frequent references to 'the King' may have given the impression that His Majesty took a personal interest in the affairs of 'his' town. That is not quite the case. In every instance it was some official – chancellor, chamberlain, justiciar, justice, sheriff, etc. – acting in the king's name. Which is not to say that the king did not know what was going on in Dunwich, some of the time.

For all the urgency and expedition, the work must have taken a number of years. The Exchequer did not give official acknowledgement of its completion until Nov. 1260:

> [Close Roll]. Since the king in the thirty-fifth year of his reign pardoned the good men of Dunwich £76 8s. 4d. which they owed in fines and amercements arising from the last justices' itinerary in the Dunwich area – so that, by the oversight of the then sheriff of Suffolk and the Abbot of Leiston, they might use that money, and other monies of the community, in repairing their port and making a certain cutting for the improvement of the port – inquiry reveals that *the work has been done,* so let them be quit.

No money was actually paid out by the Exchequer. All the 'payments' were in the form of a remission of debts. In 1261 all the debts of Dunwich were deferred, and continued to be for some years. In 1268 'for the serious losses suffered by our faithful men of Dunwich', they were pardoned four years rent, which amounted to £190 when certain adjustments had been made. In 1279 the fee-farm rent was reduced to £65 a year. That was some help, as was also the remission of a further £200 of debts in 1277, but the awful truth has to be faced – as it had to be faced by them – that the men of Dunwich were never again to be clear of debt. I stress this fact because we – I at any rate – often form the impression that the enormous financial troubles of our times are a modern phenomenon, something to do with our inability to cope with the complexity of modern life. There is nothing new or modern about them. 'Pouring money down the drain' was being practised long before drains were invented.

I do not know whether the realisation of that awful truth was as shattering to the men of Dunwich as it would have been to me. I cannot say for certain what effect that natural calamity had on the minds and hearts of Dunwich men. Disaster is said to bring out the best in some people; the worst in others. It certainly did do that in Dunwich. The never-ending conflict between the best and the worst in human behaviour was intensified from then on.

Since the evil that men do gets nearly all the publicity, and to record it – as I must – is to risk presenting a one-sided picture, I propose in the next chapter to tell first of normal life and activity in Dunwich over the next quarter-century or so. Let me warn you, though, that 'normal' did not then, as it does not now, necessarily mean 'good' or 'sane.'

16 Carrying On

Though temporarily crippled, Dunwich did not depart from the stage of commerce and politics. Her ships still sailed the seas. There were other ports. It would have taken an awful lot of disasters to stop the wine-trade. In 1250 the *Champen* of Dunwich put in at Boston with twenty-five casks exempted from seizure. In 1253 *La Blome,* master Thomas Vivian, unshipped 80 casks at London free of toll for William de Faucham. In 1258 Roger Bigod, earl marshal, was given the special task of supervising imports of wine at ports in Norfolk and Suffolk. Two years later he had to ensure that the despatchers of wine did not become receivers of bread by stopping all exports of corn, except to London.

There were obviously fewer foreign ships putting in at Dunwich for a decade or so, which meant a considerable impoverishment of the town. Some of the foreigners who did go there were treated in a manner hardly calculated to encourage their return. In 1258 one Reynold Lenfant, *citizen*

of Acre — he was a long way from home! — had a cargo worth
more than £70 seized at Dunwich; why, or by whom, or who
had the goods, was never fully established. In the summer of
1260 a Hamburg ship, laden with corn, was on its way to
Boston when it was attacked at sea off Dunwich, by Dunwich
men, part of the cargo stolen, the rest thrown overboard, and
the ship damaged. There must have been something drastically wrong with the weather, or with politics, for corn to be
imported into Lincolnshire. There must have been something
drastically wrong with Dunwich, for that sort of thing to happen – but more of that later.

The king could not, and evidently did not, expect to be
able to call on his good men of Dunwich for service on the
same scale as previously. They sent no ships at all for King
Henry's trip to Gascony in 1253, and it is unlikely that they
helped with the 'transfretation' of Queen Eleanor and Prince
Edward in the following year, although a royal agent was sent
to Dunwich on Jan. 30th to commandeer 'all ships able to
carry sixteen horses, and all other ships of any kind.' He cannot have found many. Nor can the king's clerk, John of Suark,
who paid another visit in 1255 to obtain ships to transport
certain special friends of the king to Gascony.

There was however one form of royal service which Dunwich was able and very willing to perform, namely ship-
building. In 1257 the sheriff of Norfolk and Suffolk – some
years there was one sheriff for each county, other years one
sheriff for both – was ordered to go to Dunwich and arrange
for the construction of a galley of 56 oars and a barge of 28
oars. He was to choose four of the most lawful and discreet
burgesses 'who best know how to undertake the work,' place
them on oath to do the work well, and pay them. It is satisfying to be able to report that everything in this matter was
done promptly, fairly and efficiently. Two years later the ships
had been built *and* paid for. Well, almost. William de Swyne-
ford, sheriff, had paid to the men of Yarmouth £146 13s. 4d.
for building a galley and a barge, with part of the gear; to the
men of Dunwich £132 11s. 8d. for a galley and a barge, and

part of the gear. The difference in the amounts is explained by an entry in the Liberate Roll of 1261:

> Brief to the mayor and bailiffs of Dunwich to deck [*cooperire*] the king's galley there out of the debts due to the king from the men of the town, the cost to be certified by lawful men.

But they did actually receive the £132 11s. 8d., and acknowledged receipt before the justices.

The only person who got no satisfaction was the king himself. He had wanted the galleys and barges for his expedition to Wales, which, like so many other projected moves in the war-game, did not materialise. Perhaps fifty-six – or a hundred and twelve – Dunwich men were disappointed at the cancellation of the trip to Chester; perhaps not. There must have been better ways of earning a living than rowing a galley the whole length of the English Channel and half-way round the west coast of Britain, even in summer. In 1260 the barge stationed at Dunwich was loaned to Richard Earl of Gloucester, with all its tackle; but a year later the order was countermanded, Richard having made a false move, and the bailiffs were told to keep the barge safe until further orders. As far as I can ascertain, there were no further orders. Galley and barge never sailed, but lay cluttering up Dunwich's restricted anchorage for the next twenty years and more.

Other Dunwich ships moved. A whole fleet of them made the trip to Gascony in 1264 with the object of bringing back wine. Unfortunately the political situation resulted in twenty-three of them being seized and held in Bordeaux for almost a year. Master Thomas Vivian, however, managed to slip away with *La Blome* – I wish I knew more about that wily old mariner and his ship! – and landed his cargo at Winchelsea. The master of the king's household purchased twelve casks which the bailiffs of Winchelsea were ordered to 'send at once to Sandwich, so that the king may have them there next Friday. Urgent.' The king would settle with them later as regards carriage. For some unaccountable reason – jealousy perhaps – the Winchelsea bailiffs arrested the ship. His thirst satisfied, the king then bethought him of Master Vivian and his ship, prompted perhaps by a timely reminder from the old sea-dog himself. He dictated an order to Sir John de la Haye, deputy-keeper of Dover Castle, to send the arrested ship back to Dunwich at once, because the town and district of Dunwich 'were without ships in case of invasion.' Yes, I think Thomas Vivian definitely had a hand in the affair. I can see him now, the smile on his weather-beaten whiskered face showing only in the twinkle of his clear blue eyes as he recounted his bold escape from Bordeaux, pursued by the bulk of the French fleet which was at that moment heading for the English coast.

It is true that an invasion from France was expected. Or an invasion from somewhere. It did not matter all that much, to the men of Dunwich. A state of war, or the rumour of war, meant that they could legitimately seize alien ships and cargoes. In their enthusiasm they tended sometimes to anticipate orders, or make a mistake of identity. The king had more than once sent a stern reproof for too slack a compliance with his orders, or too keen an anticipation of them. As witness this (Close Roll of Jan. 1265):

> To the bailiffs and good men of Dunwich. Remund de Ripell, merchant of our good cousin the Count of Picardy, lately came into your port with a ship laden with wine. You, on the excuse of the disturbances in the realm, took 28 tuns of wine from the ship and kept them. Give it back, and let him and his men go free.

A new kind of commerce was fast developing.

Now for something totally different; something which, I hope and believe, can be entered on the credit side of the Dunwich ledger. Though really, the more one studies medieval history, or any history for that matter, the more difficult it becomes to distinguish between 'good' and 'not so good after all.' Take the foundation of monasteries, for instance. Was it wholly an act of disinterested charity? Or was it motivated mainly by a desire to secure for oneself spiritual welfare in the next world commensurate with one's material welfare in this? Did a monastery exist for the benefit of the underprivileged and poor? Or did it exist solely for its own benefit?

Let us not dabble overmuch in controversial issues, but stick mainly to fact.

Dunwich already had four religious houses prior to 1250. Within a decade there were two more. The house of the Black Friars (Dominicans, 'Friars Preachers') was founded by Sir Roger de Holish – not a native of Dunwich, but owner of one of those odd enclaves once part of other manors – in about 1255. Their house was evidently in course of construction in April 1256, when King Henry III sent word to his steward of the royal forests in Essex that he was to let the Friars Preachers of Dunwich have seven oaks for timber, as a gift of the king. The friars of Dunwich immediately got involved in a quarrel with those of Norwich as to the boundary of their respective alms-collecting territories; it was settled that Dunwich friars should not cross the River Waveney with their begging-bowls and blessings.

The house of the Grey Friars (Franciscans, 'Friars Minor') was founded by Richard FitzJohn and his wife Alice, a fact of more than mere passing interest, as you will see shortly. The date can only be guessed at, and my guess is 1256, as near to the date of the other friary as does not matter. Both foundations were probably – I put it no higher than a probability – made as a result of the mental state induced by the disaster of 1250; a gesture to placate divine wrath and avert further disaster. Of course I realize that it could have been no more than conformity with a current fashion. It could have been the outcome of two pious wives jealously competing with each other for prestige, or trying desperately to catch the eye of the Almighty. If it was hoped – and it could have been – that the presence of two more religious fraternities in the town would contribute to a state of brotherly love and universal harmony, the futility of such hopes was to be summarily revealed.

17 House of God?

Since we are on the subject of religious houses, we will stay there a bit longer. *Maison Dieu* (*Domus Dei*, God's House, Hospital of the Holy Trinity) was well established by the mid-thirteenth century, and well endowed: houses, shops and land within the town, to a rental value of 4s. 6d., and more outside; that does not sound much, but it was not the only source of income. The hospital provided accommodation for a master and six resident brethren – also sisters, later – and comfort, of a kind, for a number of poor people. Like the Leper Hospital, this one was concerned with caring rather than with curing. The most cherished possession of *Domus Dei* was a certain cross, which apparently was reputed to be a source of miraculous healing power, attracting pilgrims from far and near; thus being a source of no mean revenue. The house was not attached to any religious order; it was under the direct patronage of the king, who appointed to the mastership, and was very loosely controlled.

Too loosely controlled. In 1251, as the Close Rolls reveal, one Robert FitzReginald had taken possession of the house and all that it contained, including the cross, and disposed of everything moveable. The reason for his action is not stated. I think it might be contained in this entry of 1243:

> Order to the sheriff that – he shall distrain on all those in the town in whose hands he shall find wool, hides and any other goods contained in a ship of Pevensey which was arrested at Dunwich to restore to Robert FitzReginald and Robert Fitz-Joce, good men of Dunwich, 50 marks, 2 sacks of wool and 40 hides, or the price thereof, which were awarded to them in the king's court for their claim which they made upon the same goods.

The wool, hides and money would certainly not be recovered. No one would admit to having received them, even if he knew where they had come from. Robert FitzReginald, I believe, was exacting his deserts in his own way. He apparently made no attempt to conceal himself or his motives. The sheriff was ordered to inquire into the affair; in particular to ascertain whether the patronage of the hospital appertained to the king or not. That in itself shows how slack the management of the hospital had become. The sheriff, Robert de Rading, found that it *was* the concern of the king. He was told to exact a pledge from FitzReginald that he would appear within three weeks of Michaelmas, 'wherever he may be in England,' to answer for his transgression.

Early in 1253 a further inquiry was ordered, without result. On April 1st the mayor, along with Robert Fulconis, king's clerk, and four lawful men of Dunwich, were ordered to make further inquiry. The missing goods, wherever they might be found, were to be kept safe. No violence or molestation was to be done 'against Robert' – Robert the thief, presumably. A fortnight later, the goods had not been found. Shortly afterwards Adam de Cestreton, clerk of the chancery, was appointed as master of *Domus Dei*. Within a week the appointment was revoked, and Robert de Rading, sheriff and king's clerk, himself appointed to the office. Obviously that could only be a temporary appointment, and on May 16th Brother William of Bliburgh, chaplain to the Bishop of Norwich, became master.

The next Close Roll entry lifts the whole tedious business suddenly into the realm of drama. Nothing has been discovered; nothing recovered. The sheriff is once more ordered to inquire, by the oaths of honest men 'into whose hands the said goods came *after the death of the said Robert.*' Two questions arise. What was stolen that was of sufficient value to merit all this fuss? The answer to that is undoubtedly, I think, the famous cross. The other question: was Robert FitzReginald murdered, and if so, by whom?

The answer to that is now a secret. It was not, I think, a secret then. For that same Close Roll contains an order to the sheriff that the goods of John de Dunewic – remember the name? – who was *charged with the death of a man* and afterwards put on bail until the justices came to those parts, be restored to him, on security given. Likewise the goods of Alice of Hemenhall, mother of the said John, having been seized, were to be restored to her. Why was the killed man not named? Why was John de Dunewic not brought to trial before the justices?

Call it speculation on my part if you will, but I think that John de Dunewic – like his forebears, a man ever ready for a fight – killed the thief, with the connivance of his mother and the approval of all who were in the know. It could even have been settled in a 'trial by combat,' only semi-legal at this date. That is by no means the end of the story, though.

In 1256, John de Sancta Maria, king's chaplain, was appointed master of *Domus Dei* 'so that he dispose the goods and revenues thereof to the advantage of the brethren and poor dwelling therein.' There was not, apparently, a lot to dispose, for in Jan. 1258 (Patent Roll):

> Robert Fulconis, king's clerk, was appointed to defend Domus Dei of Dunwich, as certain alms intended for the support of the poor there have been withdrawn, so that certain poor are dispersed for lack of maintenance, and through litigation against the wardens thereof, their means are dilapidated; and he is to recover the said goods wherever they may be, in the said town or elsewhere. He is not bound to render an account or reckoning.

House of God – or house of thieves? That is still not the end of the story.

Robert Fulconis held office as master until 1290. During his long spell of duty, nothing occurred to warrant an entry in the rolls. The fact that he was well over eighty when he died surely merited a mention, but did not get one. He was succeeded by Robert de Sefeld, king's clerk. Such sinecures as the mastership of a hospital were traditionally the reward for long service in the king's pay, which was not particularly generous for the lower ranks. (For instance, a mission from Westminster to Dunwich and Yarmouth and back would earn a clerk the sum of eighteen pence, half of which would go in expenses.)

Robert de Sefeld tried to make up for lost time, was found out, and dismissed in favour of Adam de Brom, king's clerk. In the meantime, somebody – probably Adam de Brom –

had been keeping ears and eyes open, and had discovered that there was, in the abbey of St Osyth in Essex, a certain cross, which bore a striking resemblance to— Yes, it *was* the cross stolen from Dunwich more than fifty years before! It had been 'detained for a long time,' said the report. The abbot was ordered to deposit the cross in chancery, and eventually, on the sworn testimony of good men of Dunwich that it was indeed their cross, the abbot was compelled in the presence of the Chancellor to restore it into the hands of Adam de Brom.

How had the Abbot of St Osyth come to be in possession of the cross? It had been 'brought to his abbey' by one William Litequene, *brother of Domus Dei*, who was made a canon at St Osyth.

Somebody, somewhere along that long line, was lying. Somebody made a dreadful mistake. Was it John de Dunewic?

18 Turbulent Clan

It only needs a few troublesome individuals or families to disrupt the peace of a community. Dunwich had them, just when it least wanted them, as is so often the case. One of them was the family of Scott (variable as le Escot, le Scot, de Skot, etc.) which had been established there for a very long time. The original founder of the family was probably one of the 'Scots' whom the Saxons failed to repulse, and whose descendants stubbornly refused to accept the French, interlopers in their turn, as fellow-citizens with equal rights. They figure prominently in the records through the thirteenth century as bailiffs, officials, landowners and merchants, thus indicating themselves as men of substance and initiative. Walter, John, Roger, Rowland were all apparently 'good and honest men of Dunwich' in a literal as well as a formal sense. Then, suddenly as it seems, there comes a head-on clash between the Scotts and a rival group composed entirely of Frenchmen.

It rarely is easy to determine the precise reason for family clashes, but in this case it seems fairly safe to say that it was due to commercial rivalry and a sense of injustice. The latter was not imaginary. Countless details point to the fact that there was unfairness in the system. Safe-conducts were granted to some merchants but not to others; licences to trade were issued with discrimination; lawsuits were settled in favour of the wrong persons, damages unfairly assessed, and so on. The dice were heavily loaded in favour of those who could, or would, pay most for 'justice' and privilege – despite the noble phrases of *Magna Carta;* and there was a definite bias in favour of Frenchmen. It may come as a shock to find this racial discrimination still in being nearly two centuries after the Norman Conquest, but it was there beyond any doubt, and contributed in no small measure to the disturbances which racked the whole realm.

The Scotts – Gerard, Luke and his son Richard – and their associates started off by invoking the law, bringing a suit against the FitzWilliams, FitzJohns, FitzAugustines and their supporters, which was eventually heard in the presence of the king at Colchester in 1248. The king urged reconciliation, obtained agreement to a truce, and ordered the justices to do nothing unless the FitzWilliams etc. gave them cause to do something. The Scotts, aggrieved, kept on pressing their claims for a further eight years, with such persistence that action had to be taken. A hearing took place at Dunwich in Oct. 1256, resulting in stalemate. In Dec. 1258 the earl marshal himself, Roger Bigod, was instructed to inquire into the dispute yet again, and to ensure that the contending parties presented themselves, once more, before the justices.

Luke Scott and his clan got no satisfaction from the law, and evidently stormed away from the hearing – that is, assuming that they attended it – determined to get their 'rights' in their own way. It was rapidly becoming standard practice. The first hint we get as to what was their way is in a letter addressed to the King of England by the mayor, council and community of Hamburg in June 1260:

> We beseech your excellency, as we have already done many times, for prompt attention to our humble prayers in the name of God, and justice, that you cause Lucas Scotte and the men of Dunwich to restore to Master Willekin Kranen, our fellow citizen, the goods which they violently and unjustly plundered from him in your realm. For the said Master Willekin intends to recalls the attorneys by whom he has prosecuted his case for a year and a day as best he can, unless he soon gets help of your royal clemency. Accordingly we would be eternally obliged to you and yours for action in the matter.

Their courtesy was wasted on 'you and yours'; it certainly cut no ice with Luke Scott and his. Having tasted the fruits of piracy, their appetite for more was insatiable. How many such plunderings occurred at this time is not known. Litigation was such a costly, long-drawn-out business that many merchants preferred to cut their losses and remain in aggrieved silence. The Hamburg merchants, however, were more persistent. Two of them, Salomon and Tidman, backed by their associates, 'men and merchants of Richard, King of Almain,' lodged official complaint in Aug. 1260 that:

> —they came from their parts with a ship laden with corn, etc. to England and passed by the coast of Dunwich – Luke le Scot, Richard le Scot and many others of Dunwich came with boats and attacked the ship and took a great part of the corn contained in her without measure or price, maltreated the merchants and took the ship into the port of Dunwich and broke it, and sank a great quantity of the remaining corn.

That is the most detailed account we have of what was shortly to become one of the most commonplace happenings all round the coast of England, but nowhere more frequent than on 'the coast of Dunwich.' Perhaps, therefore, we should look upon it as a reflection of the times and the place rather than as a pointer to the character of the Scott clan.

The king ordered an enquiry, one of those commissioned being Robert Fulconis, and ordered the sheriff to take the necessary action, i.e. to appoint a jury, collect evidence, warn the defendants to appear, etc. The defendants simply made

rude gestures. Another inquiry was ordered. This time the
name of Miles of Hamburg was mentioned, and further details given about the cargo: 'corn, ashes, pitch and other
goods.' (It could have been a different episode, and the two
got mixed up). A trial did take place, resulting in a conviction, in November 1260. Whereupon the 'good men of
Dunwich' entered the fray, promptly despatching an angry
protest to the king:

> An inquisition lately made in Dunwich between Tedeman and
> Salomon of Hamburg – and Luke le Escot of Dunwich concern-
> ing an offence by Luke – *was at fault* as regards the amount of
> damages and in other respects also, because it was made by
> those hostile to the said good men of Dunwich, and by such as
> ought not to have made such an inquiry, and it was *contrary to
> their charter of liberties—*

In order that 'right may be done in the presence of the parties'
yet another inquiry was ordered. Meanwhile the ship, which
had been held in Dunwich all this time, was released and
sent to London, with what was left of her cargo, and there
held as security for the correct conduct of her owners. In
March 1261 the mayor of Hamburg was informed that Salomon and Tidman had received full satisfaction by judgement
of the court, and was told to release any goods of English
merchants which had been seized in reprisal. So 'justice' was
done, not because justice was right, but because the men of
Hamburg possessed the means of hitting back. Heaven knows
what it cost Salomon and Tidman to achieve 'satisfaction.'

That, one might suppose, was the end of the careers of Luke
Scott and his son Richard. Not by any means. Their piratical
activities might have been restricted – though I doubt it –
but they prospered in other ways. In 1265 the king granted
Richard right of 'free warren' in his demesne lands in Minsmere, Westleton, Middleton, Fordle, Walpole and Dunwich.
With that amount of territory he was clearly a very rich man,
and a keen sportsman. There must have been a 'close season'
for piracy as well as for hunting. His father earned sufficient
esteem – there were various ways of doing it – to be elected
bailiff in 1266. The feud went on unabated. In 1263 Robert

le Escot – Richard's brother, I think – was murdered by a gang led by Nicholas Perceval. The details are not stated, only the bare facts showing legal machinery in motion, but it is evident that the FitzJohns were involved all the time.

For the space of several years Dunwich resembled the Verona of the Montagues and Capulets. If there was a Romeo-and-Juliet element to enliven the gloom, or heighten the tragedy, history has been pretty silent about it, recording only the violence and the hatred, and possibly only a mere fraction of that. The vendetta seems to have reached a peak of hysteria early in the year 1270, threatening a serious and widespread breach of the peace just when the country as a whole was recovering from one of its worst crises occasioned by the moves in the war-game. For six months the justiciar, the sheriff and the royal commissioners tried to ascertain the truth. They had little success then. All I can do now is narrate some of the facts they did establish.

Robert Robelin was murdered. His nephew Peter accused Richard Scott, along with twelve other people of Dunwich, including several merchants and their wives. Roger FitzJohn also preferred a similar charge against the same people; which confuses the issue and puts the record in some doubt, because Roger had just had his head removed. The commissioner appointed to make inquiry into this had no sooner done so than he was ordered to find out who was responsible for attacking the emissaries of the escheator sent to collect the tallage from Dunwich. He threw his hand in, and another commission was appointed in June. One of the charges to be investigated was that Richard Scott had murdered Peter Fitz-John. This proved to be unfounded – on the evidence of Peter FitzJohn.

But Robert Robelin was dead, and his death was eventually laid at Richard's door. In 1272 he was officially charged, and found pledges, two from Norfolk, two from Suffolk, that he would stand trial. He did, and was acquitted! All his goods and chattels were restored to him. One of the most intriguing details in the case only came to light fifteen years later. Someone – I am prepared to wager that it was a FitzJohn – reminded the justices that Richard Scott had fled after the murder of Robert Robelin in 1270. It was too late now to have 'justice' done; but not too late to extract from Richard the sum of £28 16s. 6d. on the score of a technicality. Richard paid up, and he was 'quit.'

Then Richard did a bit of investigation, somewhat late in the day. Result:

> 1287. July. Commission to R. de Boyland, R. de Toftes, R. de Basco and W. de Pakenham to deliver from the gaol of Dunwich Leonard FitzThomas, who was placed in custody there after the last eyre in Suffolk *for the death of Robert Robelin,* and he has surrendered.

They say that there is nothing more efficient than the poacher turned gamekeeper, or the criminal turned sleuth.

The Scotts of Dunwich settled down again. We shall meet one more of the clan in a scene of violence later, but for the most part the sons, nephews and grandsons of Luke and Richard appear henceforth in honourable roles as bailiffs, mayors and members of Parliament.

19 Sons of the Devil

I would have incorporated the material of this chapter in the last, had I not wished to avoid in the mind of the reader a confusion matching that which prevailed in Dunwich; for it concerns the same feud, the same events and the same period, only now I shall concentrate on the FitzJohns and their allies. In them we reach the limits of the arrogance which, along with cupidity, was at the core of the unrest that racked the realm for centuries. I have referred to it, on a higher level, as the 'war-game.' At the lower level of somewhere between baron and burgess this arrogance lost the air of pseudo-dignity conferred upon it by 'noblesse' and appeared as what it really was – stark lawlessness and brigandage. I offered in mitigation of the Scotts' lawlessness the excuse that they were acting in tune with the times. I can offer no such excuse for the Fitz-Johns, unless it be that they were determined to outdo the Scotts.

Their origin is clear; they settled in Dunwich soon after William of Normandy settled in England and, like him, promptly proceeded to demonstrate that they owned the place. Wealthy when they came, they grew ever richer, as merchants and land-holders. No other name can rival theirs for the frequency of its occurrence in the list of mayors and bailiffs, though the very earliest mentions of them occur in cases of dispute with the men of Dunwich. Some of the clan, perhaps all of them, behaved themselves quite well throughout the period of Dunwich's rise to prosperity – to which I have no doubt they contributed – and credit must be given to one of them, Richard, for founding Grey Friars in 1256. Though I cannot help but wonder if that was partly a gesture of atonement for the deeds which his relatives were already perpetrating. (There are numerous parallels; the relatives of Geoffrey de Mandeville, for instance, made several endowments of religious houses.) Let us be charitable, and say that Richard FitzJohn wanted no part in the feud which had already reached explosion-point.

We need not go over again the facts, or scarcity of facts, as to its beginning. While the justices were still trying to get to the bottom of the Scott–FitzJohn affair, the FitzJohns gave them something more to think about. In the autumn of 1258 a complaint was made by William and Augustine, sons of William FitzJohn and Augustine FitzAndrew, that:

—as they went from the house of William FitzJohn to return to their own inns in the High Street, Richard, Ralph, John and Philip Brun and their accomplices attacked them with weapons and drawn swords; and when they, to escape death, fled to the church of All Saints of that town, Richard, Edmund [sic] John and Philip followed them with the said arms and drawn swords, attacked them and wounded them, so that they killed the said Edmund and John Brun in self-defence.

Who provoked whom, who had planned the attack, and why,

we cannot know. The Bruns, incidentally, never appear in the records again; two of them for a very good reason. They were not Dunwich men. Inquiry was ordered, and the sheriff received the usual orders, with one unusual difference; 'he is not to allow the possessions of the said William, Augustine and Augustine to be touched by himself or by any other until the truth of this matter be made manifest.' That, I believe, is an example of the discrimination of which I spoke earlier.

One of the commissioners was unable, or unwilling, to attend, so another inquiry was fixed, and apparently the young FitzJohns were cleared of blame. They lost no time in incurring more; they and their relatives, that is. I have failed to establish the relationships between them all, except that they were the sons, brothers and nephews of William, who seems to have been the real villain of the piece. He, I am pretty sure, was brother to the Richard who founded Grey Friars.

Roger – could be Richard's son – murdered somebody in 1266. He was caught by the sheriff and put in gaol. Then a significant thing happened. In March 1267 the king wrote to John de Vallibus, deputy-justiciar, as follows:

Wishing at the instance of our honest men of Dunwich to show special favour to Roger FitzJohn of Dunwich, whom you took and imprisoned, we order you that, if Roger finds you twelve good and lawful men of that town to stand surety that he will appear before us next Easter to answer the charge against him, then you are to release him on bail.

Evidently the FitzJohns had friends at court. Evidently they failed him, or he was too impatient. He escaped from the Bishop of Norwich's prison at North Elmham – an escape which cost the bishop a fine of £100 – was outlawed, recaptured, and beheaded. I feel sorry for him, in a way. I think he was too stupid – or too unlucky – to keep pace with the rest of the gang. His property, houses, land and mills in Dunwich, escheated to the king – automatically in a case of felony – and were later sold to Roger Christepeny, who was a close friend and associate of Richard Scott; which would not exactly please the FitzJohns.

Meanwhile old William was playing the part of a wicked baron in convincing style. Government in Dunwich had virtually collapsed. With Robert and Michael FitzJohn as two of the bailiffs that was perhaps not surprising. The king, worried about the non-payment of the town-rent and other monies due, sent the sheriff to deal with matters. Here is the text, translated from the French and shortened, of the letter in which the sheriff reported to the Chancellor on the situation early in 1268:

Sire—

I hastened to Dunwich as fast as I could, as you ordered – And indeed *that devil William FitzJohn* was come there again. Night and day he escaped me, so that I could not make distraint for the debt owed to the king. I found the clerk (appointed as 'keeper of the town') who could scarcely fulfil the king's requirements, and I asked him how much he had received from the town. He said he had spent some of it, and his lord had had some, for which he would not answer without consulting his lord. I asked for the accounts. He said that, if I wanted them, I had better seek his lord [i.e. FitzJohn] at Norwich. When my messenger arrived there, he found this William FitzJohn, who arranged his accounts to suit himself, so that nothing was settled concerning the matter in question, which amounted to a total of £150.

—When I had been in the town for a fair while, and had made arrangements for the collecting of the debt, and thought that all was in good order, I left the town – on account of my illness, and left my attorneys to carry out my orders.

Three days later, they came to hold a session in the king's name at the Guildhall [*a le tolhous*] and do other things which I told them to do. There came William FitzJohn and John Fitzjoce. They had fully thirty armed men prepared for a fray. They told my men that they were of the king's party, and feloniously flung them to the ground, beat them, threw filth at them, and perilously wounded them, so that with difficulty they escaped into the church [that would be St. John's] and robbed them of documents of the king, and of the accounts which the keeper sent me such as they were, and three rings of gold, and part of the fines-money which they had in a purse, and many other things which the bearer of this letter will tell you by word of mouth.

So I beg you, dear sir, your lordship – be advised now that never was there so great a matter as that which must now be dealt with to raise the condition of the king, and that of the poor people on whom they batten – If speedy aid be not applied, no foreigner will dare to come here, and the townsmen with their merchandise will go to another port, and not come back here, they say.

And because you, sir, told me that I should treat them kindly, I did all I could, and nothing came of it, for fairness and courtesy will never avail here – Sire, I am too small to take charge of such malicious people. If I do not have other help – I am convinced that the king will be the loser by my fault – And those townsfolk who are peace-loving, when they see their enemies armed, dare not do anything against them, so much do they fear that vengeance will be exacted on them, because so many have often escaped.

Dear Sir, please commend me to your lord – I assure you that I am most unhappy that you have had so many complaints about my service, but honestly, sire, it is not my fault.

And indeed it was not his fault. Whoever sent him there without a small army at his back was to blame. I trust you will forgive me for making such a lengthy quotation – it could have been nearly twice that length – but I felt that there was no better way of describing the state of affairs in Dunwich at that time. It is an extraordinary bit of luck that that letter survived.

Next came the mayhem of that Christmastide of 1270, which resulted in the murder of Robert Robelin – who, by the way, was the son of a bailiff – and reports of other murders. It is clear that after the disturbances some of the Fitz-John clan had good reason to disappear. Augustine's daughter Lettice thought that her father had been killed. Old William, the 'devil,' thought that his son Peter had been killed, and made charges accordingly.

Wherever they may have gone, Peter and his brothers were back again in November, in time for the St Leonard's Fair. This, for most people was an occasion for festivity and jollification. Traders came from far and near to sell their wares. The Prior of Eye was particularly keen that it should be a success, because for the modest sum of five shillings he was entitled to collect the tolls from all the stall-holders and traders. The bigger the crowd, the better the fair. The bigger the crowd, the better the chance of creating a first-class disturbance, thought Peter FitzJohn. With his ruffianly mob he rode in on the first day of the fair and wrecked it. He would have had plenty of willing assistants, for a good proportion of the crowd present were there in the anticipation of getting something for nothing, and few situations presented a better opportunity for looting than a combination of fair and riot.

Without exonerating Peter and his brothers in any way, some blame for that episode and others must attach to the king and his advisers. They knew what went on at Dunwich; they knew who was at fault. The order issued on Feb. 8th 1271 was tantamount to a licence to transgress:

> Whereas the king by charter pardoned John de Warenne, Earl of Surrey, and his household, and others who were of his household at the time of the disturbance [this was the civil war involving Simon de Montfort] for their offences up to March 10th 1268, and whereas William FitzJohn of Dunwich, and Richard, Augustine and Peter, his brothers [a mistake for 'sons'] and Augustine FitzAndrew of the same town, were of the earl's household and fellowship in the same, as the king is informed by testimony of the said earl, the king orders that these men be not molested on account of their offences.

The 'friend at court' mentioned earlier is thus identified. Of course I do not know all the facts, but it looks to me like a cunning ruse on the part of old William to get official blanket protection for all FitzJohn misdemeanours past, present and to come. If the FitzJohns were 'of the household' of John de Warenne, why were they not at Lewes? Not because of their loyalty to King Henry, I'll be bound.

Ruse or no, it failed. King Henry died, and his protection died with him. Thomas Earl of Clare knew all about the FitzJohns – who indeed did not? – and rounded them up; Augustine, Richard, Peter, Robert and Michael, plus John Arnold. Old William must have died; the only good deed he ever did, to my knowledge. They were kept for a time in Dunwich gaol, in charge of Sir Edmund de Caldecote, keeper of the town. To his intense relief, he was ordered to find twelve men of Norfolk and Suffolk to stand bail for them, and send them packing, with strict orders not to enter Dunwich again until King Edward returned to England.

To round off the story; they all came back eventually, chastened but otherwise unchanged. Richard and Michael were among those former bailiffs who in 1289 were found to have been falsifying their accounts twenty years before. Richard got out of that by taking a long holiday abroad:

1289 [Patent Roll]. Safe-conduct for five years for Richard Fitz-John, burgess of Dunwich, *who has been long in the king's service*, trading in divers parts.

He died in 1299, shortly before one of his ships fell a victim to Dunwich pirates. His brother Peter inherited his estate for a short time. Peter's son William tried piracy as a profession for a few years, then settled down with the others to a steady sort of life as part-time bailiff, part-time pirate, full-time 'honest' burgess.

20 Still More Trouble

I do not want to pile on the agony, but there is still one more load of trouble to be reported if the picture is to be complete. Let me remind you that my source-material is such that it must deal mainly with law-breaking and trouble-making; also that my aim is to give you an impression of what life was like in thirteenth-century Dunwich. If you get the impression that life was almost unbearable by merely reading about it, what must it have been like for those who actually lived it? Of course there must have been a brighter side to it. The sun must have shone on many a tranquil summer's day; children laughed and played in cobbled streets, went blackberrying on the common, picked posies of wild flowers and listened to the trilling of the larks, as one can still do over by Dingle. Young men and maidens fell in love and either indulged in careless rapture or blissfully looked forward to the satisfaction of desire. Old men sat in the alehouse all day long and tottered to their beds unmindful of the world and all its woes. On high-days and holy-days there was dancing and singing. On all days there was gossip and drinking. There were bumper catches of herrings, and safe returns from the sea. And none of those things ever got recorded. Why should they? If there had been a newspaper circulating in Dunwich in the twelve-fifties and sixties – (intriguing thought: would it have been written in English, French or Latin, or all three; and how many would have been able to read it?) – it would have recorded the very things which I am recording now.

It would have been interesting to be able to compare accounts of the Dunwich–Walberswick disputes as seen by both sides; better still, accounts of the Dunwich and Yarmouth–Sandwich and Winchelsea 'war.' The former was fairly quiet, as it happens, just then, and was to remain so as long as a Cressy was lord of Blythburgh, and until the sea intervened once more. The war between the two Cinque Ports – it could have been all five, but only Sandwich and Winchelsea are mentioned – and the two East Coast ports flared up again just before King Henry went off to Gascony in 1253, having left the queen and Prince Richard to deal with it. They seemed to think that all the blame for the Yarmouth fair being wrecked lay with the Yarmouth and Dunwich men, and threatened dire consequences of further disturbance. 'If you disobey,' wrote Queen Eleanor, 'the king will betake himself of your bodies, wives and little ones, so that you shall feel it for ever.' The king, she said, would deal with their complaints when he was ready to do so. Unfortunately, nobody thought of writing down specifically what the men of Dunwich and Yarmouth or the 'barons' of the Cinque Ports had done; it was always 'disturbing the realm,' 'molestation,' 'breach of the peace.' Except that 'robberies' does occur once. 'Robbery' is a term loosely applied now, and may have been so then. Stealing boat-loads of herrings definitely did occur;

but it is conceivable that flooding the market with herrings, or buying in bulk at a cheap rate to sell in a cornered market, could also rank as 'robbery.' It is certain that the trouble centred on herrings, and that it usually occurred at the time of Yarmouth fair. I am inclined to think that it was a case of poaching on what each side considered was its own preserve, very much like the 'cod war' of today; only there was no thought then given to the conservation of fish. A temporary truce was established in 1257, when the Cinque Ports were subjected to the same penalties as Dunwich and Yarmouth, and soon this particular war ceased to be front-page news.

There *was* a 'newspaper' of a kind, brought out in 1280 or thereabouts; more like a Government White Paper actually, though not intended for public circulation; a kind of Domesday Book brought up-to-date. This was the *Rotuli Hundredorum* – Hundred Rolls – recording tenure of land, rights, values, etc. In some cases it gave an almost complete population-list, but not at Dunwich. It involved an enormous amount of inquiry and a lot of writing most of which is of little interest to us now except that it is the only source we have of certain items of information. These are nearly all complaints about someone's transgressions, real or imagined. The life of a government official in those days was in some ways very similar to what it is now. He had no sooner dismounted from his horse and unrolled a strip of parchment than half a dozen hopeful citizens assailed him with a barrage of complaints.

We learn, for instance, that the Earl of Gloucester was claiming 'wreck' at Walberswick, which Robert FitzRoger said belonged to him; that Augustine FitzJohn was accused of taking fines for breaking the assize of bread and ale in Middleton. That should not be taken as yet another black mark against the FitzJohns; three others – the Earl Marshal, the Abbot of Leiston, and Thomas Weyland, the chief justice – were all doing the same thing, or accused of doing the same thing; and two of them at least could have made any FitzJohn look like a mere amateur when it came to illegal extortion. Anyway, there cannot have been that much bread and ale consumed in Middleton. Moreover, reference to the

Placita de Quo Warranto – suits to determine 'by what right' certain privileges were claimed – reveals that many of these complaints were unfounded. For instance Robert FitzRoger, when it came to a point of law, could *not* claim wreck at Walberswick, the Earl of Gloucester did not try to, and the men of Dunwich did successfully claim it 'for the king'; a combination of tact, resourcefulness and guile. As for Augustine FitzJohn's 'view of Frankpledge and assize of ale,' he came into court and said that 'he did not have those liberties, never had had them and did not claim them.' Which just goes to show that one should not believe everything one hears, even when it is written down. It does not, however, rule out the possibility of Augustine having persistently got his ale on the cheap.

To return to the Hundred Rolls, we learn that:

> The burgesses of Dunwich exceed the bounds of their liberties by appropriating to themselves hunting-rights on the land of Robert FitzRoger in Walberswick.

A paltry matter of poaching a few rabbits, no doubt, but it was the first shot in the next phase of the Dunwich–Walberswick war.

And that:

> They say that William de Southwold does not allow the burgesses of Dunwich to exercise the king's writ in Southwold.

That is such a peculiar entry that I think it must have been made late at night by a half-tipsy or very tired clerk. William de Southwold *was* a burgess of Dunwich. Neither he nor any of the other burgesses of Dunwich had any rights whatever in Southwold. The execution of the king's writ there was the responsibility of Richard de Clare, Earl of Gloucester, who held the manor (and got a licence to 'wall and crenelate it' in 1259).

William de Southwold (Suold) did do something reprehensible. I do not know what, but it earned him a £20 fine when the itinerant justices came round in 1267. The king was not at all displeased, for £20 was the very sum which he owed to his physician William de Fiscampes. He instructed the Exchequer clerk to pay the doctor when William de Suold paid his fine. Unfortunately for the doctor, though, William did not pay it. I would have thought that it was a bit risky, keeping one's doctor waiting for his money like that. King Henry evidently had the same thought. In 1270 he arranged for the doctor to be paid 'out of the first monies accruing from the issues of Norfolk and Suffolk, or from the fine of William de Suold, or from another source as may seem best.' On Nov. 16th, 1272, King Henry III had no further need of a physician. William de Suold, his debt still unpaid, was an unwilling guest of the Earl of Gloucester in Orford Castle. He tolerated the somewhat spartan accommodation until January, 1274, then decided that he had better pay off that fine, and was released on bail by Sir Edmund de Caldecote. I hope the physician got his money eventually.

That was just a digression, put in for the benefit of any medical men who may be reading this. The really interesting bit in the Hundred Rolls is this:

'They say that the present Earl Marshal [Roger Bigod] came with a multitude of armed men, knights and foot-soldiers, and attacked the king's town of Dunwich, so that no one coming to the town with corn or other foodstuffs could enter it; and the said earl sent ships and barges equipped with arms and men to invade the town by water; and hindered the merchants of the king for six days; and took certain of the townsmen and imprisoned them at Kelsale; and carried off goods, jewels and other property of certain citizens of the town; and did other outrages there in the neighbourhood, in breach of the king's peace and to the hurt and serious damage of the said citizens; whereupon King Henry eventually, upon the complaint of the townsmen, sent a letter to the earl exorting him in faith and friendship – that he should cause to be amended the said gross offences – and cause to be restored what had been stolen; but the earl completely ignored that order, and at present keeps for himself the greater part of the said goods.

That is perhaps as good an illustration as one will find of the state of the country during those last years of King Henry's reign. There were doubtless hundreds of such episodes, all over the realm, and scarcely any of them – certainly not this one at Dunwich – earned so much as a mention in the national annals. Allowance being made for the 'they say,' the righteous indignation of the burgesses, the hyperbolical 'multitude' and 'outrages,' and the lapse of time between the occurrence and its reporting, it still remains an event of some importance in the annals of the town, despite the rather farcical element which one cannot ignore. Are we really to believe that the son of the Earl Marshal of England, with an 'army' at his back, and a fleet of sorts at his command, spent six days occupying the town, or blockading it or whatever, all for the sake of a few jewels and a cart-load of loot? It must have been a blockade, and the looting done outside the town. If the troops had actually entered the town they would have ransacked it, or tried to, and there would have been serious clashes and numerous casualties. None are mentioned. The event does not tie in with any of the disturbances already mentioned.

That is one of the frustrating features about it; I cannot pin-point the date. It was clearly before 1272, when Henry was still alive, and before 1270, when Roger Bigod died, and seemingly after 1266, when Hugh Bigod died. I think it most probably links up with the rebellion of the 'disinherited' knights who took refuge in the Isle of Ely after the defeat and death of Simon de Montfort at Evesham. They were being supplied with provisions from Suffolk, and any trying to escape would have found it easy to do so via Dunwich. That would be in the spring of 1266. Or it could have been a punitive gesture because the town had shown too much sympathy with Earl Simon de Montfort and his aspirations. The king had in fact sent an angry letter to Dunwich and other ports in 1263, charging them with failure to prevent the entry of his enemies. Really, the political situation of that time was so complicated that I doubt whether anybody understood it then, any better than I understand it now. That Dunwich affair was probably a stupid mistake on somebody's part.

Of this we can be certain: the stolen jewels and other goods were never returned; and Dunwich did not go hungry as the result of a six-day blockade.

114

Again something quite different: a change from wars and litigation and robbery with violence, of which one can have too much. I want to try to bring you into contact with a handful of Dunwich men about their proper business, which was sailing the seas for trade. I can only do it if granted a measure of licence to exercise my imagination; let us call it 'poetic licence' for want of a better term. There are no first-hand accounts of sea voyages at this date, and very few facts relating to them. I will be as factual as I can, and will guarantee this much of reality: all the people named here did exist, in the role and status I have ascribed to them; the circumstances of the background are true to the best of my knowledge; voyages such as the one described by me were actually made at this date, long before it even, and certainly long after it.

William FitzRichard lived in the parish of St Peter's, midway between the upper town and the lower, with an interest in both. His ships, moored beside the wharves at the southern end of the harbour, were clearly visible from his house halfway up the hill. It was a large new house, different from others in that the lower part was entirely built of flints and stones, resembling all the others in that the upper part was a timber frame with infilling of wattle and daub and a roof of reed thatch. The whole of the ground floor was the merchant's storehouse. Its contents were constantly changing, and anyone peering through the stoutly-barred windows, thereby arousing instant suspicion as to his intentions, would have gleaned little information as to what was inside. Once admitted however, in the company of Master William bearing a shielded lantern, he would have found himself confronted by a representative sample of the commerce of northern Europe.

Boxes, barrels, bundles and bales. That was what his apprentice, Hugo South, had seen on first entering there, until his eyes were opened by his first geography lesson as his master catalogued his stock-in-trade. Red wine from Gascony, old stock at the front, newest at the back; pitch from Hamburg, needed in the shipyard daily; resin from Stralsund on the Baltic; salt from Arcachon; alum from Seville; flax from Lubeck; wax from Danzig; whale-oil from the Faroes; wool from Suffolk sheep; ivory and sealskins from the distant northern isles; cloth from Gand and Antwerp; tempered blades from Toledo – how could a boy hope to retain all that in his memory? Merely to stand amid that merchandise beneath those massive oak beams and listen to the merchant's sonorous voice with its hint of justifiable pride was to travel in imagination a thousand miles of seas. The passport to that journey was the heavy iron key that dangled constantly from Master William's girdle, not even leaving it when the stout oak door was unlocked for the daily inspection or when goods were taken in and out. At night the key was underneath his pillow.

An exterior staircase of wood led up to the first floor of the house, where the master lived with his family in a roomy hall hung with tapestries and open to the rafters of the roof. Here he dined and conducted much of his business, warmed by a charcoal brazier in winter, cooled by copious draughts of ale or wine at all seasons of the year. Opposite the front door was another at the back giving access to a stair which descended to a small yard where various offices such as kitchen, buttery and privy were located. To the right of the hall was the parlour or 'soller' into which the womenfolk retired when important business was being discussed or serious drinking done. At the other end were two smallish chambers – smallish by modern standards, that is – each capable of sleeping three or four persons, provided that those persons were not all as corpulent as Master William. Above the chambers and parlour was yet a third storey reached by ladders, and in one of the tiny bedrooms thus formed, tucked under the thatch, slept Hugo South and his fellow apprentice, 'the boy.' Through the little window high up in the eastern gable of the house these two could look out across the town and far out to sea. They spent but little time on such a pleasurable occupation, though, for the first light of dawn on the horizon told them, if Master William's voice had not already done so, that it was time to scramble down the ladder, which they would ascend again only after dark.

The two apprentices had no reason to complain of their situation. William FitzRichard was a jovial good-hearted man who treated others as he would have had them treat him. He was in business to make money, like all the other merchants; but money and the getting of it was not his master. He countenanced no idleness, no waste of time or waste of anything. He tolerated no unfair practices or double-dealing. He was one of the very few merchants who had refused to follow the lead set by the merchants of Bordeaux, Bayonne and elsewhere in trying to secure a revision of the merchant-law governing responsibility for cargoes of wine and other goods in time of danger. They wanted new contracts to be drawn, whereby the ship-masters would have borne a greater share in the loss arising from the jettisoning of a cargo to save a ship. William would have none of this. In any case, his goods were for the most part carried in his own ships, the masters of which were among the few along the coast who had strict orders to indulge in no form of piracy or privateering whatever, and who obeyed those orders, despite the many tempting opportunities, rather than risk censure or dismissal from Master William.

One reason why William had taken on another apprentice was that the boy could write. Master William himself could not, and his reading ability extended no further than the checking of a bill of lading, the details of which were already firmly fixed in his memory. Ask him what would be the profit, though, on seventeen dickers of wool-fells bought at £9 6s. 8d. a 'last' and converted to parchment in six months' time; he would tell you the answer before you had sharpened your quill and found the ink-horn. Being a member of the Guild of Merchants, an exclusive body licenced by the charter, he was entitled to his own seal. In actual fact he was using the seal of his grandfather William, made fifty years earlier. It was of lead, circular, about one inch in diameter, inscribed with the legend S.W.LE FIZ RICHART; in the centre was a neatly engraved ship with furled sail, rigging and steering-oar all clearly to be seen. If you would like to see it again, turn back to Fig 5, p. 59, where it is illustrated. The seal was picked up at Dunwich some three hundred years after Master William made his last voyage, on which it was not needed. Of all the many fascinating possessions of his master, that seal most fascinated the boy. He was never given the privilege of using it, and would never have dared to ask for such a privilege, but when the merchant pressed it on the blob of soft wax at the bottom of a sheet of parchment on which were painstakingly written words dictated to him, then the boy felt all the importance of his master's position, and something akin to pride in his own.

The boy was seventeen or thereabouts when William Fitz-Richard in the summer of 1278 decided that the time had come for another major commercial venture. Not just another of the routine trips to the other side of the sea, which were made at roughly three-week intervals throughout the year; something exceptional, involving a really big risk and a proportionately bigger gain if it succeeded. Every sea-voyage was a gamble. The bigger the gamble, the more calculated it had to be; the more one had to weigh up all the factors involved – political uncertainty, economic conditions, risk of war, the weather, the temper of the men, their skill and experience; above all, the availability of money. And when all that had been taken into consideration, it was still a gamble. At any given moment there were in Dunwich several hundred men, and perhaps three times as many women, whose eyes and thoughts were anxiously turned towards the sea; who night and day could not escape a nagging fear; whose only source of comfort was to put their trust in God and hope that the pathetic tokens of their faith might serve some purpose, his or theirs.

William had taken everything into consideration. His friend and associate William Barnard had recently been drowned in a storm on the return voyage from Gascony, but he had readily found another associate in John Cock, a man who did not place his money wildly. Trade with Flanders was at a standstill as a result of the recent embargo. There was talk of the requisitioning of ships on the southern trade-routes, and indications of increasing piracy in the Channel. The provision of whale-oil had sunk very low; lamps would still be wanted in the coming winter, and every winter yet to come. Walrus-ivory and whale-bone were fetching good prices now that the demand for carved pyxes and other devotional objects was on the increase. He had three sound ships and thirty good men standing idle. The weather seemed set fair. A venture to the northern isles was decided upon.

Accordingly, towards the middle of June, measures were taken to equip and man the three ships *Margaret, Holy Mary* and *Welfare,* with Henry Ringulf, William Helbe and Roger Jeycors respectively as masters. All three were cogs of about fifty tons, normally manned by six men each, though capable of carrying many more than that, in extreme discomfort. Built at Dunwich, they resembled vessels built at any other port in northern Europe, differing only in the decorative features adopted by the Dunwich shipwrights as their hallmark. The stout straight keel of Suffolk oak, some forty feet in length, curved up fore and aft to form a 'prow' at either end, which made for easy manoeuvring in narrow harbours. The hull was carvel-built of thick planks on sturdy ribs and caulked with pitch. Broad in the beam, a good sixteen feet amidships and not much less at prow and stern, the cog was a strong ship capable of weathering all but the very worst of storms, provided that the coast was not too near on the lee. It rocked and bucketed like a walnut-shell in even a gentle swell, but that was a feature of sailing which generations of mariners had been brought up to accept. The greatest defect of design was a tendency to be top-heavy when unladen, owing to the weight of the mast and main-spar carrying a single large sail, and the main-top lookout-post perched atop the mast. Added to that source of instability was the encumbrance of the lofty forecastle and aftercastle, imposed by the frequent adaptation of merchant-ships for use as ships of war. In times of peace the defect could be remedied to some extent by removing the upper part of both 'castles,' and further stability obtained by ensuring that the vessel did not sail unladen.

It was these measures that occupied the last two weeks of June and the first week of July, and kept the boy busy running back and forth between ship-masters, shipwrights, corn-merchants and his master's house. The outward cargo was to consist mainly of grain, not easy to procure at this time of year; the stocks that were left were of mediocre quality, and uncertainty about the coming harvest made merchants reluctant to part with them. At last however the three cargoes were made up, the refitting completed, provisions laid in, spare sails, ropes, anchors all safely stowed. All that was needed was a southerly wind.

Walter FitzRichard, William's son, was in charge of the commercial side of the venture. William had done the trip twice before, and would have gone this time, but his sea-legs were not as good as they used to be, and his wife's arguments stronger than they used to be. Hugo South was to have gone as assistant to Walter, but at the last moment he was taken ill, and so the boy was granted his dearest wish and allowed to join the expedition. Master William was reluctant to let him go, partly because of the lad's extreme usefulness at home, partly because – though he did not say this openly – he feared for his safety and doubted his ability to withstand the rigours of a long and hazardous voyage. The boy had proved himself to be a good sailor, but he was still very young. However, Roger Jeycors was keen to take the boy on the *Welfare* with him, and so he was signed on as master's mate, and shared the master's cabin in the aftercastle.

The departure of ships on the morning tide out of Dunwich was such a commonplace event that few people on the quayside paid any particular heed as *Margaret, Holy Mary* and *Welfare* were warped slowly from their moorings, then towed by twelve-oar long-boats through the narrow haven-mouth into open water. Half a mile off-shore the long-boat men cast off and returned to take the next ship in tow. If Master William, who came out on the third long-boat trip, felt any emotion, it was not evident to the twenty-four men aboard the ships. They knew as well as he did that something like a thousand pounds of his money was at stake. He knew as well as they did that their lives were at stake. That was what commerce meant, and one did not wax emotional about it. There was, for all that, a note of real concern in Master William's voice as, standing in the stern of the long-boat already heading for the harbour, he called out: 'God speed and keep you!'

The boy was too busy helping to unfurl the sail and trim the ship to consider how he felt. When he did have leisure to stand and stare, the town of Dunwich was already receding in the haze, and he felt a momentary pang at the thought that he would certainly not see it again for at least two months, perhaps never. As for the mariners who were to be his companions, he had given little thought to them, or they to him, beyond mutual satisfaction that John Gonomanaway was of the party. For John was an old friend, simple but sincere, who knew a great deal more than people gave him credit for.

The crews had been selected and allocated to their ships on the basis of their experience and ability to work together as a team. They knew each other, the ship and the master, and he knew them. The boy would have to fit in with the team, as Roger Jeycors made clear to him before they had put many leagues behind them. The crew's 'quarters' was a cabin beneath the fore-castle which would just about have held all six of them if all had lain still in their bunks. They never did, for whilst at sea three of them were always on duty at any one time; one in the main-top, one at the helm, and one patrolling the narrow deck to ensure that ropes were secure and report any incident however minor – a small shift in the wind was a major incident – to the master. Every four hours, day and night – measured on the hour-glass in the master's cabin – the watch was changed. Those coming off watch would crawl into their bunks and be asleep within minutes; not so soundly asleep however that they could not be out again within seconds if the need arose. A freshening wind, a sudden squall, a headland projecting too far across the bow would cause a shrill whistle to sound, a sharp order to ring out, and every man would be on duty to shorten or let out sail, tighten ropes, man the pump, double-man the helm and bring the ship to where the master wanted her, instead of where the wind wanted her.

Ashore, the mariner ate all he wanted, drank all he could and slept when he would. Afloat, his appetites and needs were subordinated to the will of the wind and the master. With any luck, the two were reconciled. Navigation was a matter of the moment, the here and now. The ultimate destination was known. That was all, as regards sailing. There were no charts, no sailing instructions, to be consulted. The compass in the master's cabin was there for emergencies which, it was hoped, would not arise. The ship's course was quite simply northward along the coast from one landmark to the next; not so near to it as to risk being driven ashore or running aground; not so far from it as to lose sight of it for very long. Everything depended on the master's knowledge of the coast as seen from the sea. Maintaining such a course meant a constant re-adjustment of sail and steering-oar. The latter was frequently rendered almost useless by the rolling of the ship. Offshore winds provided the safest conditions, but the only real safety lay in constant vigilance and the knowledge which all ship's masters possessed from a life-time of experience. Some of this knowledge was passed on to the boy and relieved the tedium of what seemed a painfully slow journey as the *Welfare* and her sisters ploughed steadily through the blue waters.

At sunset on the first day the north Norfolk coast was a purple streak separating the fire-flecked sea from a sky of turquoise. The sail was shortened, and lanterns suspended from the main-top and stern; the off-duty crew, after a meal of cold meat, bread and cheese and ale, dossed down in their cramped quarters. The boy was sound asleep in his bunk when the master came in to snatch a few hours sleep also, confident that, if the breeze held steady, the Lincolnshire coast would be visible at first light.

The next day they saw Ravenser slip slowly astern, then Withernsey and Hornsey. At night-fall the ships dropped anchor in Bridlington Bay, the masters preferring not to attempt to round Flamborough Head in the darkness. The wisdom of their decision was emphasised before dawn by a sudden freshening of the wind and a shift to the north-east which held them prisoner in the lee of the headland all next day and the day after. The boy began to think that sailing was not quite such fun after all, as the ship swayed and rocked with the great grey cliffs always there. Roger Jeycors, having foreseen just such a situation as this, produced from the chest in his cabin a chess-set carved out of walrus-ivory and taught the boy to play chess. As quick at learning this as at everything else he tackled, the boy was soon capable of giving the old man a worth-while game, and decided there and then that he would make a set of chessmen of his own. Several of the crew also played, though they preferred games with more of a gambling element in them. They were nearly all engaged in carving some trinket or ornament, and John Gonomanaway promised the boy that he would teach him the knack of carving ivory when they had some tusks.

During the night the wind dropped, and at daylight the three cogs weighed anchor and cleared the headland, then struck northwards again, tacking and veering all day slowly past Filey and Scarborough, sheltering at night in Saltwick Bay, with St Hilda's abbey perched on the cliffs behind them. For two days and nights they were able to keep a steady course some five miles off the coast. The landmarks were nearly all churches, and the boy came to understand more clearly the sailor's attitude towards religion, more practical than that of the womenfolk at home. Mouths of Tees, Wear, Tyne and Blyth were passed. Blue hills in the distance stood well back from a dimly-seen shore, and could still be seen when the master steered out to sea to avoid the treacherous Farne Islands. For two whole days no shore landmarks were seen, only the distant hills, which disappeared when the vessels moved in again north of Aberdeen.

They dropped anchor in Cruden Bay and boats were sent ashore to refill fresh-water casks, procure fresh bread, and meat if any was to be had. The boy was surprised to see that the men in the boats were all armed with knives, staves and crossbows, as though landing on a hostile shore. They were, for any shore a hundred miles from home was hostile, whether a state of war existed or not. One let it be known that one's intentions were honest, making payment for what one had, and emphasised that interference would be met by resistance. An hour sufficed to do all that was necessary, and allowed no time for the gathering of any ill-intentioned gang which might be in the neighbourhood.

Once again all sight of land was lost as the ships sailed due north for two whole days and nights; as nearly due north, that is, as the erratic compass and occasional glimpses of the sun and stars allowed. When land was again sighted, it was by the boy himself, perched in the main-top. For the first time, land to starboard. Fair Isle rose out of the mist, then faded back into it. Course was altered more to the north-west. The wind freshened and veered round to the west, presently blowing with almost gale force, driving squalls of rain before it, and surprisingly cold. The crew donned their thick leather surcoats and fur-lined hoods, and changed their canvas shoes for high leather boots.

Such weather was the very thing the ship-masters did not want just then. But they had to accept what came. There was no question of putting back to sheltered waters; nothing to do but give way to the power that ordered such things; perhaps put in a silent petition, if they were that way disposed. To have attempted to make headway against wind and sea would only have resulted in swamping the cargo, protected only by tarpaulins, and risking the loss of their ships. Accordingly all sail was taken in and the vessels allowed to drive before the wind. With luck they would find shelter among the islands of Zetland; failing that, if they stayed afloat, they would reach the coast of Norway. Any real danger would only arise when they reached one coast or the other. It all depended on God Almighty and the saints. Roger Jeycors was prepared to co-operate to the best of his ability, and ensure that his men did likewise. He said so, quietly, to the boy. There was no point in shouting it to God, for his words would have been swept away in a direction where God was not very likely to be found.

He was heard, nevertheless, or so it seemed. The wind abated just as the most northerly island of Zetland came into view, and that night the three ships were riding safely at anchor in the lee of Mid Yell. Next day the weather was all that could be desired; a steady breeze from the south-east filled the sails and drove the ships straight to the Farra Islands, two hundred miles in two long days and one very short night. This was sailing as the mariners and masters would have had it always; a clear bright sky, a sparkling blue sea, and a frothing white bow-wave breaking to either side of the prow. The air was cool, crisp and clear, so that the island of Suthuroy was sighted by the look-out man a good twelve hours before the *Welfare*, followed shortly by the *Margaret* and *Holy Mary*, glided proudly into the harbour of Thorshaven on the last day of July.

Walter FitzRichard and the boy were kept very busy during the next few days, while the masters and mariners, when not on guard duty, took their ease in the taverns of the town. The cargoes of wheat and barley were quickly disposed of at a fair price, but the return cargo, which was the prime object of the voyage, presented some difficulty. There was plenty of walrus-ivory, but the immediate stocks of whale-oil had all been taken a week before by ships from Denmark and Germany. Such an eventuality had been foreseen, and instructions given to the masters that they should proceed to Iceland if no oil was to be had in Farra. They were preparing to do this, and had already loaded one of the ships with a ballast of rocks for the journey, when the smoke of a beacon was seen rising from the hilltop on the island of Nolsoy, four miles away to the east. That could only mean that a boat had been sighted flying a tunic from the masthead, and *that* could only mean that a school of whales had been sighted.

The cry of '*grindabodh*' arose on every side; all other work in and around the harbour came to a sudden halt as boats were manned in haste. Runners were despatched in all directions, mainly northwards along the rough tracks of Streymoy, and soon other beacons sent glad tidings skywards in columns of black smoke. For this was a harvest-day in Farra the day of a whale-drive, such as might happen any time, but never with the promise of a better yield than on a fine hot day in early August. The crews of the Dunwich ships did not need to be summoned from the taverns. They were carried out on a wave of surging humanity which swept them to their small boats moored at the quayside and then rowed out to join the fleet of craft heading for the northern tip of Nolsoy. The boy had barely time to leap on board the *Welfare*'s boat as it came alongside to pick up harpoons then pushed off rapidly in the wake of the others.

More and more boats put out from the Streymoy shore, yet more from the village of Nolsoy on the narrow neck of land between the main island and its northern tip. By the time the rowers reached the point there must have been five hundred boats, two thousand oarsmen battling with the swirling tidal-race. Their quarry, a school of some three hundred caaing whales, made lighter work of the currents than did those intent upon their slaughter. Had those sleek monsters only known, they could have even then escaped to freedom and the safety of open water, for there were not yet enough boats out from Nolsoy to cut off their retreat. Not until another fifty boats had reinforced the cordon and closed in with it. Perhaps a third of the school, in particular the larger whales, strong creatures twenty feet and more in length, did turn and thrust their way through the menacing line despite barbaric baying from the pack of hunters. Great lashing tails stirred up the waters, flinging boats and crews aside like so much useless jetsam. The line of boats slowed down while those nearest to the unlucky crews pulled over to rescue their fellow-hunters, then reformed once more and moved inexorably on.

Escape to the east for any more whales was barred. Escape to the south was barred by a continuous line of boats from Thorshaven to Nolsoy. No orders had been given, for none were needed. The men and boys of Farra had seen and done all this a hundred times and more. They had no more need of being told how to hunt whales than a Suffolk man had of being told how to reap a field of corn or net a catch of herrings. The whales turned northward into the narrow strait between Streymoy and Eysturoy; there was nowhere else they could go. The two-mile line of boats behind them stretched from shore to shore. Panic seized those simple creatures as the air was rent by raucous cries that echoed from the cliffs on either side and a thousand oars beat madly on the water, hastening the quarry gliding to its doom.

The whales were trapped. The beacons spread the news along the strait, bringing men from Haldarsvik, Streymenes, Oyri, Hosvik, Hvalvik and other hamlets to block the strait at its narrowest just north of Hvalvik, where a quarter mile of sandy beach was waiting to receive the harvest of the sea. By tens and twenties the blue-black caaing whales were thrust by their own impetus upon the sand, where savage harpoons stilled their quivering amid streams of blood. The boats closed in, a solid barrier now, and any whale which tried in desperation to escape was pierced with harpoon, spear and sharpened anchor-fluke, so that the waters of the strait seemed turned to bloody turmoil as one by one the thrashing tails stiffened and a hundred carcasses lay still. Triumphantly they were dragged ashore to join the others. As the sun went down behind the western cliffs a count was made. Two hundred and five whales. The best haul of the year; the best for many years.

The excitement was by no means over. The sharing of the spoils gave rise to scenes almost as wild as the hunt itself, as landowners, boat-owners, harpoon men and rowers each laid claim to what they thought was their fair share. A hundred arguments were going on at once. At last affairs were settled more or less, and the work of 'flensing' began. Men with sharp axes hacked through the outer skin of the carcasses to reach the layer of blubber beneath. This was cut away in large pieces, carried in baskets to a stretch of level ground and cast into iron cauldrons brought from far and near. Wood-fires were lighted underneath the cauldrons, around which sat a merry throng attracted by this ritual of fire and blood. There was roasted whale-meat for all comers, as much as anyone could eat, and still enough for distribution in the traditional manner to the churches, religious houses and the poor of all the islands. When work was well in hand, and appetites satisfied for the time being, then the dancing and singing began, to continue all through the rest of the short summer night.

A similar scene was enacted twice more whilst the Dunwich ships were there during the next three weeks, but their crews took no part in them. They were too busily engaged in taking the ships from point to point in leisurely fashion to pick up barrels of whale-oil from the various owners. In between trips there was much hospitality to be enjoyed; the mariners would have been content to stay there longer, but it was time to be on the move homewards. Storms were becoming more frequent; a calm day often meant a day of mist and fog. So, towards the end of the third week, the wind being right, the laden vessels slipped away.

For two days and nights the weather was squally, the seas boisterous, as was only to be expected, though progress was fair. Towards evening on the third day, when Zetland had already been sighted to the south-east, the westerly wind increased with startling suddenness, whipping up the waves to what seemed mountains high. Seen from the deck of the *Welfare*, when seen at all, the sister ships appeared to be swallowed by the waves every minute. The look-out man in the main-top was ordered down; the sail and main-spar lowered, firmly lashed on top of the cargo; the ineffective steering-oar secured in a neutral position, and the *Welfare* committed to the will of wind and waves.

It was a situation in which Roger Jeycors had found himself placed a score of times. He showed no sign of fear, for he felt no fear. He knew that the storm would drive his ship before it, and that a hundred leagues of open water lay ahead. That is, if the wind did not change direction. Roger was not a deeply religious man. He knew his trade. He knew the northern seas, and the capabilities of his ship. He knew where his own capabilities ended and where God took over. That moment was now. The prayer he uttered was almost a command, differing only from the commands given to his crew in that it was spoken quietly: 'Westerly – keep the wind westerly – else let it drop.' To the south lay the rocky shores of Zetland.

The wind shifted imperceptibly to the north. Roger Jeycors

sensed it. His compass tended to confirm what he suspected. The sky above was black with driven cloud. The sky ahead was indistinguishable from the sea. It would have been hard to distinguish sea from land, if land had been there. Was land ahead? How far to the east had the ship been driven before the wind had changed? Listen! Above the howling of the wind, the creak of cordage and the hiss and rattle of the spray, he thought he heard another, deeper sound. One often hears that which one hopes, or fears, to hear. His eyes strove to pierce the murk that lay beyond the tossing prow. Again he thought he heard that sound. Only the watchman was on deck, clinging to the forecastle brace. The rest of the crew were huddled in their cabin, with the door open, waiting for orders. Roger opened the cabin door behind him and called to the boy, lying on his bunk. The lad got up and stood beside the master, clinging to him as the wind tried to sweep them both into the hold. Roger pointed ahead, turned to the boy and shouted in his ear: 'What d'ye hear, boy?'

The boy listened, one hand shielding his ear. 'Thunder', he shouted, 'Distant thunder'. So Roger had not imagined it. There was another sound; the sound of breakers pounding on a rocky shore. There was land ahead. Not very far ahead. Maybe half a mile. The master knew only too well what that meant. He had been wrecked twice before, once on this very coast, if it was the coast he thought it was. Leaving the boy, he stumbled forward along the narrow heaving deck, seeking a handhold at every step, and mustered the crew. Two men were ordered to stand by the anchors, ready to cast them overboard with double cables. The likelihood of their striking bottom in this depth of water, or of holding for more than a few minutes if they did, was slender in the extreme; but it was one hope. Two others were ordered to unlash the boat. To launch it in such a sea would be virtually impossible, but it was there. If it were launched, it would be smashed to pieces on the rocks more surely than would the ship. But it might not be. If it were, there would be that much more wreckage to cling to. The other two men unlashed the steering-oar and stood by it; clung to it rather. The oar was useless, but it might serve, if a cove or channel presented itself by some whim of fate. There was no question of casting any of the cargo overboard. It would have made no difference to the safety of the ship or crew, even if it had been possible to get at it beneath the tarpaulin, encumbered as this was by the heavy sail and spar. Not only that; Roger Jeycors had a rooted objection to throwing away a cargo which was the sole reason for his being there. While the ship floated, the cargo would float with it. There were no more orders to be given, for the moment. The master made his way back to the after-castle. Grasping the boy, he dragged him into the cabin.

The feeble light of the swaying lantern fell on the old man's face as they sat on their bunks, facing each other. The boy saw no hint of fear in the eyes which confronted his, nothing of the feeling which gripped his own heart. The man's voice was firm.

'Do you listen to me, boy,' he said. 'We may be done for. We may be not. Only a miracle can save us. I know of none better, when it comes to miracles, than our Saint Edmund, a Suffolk man. I'm not a man for praying, but do you mark this, boy. If we come out of this alive, I vow I'll make an anchor out of solid wax, and give it to the saint. That's a bargain, and you're my witness on't.'

Man and boy went out once more into the raging tumult. Showers of spray drenched the ship and blotted all sight of safety and danger alike. A thunderous roar assailed the ears. The boy felt numbed, helpless; too helpless either to think or pray. He looked at the shadowy forms of the two men clinging to the helm. Their faces were turned upwards, as it seemed. He thought he heard a hoarse cry from one of them, sounding like 'Saint Edmund save us!' He thought of the St Nicholas token which he wore around his neck. He tried to pray. Perhaps he did pray. Perhaps he merely hoped, with eyes closed tight.

The sound of the breakers was now terribly near. But there was something different about it. The boy opened his eyes. To starboard he could just discern a whiteness below a line of intense blackness. The thunderous sound came only from that direction. There was no whiteness ahead. The shore was on the starboard side. They had cleared the headland. Joyously he turned to face the master, who, to his surprise, was not exuberant.

Yes, they had cleared the headland. But what headland? Zetland was all headlands. They could be driving into any one of a half a dozen inlets or channels which separated the islands. The next half-hour would reveal the answer.

Roger Jeycors had not moved from his station on the deck. The boy stood beside him. In the dim light he thought he saw a look of quiet confidence on the old mariner's face. For a time they both strained eyes and ears without speaking. The eastern sky grew lighter. The wind was diminishing in force. The booming of the breakers had not been heard for twenty minutes or more. Roger laid a hand on the boy's shoulder.

'We're clear, boy,' was all he said. The expression of thanks to the saint which the boy had expected did not follow. As if reading the boy's thoughts, Roger said simply: 'I shall keep my bargain.'

An hour later, in broad daylight, the isle of Fetlar was seen and recognised a league to starboard. To complete the joy of all on board, the *Margaret* was sighted a mile astern, with *Holy Mary* close behind her. Both had hoisted sail and were making rapid headway. The *Welfare*'s master allowed them to overhaul him and come close enough for a shouted consultation as to their course before putting sail and steering-oar into commission. It was agreed that the three ships should take advantage of the steady northerly wind as long as it lasted, making landfall where they might.

Three days of uneventful sailing brought them once again to shelter in Bridlington Bay, where they rested for two days before setting out on the routine coastal crawl. The weather was so fine that it took them four whole days to reach Dunwich, and the boy had time to start carving his chess-men, with the help of John Gonomanaway.

22 Saint Edmund

While Roger Jeycors had been busy conducting the *'Welfare'* across a thousand miles of sea and back again, his bees had been just as busy in their own way. He possessed a dozen hives or 'skeps' which throughout the summer and early autumn were lodged in the hamlet of Dingle, about a mile north-west of Dunwich. They were in the small close of old Alice Wygmer, who kept a watchful eye on them during the enforced absence of Roger, and talked to them when she felt the need of conversation. Roger spent as much time there as his duties would allow, disregarding the pointed remarks made in his hearing about his relations with the elderly widow, and regarding with genuine appreciation the cup of elderberry wine which she never failed to produce for his refreshment. Bees were the only passion in his life. He worked on the sea, but he had no affection for the sea. His heart was here, in this fragrant little meadow. All around were other meadows rich with wild white clover and a host of flowers whose names he did not know, but whose fragrance he shared with his bees. To one side lay the marshland with its ditches full of meadowsweet; inland lay the heath. From the blossoming of Alice's apple-trees to the last days of the heather Roger's bees were busy all the daylight hours.

He too was busy in the fortnight after his return from Farra, collecting and preparing the honey and the wax. For he had a bargain to keep. When he had collected some twenty pounds of wax, he made a wooden mould in the shape of an anchor and poured the molten wax into it, then left it to harden well before removing the sections of the mould. It was not a work of art. It was not meant to be. But it said what Roger had to say; better than any words he could have found. The boy helped him. Roger seemed determined that he should, and equally determined that the two of them should go to St Edmundsbury as soon as possible. William Fitz-Richard fully approved of the proposal, adding a small barrel of oil as an additional thank-offering to the saint on his own behalf, and promising to lend them his horses for the journey.

On the following Monday morning they set out in the company of a score of others, mostly men who were combining business with pleasure or devotion, all bound for St Edmundsbury. It was a merry party which rode through the Bridge Gate, past the Hospital of St James with its ancient church, and out along the sandy lane to Westleton. A few miles further, and the boy found himself in a land hitherto unknown to him, for Blythburgh was the furthest limit of his journeying by land until this day. The ten hours of riding to the other side of the county was to provide him with as much experience and instruction in one day as had his long journey to the northern seas, and infinitely more pleasure. The road of grass and gravel meandered with no apparent aim, climbed out of one delightful valley only to drop down into another equally charming a few miles further on, becoming a village-street for a time, then once more a narrow track through open fields and woodland. Not many people were to be met with in the villages; the inhabitants were all in the surrounding fields busy getting in the harvest. The boy, seeing the sun-tanned faces of the peasants, and noticing how all the girls paused in their work to stare, and frequently to wave, remarked to his companion that he would like to live that life.

'Ah, boy, 'tis good now,' replied the mariner. ' 'Tis harvest, and the sun do shine. But do you come in winter, you'll see a difference. Life for them is hard then. They are not free as we Dunwich folk. They are bound to the lord of the land. No better than slaves they be.'

This did not in the least diminish the pleasure which the boy derived from the contemplation of the fields of golden corn, the woods, the flocks of sheep on the upland pastures, the villages clustered round their churches of stone and flints. There were frequent encounters with bands of travellers like themselves; then greetings were exchanged, and a topic of conversation provided for the next half-mile. Several times in the course of the journey they came upon a couple of figures clad in grey or black cloaks, barefooted, one hand clasping a stout staff, the other raised in greeting before being out-stretched in an appeal for alms. The reception accorded these wandering friars by the members of the party varied consider-ably.

Some answered the valediction of the friars with a reciprocal *'Pax vobiscum'* and pressed a halfpenny into the outstretched palm. Others affected not to notice them, and became en-grossed in their own conversation. Others broke off their con-versation to make audible remarks about 'idle beggars'; re-marks which the friars in their turn affected not to notice. The boy was uncertain what attitude to adopt. He had in his wallet a few pennies, one shilling and two groats which he knew would be needed later, but he did not wish to appear niggardly. Roger Jeycors solved the problem for him, after the first encounter which had cost him a penny, by changing the position of his horse whenever a pair of the religious brethren appeared, and directing the lad's attention to some more in-teresting feature of the landscape. Not that Roger was nig-gardly. He just felt no obligation towards these itinerant beg-gars who, he felt, might have served God better if they did some regular work, and who, he was convinced, would have known a great deal more about God if they had spent a couple of months at sea.

At noon the cavalcade halted for refreshment at Stonham. Most of them had brought their own food in their saddle-bags, but all partook of flagons of ale served by the ale-wife at the wayside tavern; while the horses, after a long cool drink from the stream, nibbled the grass beside the dusty road. About an hour after the resumption of their journey they caught up with another smaller party of travellers. Four men and a woman accompanied on foot a litter borne by two rather sorry-looking nags, proceeding at a painfully slow pace. Their slow-ness was explained when Roger and the boy, recognising the men, reined in their horses and inquired the purpose of their journey. The boy half guessed it as he looked at the pallid face, expressionless of all but pain, of the man lying in the litter, and heard the name of Nicholas Gonomanaway men-tioned. He remembered how, one day in the previous week, he had been passing the Gonomanaways' shop in the market-place and had seen a group of sad-faced people gathered round the shop-door discussing the desperate plight of the tenant.

The details of the story were filled in now on the road between Stowmarket and St Edmundsbury. The sick man was thought to be suffering from dropsy, and had been treated accordingly, with no effect. His stomach swelled until he looked like a woman in an advanced state of pregnancy. The doctors had abandoned all hope; as had nearly everyone else, including the patient himself. Not so his wife. She had hope of a cure. Only one hope, namely that her husband could be persuaded to seek the aid of St Edmund. He had agreed, and the party had set out on the previous day upon the agonising journey, hoping to reach St Edmundsbury by the end of the second day.

Hurriedly wishing them well, Roger and the boy left them to catch up with the other riders, and two hours later they were passing through the South Gate of the famous town. The members of the party went their several ways. The boy and his companion sought out the modest inn which had been recommended to them, situated in a narrow street just off the market-place. Their horses being safely stabled, they themselves took a short walk in the town whilst a meal was prepared for them. Entering the Abbey by the great gate beneath the Norman tower, the boy stood amazed at the solid magnificence of the abbey church. Never had he seen such a building. It seemed to him not one church, but three placed side by side, each one larger and loftier than the biggest church in Dunwich. Even Roger, who had seen many fine buildings in the course of his travels, was impressed; but his appetite would not let him stand and stare too long, and the two sightseers returned to the inn.

They ate their meal to the accompaniment of an exchange of comment and information between the taverner and the numerous customers who dropped in for a brief spell. No questions, and very few inquiring glances, were directed at them, for visiting strangers were common in this town. The boy, content to look and listen, learnt two things which surprised him. One was that all the Jews in the town had been arrested on charges of clipping and debasing the coinage, and taken to London for an inquiry. The circumstance had apparently caused embarrassment not only to the Jews but also to many shopkeepers and traders; it accounted for the extra care with which the taverner scrutinised every coin placed on his counter. The boy secretly extracted the coins from his wallet and felt the edges, reflecting that if halfpennies and farthings were clipped they would almost disappear.

The other discovery which surprised him was the obvious ill-feeling which existed between the townsmen, or at least some of them, and the inmates of the abbey. He became less surprised when it was pointed out to him that the town was virtually ruled by the abbot, and that that dignitary was as harsh and greedy as any feudal lord, indeed more so than many. He ventured to say that he thought the abbey a most magnificent and holy place. The taverner agreed that it was, but one of his customers asserted that those sumptuous buildings were not built for God or the holy martyr St Edmund, rather as a means of attracting pilgrims from far and wide in order to extract money from them to maintain the abbot and monks in a life of luxurious idleness.

Such thoughts however were far from the minds of the boy and Roger when, early the next morning, they entered the great church along with a crowd of others and listened to the office of prime celebrated by the monks. Roger leaned against one of the massive pillars of the nave, carefully holding his anchor of wax wrapped in a clean linen cloth. Through the narrow entrance to the choir he had a glimpse of the high altar on which stood a splendid crucifix of carved ivory. He thought of the perilous journey that some mariners had made to procure the walrus-tusks destined to be thus transformed into a thing of lasting beauty, and felt himself worthy to be there.

The office concluded, the monks filed out to their appointed stations and duties. One of them conducted Roger, the boy and a dozen others similarly bearing gifts, along the nave, into the north transept and so to the chapel of St Edmund. The old mariner kneeling at the entrance to the chapel, dumbly handed the anchor to one of the attendant monks. He was totally at a loss for words, so it fell to the boy to recount briefly the circumstances of their miraculous deliverance from a watery grave on a distant shore, the story being written down even more briefly by another monk to be later recorded for posterity. Then the gift of wax was placed on a low table in front of the shrine within which the saint's bones rested. Roger did not know – or perhaps he did – that at the end of the day his gift, like all the others, would be removed and either converted into cash or put to a practical use. No matter. He had kept his bargain. He, and his beloved bees, had done it.

The pair of them turned aside and were on their way out when they met a large crowd of people coming in, preceded by four men bearing the litter on which lay Nicholas Gono-manaway, looking a day's march nearer to death than when they last saw him. The chance of seeing a miracle performed was too good to be missed. They turned and walked beside the litter, which was gently set down inside the chapel. The attendants, for whom the spectacle was no novelty, went about their business with a dignity in marked contrast to the vulgar curiosity of the onlookers. One of them produced large bowls and a clean towel; another took a silver goblet from a cup-board; extra attendants were summoned from the adjacent cloisters.

The sick man was raised to a sitting posture and supported by two of the bearers. His wife tearfully supplied the details of the case, which were written down. Nicholas Gonomanaway asked, in a barely audible voice, that he be given to drink from the goblet of the saint. Filled with holy water from the stoup contrived in the side of the shrine, the silver goblet was handed to him, and he drank. What happened then is best told in the words of the official chronicler of the abbey, which were to survive long after all else connected with that September day in St Edmundsbury had been forgotten:

'The great power of God was put into operation through the intermediary of the merits of the gracious prince, as the man vomited forth a great quantity of poison, and in the same instant the huge swelling of his belly subsided. His stomach was reinvigorated within his strengthened body; the watery humour perished and, restored in a fresh skin, the man became well again. The two bowls were filled with a kind of vipers which he had spewed from his mouth shortly before, and the poison which had been confined within him spread abroad its putrid vapours. As the recipient of the divine antidote made his confession, in the same hour that he tasted the cup he felt himself relieved by heaven of his discomfort. And so, the consecrated host having been offered as an oblation to the Almighty and to his precious martyr, the man returned home with his wife and friends, and in a short space of time was wholly freed from the trouble of his sickness.'

Amongst the wide-eyed onlookers, most of whom held their noses, there might have been one or two who wondered secretly what magically potent emetic had been placed in that goblet. None dared express the thought aloud; nor would he have found a ready hearer if he had. The hard-pressed monks, assisted by the craving for fresh air, at last cleared the throng from the church, and normal business was resumed. Out in the street once more, Roger and the boy debated whether to stay another day and share in the excitement on the spot, or to hasten home and be the first to impart the news of the miracle in Dunwich.

They decided on the latter course, the more readily in that their inn was overcrowded and not very comfortable, they were expected back on the Tuesday evening, and money was running short. So they collected their horses, thoroughly rested and well-fed, and rode back the same way as they had come, reaching Dunwich before nightfall. Nicholas Gonomanaway and his party arrived two days later to find the whole town talking of the event.

There *is* poetic licence in that chapter; that granted to me , and that which we must allow to the unknown chronicler of St Edmund.

23 Reconstruction

Archaeologists can reveal the ground-plan of a vanished Silchester beneath green fields. History and imagination can rebuild the houses, people them, and re-create a town. The re-creation of Dunwich as it was before the first, and last, map drawn (in 1587) is a task to which the archaeologist can make no contribution, the historian supply only a few handfuls of facts, many of which turn out to be assumptions or deductions, thus leaving the bulk of the work to be done by imagination. I want you to bear that in mind and grant me, if you will, an extension of the licence already exercised.

One can still stand on what was the highest point of land in medieval Dunwich. To do so involves a slightly hazardous scramble and a cliff-top walk not without its risks. The only remaining landmark visible is a solitary gravestone, less than ten yards from the crumbling cliff-edge and perhaps no more than ten years from the inevitable topple. The view in one direction is totally obscured by thickets of briar and blackthorn. One hundred years ago the view eastwards would have been interrupted by the gaunt ruins of All Saints church. Seven hundred years ago, to have stood on that spot on a fine morning of late summer would have been to enjoy a prospect, if not unique, certainly difficult to match elsewhere in England.

The view westward then would have been blocked, not by briars, but by the solid fence of wooden stakes which gave Pales Dyke its name, set along the crest of the rampart, until one climbed up on to the wooden platform, already badly needing repair, on the inner side. Then, looking out over the pointed tops of the pales, one's eye would range over the cultivated strips of West Field, beyond which lay an expanse of heather, gorse and bracken such as is to be found there still. Immediately below was the ditch, much overgrown for lack of maintenance, and needing but another decade or two for nettle and briar to have taken control on this light sandy soil. The ditch when first constructed had been forty feet wide and fifteen deep. It was still, more or less, though width and depth would not have deterred another Bigod so much as the difficulty, having once got in the ditch, of seeing how to get out.

From this vantage-point the Dyke to one's left curved downward and seaward, interrupted by Gilden Gate and South Gate at quarter-mile intervals, until it became lost in the tanglewood that flanked the shore. Beyond it lay Sea Field, with a windmill standing out among the strips of stubble beside the Minsmere road, and two mills with whirling arms outlined against the sky. Northward the Dyke ran even more sharply downhill, past Middle Gate and Bridge Gate, to merge with the mud-flats of the river half a mile away. Along this stretch were houses built outside the rampart, mostly in the vicinity of the gates, and not very visible. The one building outstanding by virtue of its size and form was the leper church of St James, and even that was almost hidden by the shoulder of Leet Hill and the trees beginning to break its rounded profile. Beyond that, on the skyline, was the dark green of Westwood. Due north the river harbour stretched to Walberswick and the dimly-seen hamlet of Southwold; a mile-wide expanse of smooth grey water dotted with ships and fringed by cattle-speckled marshland. Seaward of it lay King's Holme, featureless in the distance and the summer haze, save where the dunes contrasted sharply with the blue-green sea beyond.

Eastward, traversing from right to left, the eye could scan the whole of Dunwich town; a network of streets and alleys appearing from this angle as a mass of buildings, less than half of them distinguishable because the houses and fences on one side of a street obscured all but the roof-tops of those opposite. Windmill-sails betrayed their presence as the only objects moving. Church-towers stood out among the roofs until the shadow of a passing cloud merged their weathered flint and stone with the dark grey of weathered thatch. The seeming solid mass of roofs was seen on closer scrutiny to be interspersed with hundreds of yards and gardens, in most of which a fruit-tree overhanging a wattle fence was all that could be identified. The occasional larger space enclosed by wall or fence denoted monastery, that of the Temple in the right foreground most prominent of all, distinguished by the circular roof of the chapel. In the centre of the scene a larger space than usual, between the lofty Guildhall and the tower of St John's, denoted the market-place.

To the north the downward slope of the town was broken by a series of conical hills, from one of which a slender wooden tower rose skyward. Further on, to the right, the concentration of houses, sheds and barn-like buildings was so dense that the shipyards and wharves were discernible only as a winter wood of masts and spars, some draped with red-brown sails. The haven-mouth was quite invisible, but a mast and main-top moving slowly through the roof-tops marked its line. Likewise the sea-wall was not seen; one knew that it was there because the town ended abruptly along a line stretching all the way from the end of the quay to the point where the Pales Dyke began. Beyond that line the waves broke ceaselessly upon a pebbled shore, while further out the grey-green waters stretched to where the sky began.

Eight hundred houses apprehended at a glance; a dozen abodes of prayer and worship; windmills, workshops, taverns, shops, storehouses, ships. There must have been three thousand people at that moment contained within the square mile or so of space enclosed between the Pales Dyke and the sea, though very few of them were visible from up there on the hill. Three thousand merchants, mariners, their wives and children, shipwrights, carpenters, sail-makers, tanners, blacksmiths, shoemakers, fishmongers, dyers, friars, pilgrims, alewives, housewives, bakers, brewers, beggars, idlers and at least one rat-catcher. What a hive of industry and contentment! What a model miniature world in which to live, flanked on the one hand by the bounteous earth and the other by the bounteous sea! How right that high above it all the sun should shine, and soaring larks should sing! What peace and harmony, what happiness was there!

Let us not shatter the illusion by recalling what has been recounted in preceding chapters, nor ask too many questions as we stroll down the hill, as tourists would have done in later

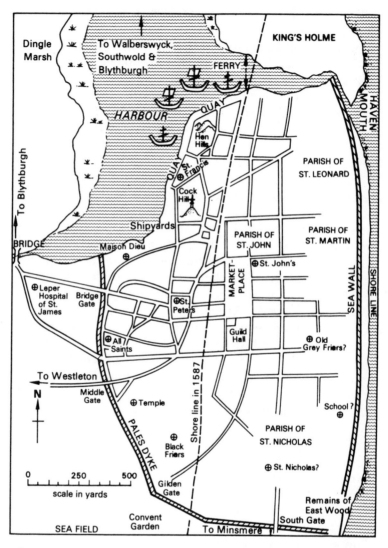

Fig 9 The Town and Harbour c.1280. Western half based on map drawn by Ralph Agas in 1587 and published in Gardner's 'History of Dunwich.' Eastern half of map is conjectural, but relative positions are believed to be accurate.

days, into the great open space that was the market-place, the centre of the town, the heart of Dunwich.

A dozen streets led into it from all directions, though only five of them were main thoroughfares; these came from the quay and from each of the town-gates. All carried a steady stream of merchandise borne in carts, on pack-horses or in baskets of all shapes and sizes, especially in the early morning and around noon. The rest of the streets were little more than alleys, wherein one fat lady carrying a basket on each arm would have been unable to pass even a thin lady similarly burdened until one or both had turned sideways. The ladies of Dunwich saw little inconvenience in this; it afforded many an excellent excuse to stand and gossip for a long five minutes. Those other inhabitants whose progress was thus impeded rarely showed any annoyance, for that was how one picked up news which otherwise one might have missed, or imparted news superior to that one heard.

In the north-east corner of the place – an oblong rather than a 'square' – and set back from it, stood the large cruci-form church of St John the Baptist surrounded by its grave-yard. One would have said that the graveyard encroached upon the market-place, except that it was there first. In the opposite south-west corner stood the Guildhall – many still called it 'Tollhouse'; the bailiffs called it Court House – a large building in the upper chamber of which the government of the town, if that is the right phrase, was carried on. In the centre of the open space, normally a prominent feature but almost hidden by stalls and customers when the market was in progress, stood the recently erected market-cross.

Apart from the graveyard fence, the Guildhall frontage and the gaps made by streets and alleys, the whole facade of the market-place on all its four sides consisted of shops, to a total of nearly fifty. At a casual glance they all looked alike, each one a rectangle of dirty white relieved by greyish beams and pierced by door and window – not what we think of as a 'shop window'; a two-foot square opening with bars across it – surmounted by a triangle bordered with thatch some two feet thick. Seen from across the place, they resembled a strip of crochet-work done by an inexpert hand and then slightly rumpled. A closer inspection would have revealed that those thatched roofs were all wearing 'hair-nets' of stout twine weighted at the edges with heavy stones to prevent the wind from removing them. It would also have revealed significant differences between shop and shop, other than that afforded by name-boards and signs. Whereas the majority conformed to a standard pattern, here one found a shop with two doors, two windows and two gables; there two shops with but a single door and gable shared between them; at one end, near the Guildhall, the shop of Alexander Calf had three gables and three doors. These differences would have been further under-lined and explained if one had consulted the rent-list in the bailiff's office, which showed that most shop-keepers paid one shilling rent per year; a few paid two shillings; some paid three or four pence; Henry Ringulf fourpence halfpenny, and Alexander Calf thirty-one pence. The same list would have revealed the existence of twenty-one permanent stalls and stall-holders, a third of them paying sixteen pence a year, the rest ninepence or a shilling. Which suggests that keeping a stall was as lucrative a business as keeping a shop.

And so it ought to have been, for every day was market-day in Dunwich – including Sundays, when trading began an hour later, after mass – and Dunwich market supplied not only the town itself but a wide area of countryside with both what it needed and an outlet for what it produced. It would be diffi-cult to think of an every-day commodity in existence in the late thirteenth century which was not obtainable in Dunwich market-place, either immediately or 'when the next ship comes in from' Copenhagen, Hamburg, Barcelona or wher-ever. There were bakers, butchers, grocers, spicers, mercers, cutlers, saddlers, hatters, potters, chandlers – the list ended only when the tour of the market ended. Foodstuffs naturally predominated among the commodities sold, with fish very high on the list, even though there was a separate market for that down by the quay. One could have bought butter, eggs, bacon, cheese, game, poultry, fruit, wine, malt, beer, shellfish, salt, mustard, vinegar, pepper — skip through a list as long as

you like; it was all there, one day or another. The heart of
Dunwich was very near its stomach.

I would have liked to linger for a picture of the scene, say,
just before Christmas. But only a Breughel could really have
done it justice; and by the time that a Breughel had come
along, this Dunwich had gone. We must press on, neglecting
as we go many a fascinating corner of the town, particularly
along that mile or so of wharves, shipyards, sailyards, rope-
walks, etc. where smells and sounds spoke just as eloquently
as sights. One feature, however, must claim our attention, as
it claimed that of everyone in Dunwich and for several miles
out to sea. That is the 'conde' perched on the top of Cock Hill
like a miniature Eiffel Tower or an outsize gallows. Cock Hill
was the largest of those peculiar hillocks standing between the
upper town and the harbour. It was of natural origin – I
think; we shall never know for sure – being of the same substance as the rest of the town, namely sand and gravel, but
had probably been enlarged by the addition of further
material from the dredging of the harbour until it stood fully
fifty feet high; as high, that is, as the point from which we
began our survey. It had a flat circular top of some twenty
feet in diameter. On this flat area was erected a wooden tower,
the 'conde' – a Saxon word; cf. 'conning tower' – rising to a
further thirty feet in three stages, each consisting of a wooden
platform reached by a ladder, and each smaller than the one
below. Its purpose was to provide a vantage-point from which
the movements of the herring-shoals out at sea might be observed. These herrings were not visible, of course, but the
gulls wheeling and diving above the shoal could be seen at a
distance of several miles (as much as ten miles, I am told, but
I find that hard to believe) and any change of direction could
be signalled to the fishermen by the 'conder' using leafy
boughs, or something similar. I understand that a similar
practice is still in vogue in the remoter parts of western Ireland, where there are very high cliffs. The topmost platform
was surrounded by guard-rails to prevent the conder from
being blown off in a high wind, or falling off in excitement.
There is not very much documentation of this interesting

feature. Gardner quotes an item from the bailiffs' accounts
of 1288 – *De signis datis ad Portas ejusdem Villae,*
£4 16s. 3½d. – which he interprets as 'For Beacons and conder.'
But I think he was mistaken; it looks to me more like a reference to some kind of official stamp on merchandise passing out
of the gates (*porta,* not *portus*) to signify that customs duty
had been paid. The conde could not have been a source of
revenue, rather the opposite. At Walberswick, for instance, in
1451, more than £6 was expended on nails and timber 'for
the Conde' and 'to make an End for the Conde.' There was at
Dunwich a 'tenement Cond.' owned by Richard Skot in St
Nicholas's parish in 1334, paying 6d. rent. So either there
were two condes in the town, or the word was used for a
beacon as well. Sorry, I get carried away by these interesting
oddities. We were on our way to the quay.

At one of the wharves we hail William the Ferry, who for
one halfpenny per person will row us across the harbour and
land us on the shore of King's Holme. Not at all the sort of
place to take tourists; not many of the townspeople ever went
there, or went beyond the first forty yards or so. Those who
did were mostly searchers after wild birds' eggs, wreck-seekers
or people up to no good. This desolate stretch of marsh was
an ideal place for that. King's Holme – it was also known as
King's Marsh, later Church Marsh, Leonard's Marsh and
Levald's Marsh* – was not really a 'marsh' in the normally
accepted sense of the word; 'waste' would have been a better
term. I described earlier how it came to be there.

Seen from above by an unusually imaginative sea-gull, or
seen on an accurately drawn chart, such as no one had ever
seen at that date, it would have had something of the appearance of a gigantic outstretched claw poised to wrench the town
of Dunwich from a perch which it had chosen for itself; a
'thing of doom and destiny, biding its terrible time'; which
indeed is what it was, and which alone justifies my inclusion
of it in this rapid sightseeing tour.

---

*Actually, there is some doubt as to what it was called at this date, or
whether indeed it was called anything. I was relying on Gardner, who evidently had not seen the Close Roll entry of 1408 (See p. 252). For simplicity's
sake I have decided to retain the name King's Holme all the way through.

It may surprise you to know that you can still see a great deal of King's Holme; of the substance of which it was composed, that is. If you walk from Dunwich to Walberswick and back you will be walking along a two-mile stretch of shingle; that was once King's Holme, much further out to sea and very different in appearance from now. You will also have very sore feet when you get back, so perhaps you would do better to walk Scolt Head or Blakeney Point in North Norfolk, both fair examples of what King's Holme was once. As bits were added here and subtracted there, the outline of the spit was constantly changing, likewise its surface. On the seaward side the winds had raised sand-dunes to a height of twenty feet in places, whereon grew marram grass, slowing down to some extent the movement of the restless sand which nonetheless continued to advance, now inland, now southwards towards the town.

The central zone of sand and shingle was a curious mixture of garden and desert, depending on the weather and the season of the year. For many months it looked as though nothing had ever grown there, or ever could. Then, quite suddenly as it seemed, the area came to life with patches of seablite and sea-campion, and colonies of docks and nettles. On the inner zone, the strip of real marsh where river and tide held equal sway, there was nature's garden. There sea-lavender, plantains, sandwort, sea-asters and thrift elbowed each other and wove their coloured patterns among dense clumps of reeds and rushes marking the water's edge.

No man had ever thought to build on King's Holme; not even a hermit's cell, or chapel like the isolated one on an island in the marsh of Minsmere; not even a shepherd's hut. No sheep or cattle grazed there then. (They did much later; in the seventeenth century the grazing there was valued at £200 a year, according to Gardner; but I doubt that valuation.) For though in times of desperate shortage animals might have been taken there to snatch such scanty bite as did exist in summer, it would have meant either a perilous short trip by raft across the harbour or a long roundabout route of eight miles via Dingle and Walberswick Bridge, not to men-

tion the unwelcome attention which the men of Walberswick
and Southwold would have paid to such a prize. The only
permanent occupants were birds; oyster-catchers, avocets,
sandpipers, terns, stone curlew and ringed plover nested there;
sometimes a colony of gulls, and always duck of several va-
rieties, especially on the inland side. The nesting-season was
the time of greatest human activity on King's Holme. That,
and the rare occasion when a wreck was cast ashore there.

24 Wreck

The very word 'wreck,' along with a few others such as 'fire,'
'murder,' 'treasure,' has an evocative, emotive quality. Not so
much nowadays as used to be the case. Wreck (*sae-upwarp*—
'what the sea throws up,' it was first called), i.e. the right to
claim wreck, figures in the laws of England from earliest times
as a perquisite of kingship. Kings soon found it an embarrass-
ing asset, and preferred to give it away – at a price – especially
as it included 'whales, grampuses and other great fish' which
by the time they reached the king or he reached them were
fit only to be hastily thrown back whence they had come. To
those inhabiting a stretch of coast however the privilege of
claiming wreck was eagerly sought and jealously guarded, by
law if possible; if not, by any other means available.

It is well known that 'wrecking,' i.e. deliberately ensuring
that a ship should be wrecked in order to profit from the looting of the cargo, was a regular occurrence on the rocky coasts
of Devon and Cornwall, or any rocky coast, until the late
eighteenth century. I am not writing here about 'wrecking,'
but about the disposal of what was wrecked without human assistance. I have no reason to suppose that the men of Dunwich,
in common with those of Yarmouth, Orford, Goseford and
other East Coast ports, ever deliberately caused a wreck, with
false beacons, obscured markers, lanterns tied on cows' horns,

and the like. They had no need to resort to such subterfuges; the shifting sandbanks and variable currents ensured that wrecks occurred with great frequency and without human agency. It may surprise landsmen to learn that the coast of East Anglia in the early nineteenth century – and therefore presumably at a much earlier date also – was every bit as fruitful of wrecks as was that of the south-west peninsula.

It is perhaps less surprising that, despite the countless references to 'wreck' in official records, references to actual shipwreck in the Middle Ages are relatively rare, for lack of publicity was essential if 'right of wreck' was to be of much value. There would be ample scope for the imagination in an account of shipwreck on, say, the shore of King's Holme. I shirk the task, not so much from reluctance to exercise poetic licence too often, or from doubt of my ability to achieve realism, as from a fear that, if I did, the result might be too repulsive. There would, I think, have been little heroism or humanity displayed. The men of Dunwich may not have deliberately engineered a wreck; they never, I am sure, made the slightest effort to prevent one, and never failed to profit by those which occurred.

Everybody, including the law-makers, took it for granted that there would be wrecks, and that people would be drowned. No provision whatever was made on shore for the safety of those at sea. 'Safe keeping of the sea,' a task entrusted to Dunwich men in 1242 for a number of years, clearly meant protecting ships against piracy, and more particularly protecting those on land against attack from the sea. The various beacons set up at intervals along the coast – one at Cachecliff, two at Dunwich, one at Walberswick, one at Southwold, etc. – were likewise primarily there to warn the inhabitants on land of the approach of enemies by sea. Shipwreck was a fact of life; an act of God. To have done anything – not that one could have done much – to prevent it or minimise it would, in the eyes of many, have been tantamount to sacrilege. From the point of view of those ashore at Dunwich, it would have been 'robbery.'

The sole aspect with which the law was concerned was the ownership of 'wreck.' The territorial limits had all been fixed centuries earlier; and still provided scope for argument for centuries to come. Ships and cargoes cast up on King's Holme belonged to Dunwich, 'in the name of the king.' At some date very near to the time of which I am writing – it was first enrolled on the statutes in 1275, to the best of my knowledge – an important modification was made to the law governing wreck. If a man, woman, child, *dog or cat* escaped alive, then the wreck was not technically 'wreck.'

I am able to quote two relevant entries in the Close Rolls:

1260. Order to Robert Neville, keeper of Bamburgh Castle, that, if John Sparcunte shall adequately prove three pieces of wax, now in Robert's custody, which were found in a certain wrecked ship of Dunwich, to be his, and not rightly to be classed as wreckum' *because the men of that ship escaped alive*, as John maintains, then the said wax is to handed over to John at once.

1265. Letter to the bailiffs of Romney. Three merchants of Pampelona, with a certain ship of Dunwich in which they and their goods were travelling, were in danger of being wrecked off Romney. Twelve men of Romney and others kept the cargo, which the bailiffs are ordered to restore at once to the said merchants.

In that latter instance it seems very probable that the Romney men did by their own efforts assist the work of the Almighty; and quite certain that they ignored the modified law.

I cannot help wondering how many unfortunate mariners – to say nothing of ship's cats and dogs – were callously murdered, or left to die when they might have been saved, as a result of this modification of the law. It would be so easy to administer a sharp blow on the head, a gentle squeeze of the throat; or simply do nothing, but look the other way, and get on with the really important business of securing the cargo. I know that is a terrible assertion to make. I have not one scrap of evidence with which to back it. How could there be any evidence? Without wishing to appear too cynical, I think I would rather have perished at sea than have taken my chance on King's Holme with a wrecked ship behind me.

A ship did not even have to be wrecked for its cargo to be treated as 'wreck.' In 1274 William Barnard of Dunwich left Bordeaux with two of his ships laden with, amongst other things, fifty bales of alum. He and the Spanish merchants who owned the cargo sailed in one ship, which was wrecked in a storm and lost with all on board. The other ship, with the alum, reached Sandwich. The bailiffs there sent the cargo on to London. The tax-collector in London, on the excuse that William Barnard had been tax-collector in Dunwich and was in arrears with his returns, retained six bales and sent the rest to Dunwich. Actually Robert Barnard, not William, and Henry de Southwold were the tardy tax-collectors. At Dunwich most of the alum 'came into the hands of the men of Dunwich.' Margaret Barnard, widow of the drowned merchant, faced a claim from the partner of the drowned Spanish merchants for compensation of his loss. He claimed in fact fifty-two bales of alum. Margaret had to hand over what was left. The end of the story comes in 1280, when Margaret claimed successfully

'—certain goods at Dunwich, formerly belonging to Isaac son of Benedict of London, Jew of Norwich, who was hanged for an offence against the coinage, and all his goods forfeited to the king.

Hardly a happy ending. It was hardly a happy story. I am still not sure who 'won.' The moral seems to be that, if Paul was to be paid, then Peter must be robbed.

25 Storm and Strife

The frequent introduction of the lords of the manor of Blythburgh into my story is necessitated by the fact that they played a vital part in shaping the course of Dunwich's history. So long as Blythburgh remained neutral or submissive, Dunwich men usually got their own way and arranged things to their own advantage. It would appear that Blythburgh did accept a subordinate role throughout a whole generation of Cressy rule. Then the male line came to an end, leaving only Ermentrude, widow of Stephen de Cressy, to survive on an annual allowance of £10 from the king. The whole of the Blythburgh lands and the rest of the revenues were held by Robert Fitz-Roger. Ermentrude therefore had a very good reason for marrying Robert. Several good reasons in fact. She may have been in love with him, or he with her, but that is not likely to have affected the issue very seriously. He was descended from the Claverings of Corbridge in Northumberland. The direct line of the Clavering males had ended, and Robert FitzRoger, while still a baby, had inherited the lands and fortune of the Claverings, scattered throughout the counties of Northumberland, Essex, Northants, and Norfolk. The king had held them throughout young Robert's minority, but at last he was old enough to enter upon his inheritance, and marry. A very good match indeed for Ermentrude; the more so in that a young husband with northern blood in his veins and a tradition of Border feuding in his ancestry would be the very man to put those Dunwich upstarts in their place.

Robert had been long enough on the Suffolk scene – some of his kinsmen lived in Dunwich – to have learnt where Dunwich could be hurt most effectively. Not content with his legitimate fair and market at Blythburgh, he set up another market at Walberswick and instructed 'his men of Walberswick' to ignore the Dunwich regulations as to tolls and customs, row up the river to 'his port' and sell their fish there, paying all tolls to him – 'to the loss of Dunwich.' The reaction of the Dunwich men seems to have taken Robert by surprise, and indicates that he did not know everything about Dunwich men. They struck back with speed, force and guile.

A party of them sallied forth up the river in April 1281 and made an organised raid on Walberswick, 'seizing oars, sails, anchors and other goods' which they carried back to Dunwich. That 'other goods,' without doubt, hides a multitude of thefts both great and small. FitzRoger complained to the sheriff, as they knew he would. Three justices were appointed to hear and terminate the affair. One of them was Sir Richard de Holbrook, keeper of the town of Dunwich for the time being. It suited the burgesses to have a keeper in charge of the town, even though they did have to pay him 6s. 8d. a week maintenance. He took the responsibility from their shoulders; and he could be 'squared.' He evidently was on this occasion, for in November the three justices pronounced that 'the burgesses had distrained in the usual way for toll and custom due to the king.' They had not robbed anybody of anything; they had acted according to the law. Oh law, what crimes have been enacted in thy name!

Robert FitzRoger had to retire in discomfiture and think of something better. Sir Richard was back in Dunwich the following May with orders for the bailiffs to provide men and ships to defend the coast against pirates of Holland, Zeeland and Friesland, and 'such as they intercept to keep in safe custody until further orders.' Since the order was not repeated, I take it that the Dunwich men, along with those of Ipswich and Yarmouth, responded willingly, and I have little doubt that they kept safely anything that fell into their hands. Legitimate trade continued. Robert and Richard Ille obtained 'simple protection' for two years. Others managed perfectly well without it. Augustine FitzJoce, a friend of the FitzJohns, ran into a bit of trouble. He brought 125 tuns of wine from Libourne in Gascony in his ship *All Saints* and landed the precious cargo at Ipswich, but when he demanded payment for the freightage of £57, the three rascally wine-merchants refused to pay. It was too much, they said. I think they were probably right. He sued them. They 'surreptitiously' obtained a writ for a certain John Bek to try the case. John Bek was 'engaged elsewhere.' Lawyers with hypersensitive palms were never unemployed. So Sir Richard de Holbrook and his colleagues were commissioned to deal, and Augustine got his money – at a price.

Then came a lull in the affairs of Dunwich. The pirates were successfully subdued; no major menace darkened the political horizon; no untoward disturbance marred the autumn round of activity, and Dunwich settled to the calm, dull winter of 1285–86. People slept soundly in their beds, looked forward hopefully, as ever, to the coming of the spring. Not without some slight trepidation, though, as always. There was always one element in the complexity called life in Dunwich that was beyond all human manipulation. The sea. It was always there; always would be. Dunwich was there because of the sea; depended on it in every sense for its existence. Did it ever occur to Dunwich men that what the sea had done, it could undo? That what the sea had given, it could take away?

Such thoughts must surely have occurred, to the older people especially, sometimes as they lay abed on those long winter nights and listened to the ceaseless murmur of the surf. The sound did not keep them awake; lulled them to sleep rather by its familiar presence. They might perhaps have had a restless night if that sound had ceased altogether, to be replaced by ominous silence. There was always a certain routine anxiety in any case as the moon completed its twenty-eight day cycle and the next spring tide came due. The inhabitants of the lower town, those nearest to the sea, hardly ever got through a winter without at least one alarm, waking in the morning to find the sea in their back-yards, if it had not already got them from their beds. But even that was routine. Having lived through it many times before, they would live through it again. Get the winter over, and there was nothing to worry about. Next winter was a long way ahead.

The people of Dunwich knew when the winter was over; but did the sea and the wind know? People began to have their doubts as the high tide of New Year's Eve, March 23rd 1286, rose higher, pushed and stirred by a bitterly cold east wind. High tides, being routine, took no one by surprise. Furniture and bedding had been moved into chambers and lofts in the houses bordering the quays and what was left of the sea-wall. Fishing-boats were drawn up into the alleys and back-yards; larger vessels securely moored and lashed together. Whatever precautions could be taken had been taken. What the sea would do, left to its own devices, was predictable. It would rise, then fall. What the wind would do, no man could tell.

What the wind did do was to set firmly east and blow with fury all that day and all the next night, so that the sea could not fall. In the early morning of New Year's Day the waves were pounding against the sea-wall and sweeping right over it in torrents of foam beneath showers of spray. The occupants of those dwellings nearest the sea removed in all haste their belongings which, aided by their more fortunately placed neighbours, they carried to the churches of St Martin, St Leonard and St Nicholas, where it was confidently expected they would be safe. A guard was set to watch over them, nevertheless. No business was transacted in the market that day; no drinking in many of the taverns, for they were three feet deep in muddy water, and not even a horse would have drunk that. Barrels, crates and baulks of timber jostled each other on the quay. Ships strained at their moorings, buffeted the submerged wharves and other ships until the inevitable parting of timbers resulted in their gently settling in the swirling mud. Some whose ropes were worn and chafed broke free, shortly to lose their freedom by being driven aground upon the marshy side of the harbour. Waves swept right across King's Holme, a sight which most of Dunwich folk had never seen before. Church-bells rang out an intermittent clangour of alarm; a futile gesture with no reason in it but traditional usage and the belief, perhaps, that God might hear. A constant watch was kept, though there was nothing that watchers could do, except watch. And pray.

The Grey Friars brethren were in a serious plight; their monastery stood very near the sea at the south-east corner of the town, The first onslaught of the waves had demolished the sea-wall here and replaced it with a low cliff which crumbled every minute and receded before that irresistible force. The anguished brethren knelt all night upon the chapel floor and prayed; no count was kept of paternosters told that night with fingers cold and numb, though hope was not abandoned that their prayers might yet penetrate the never-ending tempestuous roar. By morning half the monastery had gone.

The situation in the lower town eased slightly towards noon, as the tide receded just a little and the wind shifted more to the south-east. Attempts were made to mend the breaches in the wall. There was no lack of material; no lack of willing hands. What they most lacked was time. As darkness fell the hopeless task was abandoned. That night the wind again reached gale force. The sea rose higher still. When daylight came at last, after the longest night the Dunwich folk had ever known, the scene which met their gaze brought cries of anger and despair to lips already parched with prayer, and eyes incapable of further tears looked blankly out on desolation.

It was as if some giant reaper had swung his scythe and mown a hundred-yard-wide swathe along the seaward side of the town, leaving it in tangled heaps at the end of each successive stroke. One heap of debris, by a whim of fate, had saved the harbour-mouth from being blocked. The sea-wall had disappeared completely. The borderline between land and sea was now a cliff of sand and gravel ten feet high, upon the jagged brink of which a score of houses balanced drunkenly, partly on land, partly on nothing. Several slipped gently over the edge even as one watched. The little monastery of the monks of Eye, with its schoolroom, had gone for ever; the last link with St Felix had been severed the day before, when the precious 'Red Book' was moved for safety to the library at Eye. Grey Friars house was utterly destroyed; the west wall of the chapel stood; that and the graveyard alone remained.

The parishes of St Michael and St Bartholomew no longer existed even in name, while those of St Nicholas, St Leonard and St Martin were somewhat smaller than they had been two days previously. St Anthony's chapel was a pile of flint rubble half-buried in shingle thirty yards out from the cliff. Along the quayside and on the river frontage the damage to buildings was much less, though still considerable. Several houses had been buffeted into collapse, but most of the material was still there to be salvaged and re-used. The king's galley was driven from its moorings beside the wall of Maison Dieu and carried across the harbour almost to the bridge, where it was left high and dry by the receding flood, never to float again.

Poetic licence? Well, it had to be. Gardner, basing his report on the chronicles of Stowe and Holinshed, says only:

1286. On the Night after New Year's Day, through the Vehemence of the Winds, and Violence of the Sea, several Churches were overthrown and destroyed in divers Places; *Dunwich* was one of the sufferers.

A story needs more than that! Official records, at a much later date – I shall quote them presently in illustration of another aspect of the disaster – speak only of 'an inundation of the sea,' 'a storm of the sea,' and do not even give the date.

All that was bad enough. Worse was yet to be revealed when a week later men were able to get out on King's Holme to see what had happened there. King's Holme was an island once more, for the second time within the memory of many then living in Dunwich. The sea had broken through at the same spot, or very nearly the same spot, as it did thirty-six years earlier, opposite the Blyth River. The obstruction placed there then by Dunwich men had been largely swept away, leaving a gap through which the swollen river now swirled merrily out to sea, thus providing Walberswick, Blythburgh and Southwold with a natural haven as good as that of Dunwich. Better than that of Dunwich, for this haven was wider, straighter, unencumbered by debris and scoured by the river as well as by the tides. If the situation were left like that, then the days of Dunwich as a port were numbered. The collection of tolls from Walberswick boats would be impossible; the payment of tolls to Robert FitzRoger was an awful possibility.

Too awful to be calmly contemplated or accepted. It was one thing to submit to the will of God – though a blow like that could not be the will of God; it must be the work of the Devil. It was quite another thing to sit back and let others – let FitzRoger of all people – take the bread from one's mouth, reap a harvest which they had not sown, deprive honest men of their rights and liberties. They had fought back in the past. They would fight back again now. Hard times lay ahead, no doubt of that. But they would fight, with courage, effort, determination – and money. So thought – or so I think they thought – those burgesses and bailiffs as they stood and watched the muddy waters swirling through the gap. A similar group no doubt stood on the further bank, and what they thought I cannot guess. Their faces, I am sure, were innocent of any trace of sympathy for Dunwich.

In considering the reaction of the mass of townsfolk, as distinct from the officials and leading men of commerce, it must be borne in mind that the actual damage to the town was localised both geographically and socially. Three quarters of the town's area suffered no damage at all. Those who suffered most were the poorer people in the lower town, between whom and the residents of the upper town there had never been any great amity. Lower town and upper town depended on each other, but that did not mean that they loved each other. A disaster affecting the whole community equally would undoubtedly have produced a communal re-action. This one, as the recorded facts amply demonstrate, did not. If there had existed the social machinery to spread the loss, and the individual will to share it, then the social structure might have been strengthened. Instead, it was drastically weakened.

The immediate reaction would of course be one of consternation and pity. Help would be given where it was most desperately needed, to those least able to help themselves. But charity and sympathy are rapidly eroded by time. Within a few weeks of the disaster the majority of the people adopted resignation as their stance; settled down to make the best of a situation which, after all, might have been much worse. A minority opted for anger; and anger needed a target. Somebody was to blame. Who else but the 'government', the mayor and bailiffs? They ought to have foreseen such a disaster and done something about it years ago. They ought to have built the sea-wall higher and stronger, and kept it in proper repair. They ought to have made a proper job of stopping up the Southwold haven; or they ought never to have stopped it up at all, then the sea would have flowed in there and made a mess of Walberswick. Instead of spending money on the town they had spent it on themselves, on their ships and wharves and warehouses. What was wanted was a new government.

That view must have been fairly widely held, for they got a new 'government'. That year's elections brought into office as mayor Simon Baldock, who had been bailiff eleven years before; as bailiffs Walter Almayn and Henry Allepine, newcomers to office; Roger Turold, bailiff for the third time, and Luke Scott, bailiff twenty years before, and pirate in the meantime. Apart from him, none of the traditional officeholding families was represented. They accomplished nothing. The tide of resentment swelled. The next year's elections saw an even cleaner sweep; Andrew Fressel as mayor, having been bailiff twelve years before, a normal procedure; Henry Snayl, Roger Korchest, Simon Cariock and Walter Silknet as bailiffs for the first, and last, time. The traditional rulers evidently stood aside and left the newcomers to get on with it, while they themselves put their faith and energy – and money – into other things.

The newcomers, one must suppose, talked. They did nothing. It was evident to some of the town at least that nothing would be done unless somebody took drastic action. Which is just what somebody did. The Patent Roll of Oct. 12th 1287, relieves me of the burden of reconstruction. It is one of the most explicit records of its kind:

'Commission to Richard de Boyland and William de Pakenham [knights of the shire], upon complaints made by the mayor and bailiffs of Dunwich, to inquire into the contempts committed by these *mariners* of Dunwich, viz. Robert Sparrow, Robert le Poer, John Joce, John le Barewer, Geoffrey Codun, Edmund Codun, Geoffrey Fykett, Richard Morebred, Robert de Eyse, William de Southwold, William le Official, John le Palmer, William Totepeny, Geoffrey Blackat, John Fike, William de la More, William Belamey, Valentine Richman, Richard Ille, Nicholas Honeman and Andrew Terry, in *entering into a conspiracy* whereby they have taken their oaths *not to permit the court of the said mayor and bailiffs to be held,* the king's dues from themselves to be levied, or execution of the king's writs and judgements of the king's courts to be carried out; in levying to their own use fines imposed upon the burgesses by Salomon de Roff and his fellow-justices last in eyre in Suffolk, and in not permitting the peace there to be kept by the mayor and bailiffs. All persons found guilty are to be guarded by the sheriff, to appear before the king a fortnight after Martinmas.'

It sounds like a rebellion, as in a sense it undoubtedly was. But there was no rioting, no violence, no drafting of a new constitution, or anything like that. A band of determined men said to their rulers: 'If you don't do something, we will.' They were not the feckless, lawless element of society, though their ranks did include two men who had seen the inside of a gaol. Some of them – Poer, Joce, Codun, Fykett, Ille – were well-to-do respectable merchants. Some were very old, some young. All, in a sense were 'mariners'; men of the sea; men accustomed to doing rather than talking. Their tactics were strangely in advance of the times.

They evidently did a lot of picketing over a lengthy period. Just how peaceful it was we cannot know; but, had there been serious violence, the complaint of the bailiffs would surely have mentioned it. They must have had the support of all the poor in the town, and at least half the better-off householders and shopkeepers. This is indicated in the bailiffs' accounts for 1287–88, which have survived by a strange chance (or simply thanks to Gardner) and which show that the rents collected that year only amounted to £12 8s. 4d. as against a normal £30 odd. The confiscation of the fines imposed at the last session of the justices was a risky thing to do. To me, the mere fact that they did it affords some indication of their good intentions, for they clearly made no effort to conceal their identities.

In the light of subsequent events, it looks as though their objective was twofold. Firstly, they demanded a thorough and impartial inquiry into the municipal finances over the past thirty years. The reforms ordered fifteen years previously, when Thomas de Clare had come to clean up the mess created by the FitzJohns and their faction, had never in fact been put into effect, or only partially. The conspirators did not believe – and they were proved right – that the town's finances were in such a bad state as the bailiffs said they were. Secondly, they demanded that measures be taken forthwith to improve the state of Dunwich harbour. This implied, as a matter of logic, that Southwold haven be put out of action. Either Dunwich was the only port on that particular stretch of coast, or it was not. If it was not, then those sheets of parchment locked in the town chest, with all their fine words about 'liberties' and what not, were just a lot of useless ornaments.

There is no record of the inquiry actually taking place; no aftermath of any kind in the records. I assume that it did take place; that no one on the list of 'conspirators' was found guilty, and no one put in gaol. In August 1289 an inquiry was ordered into the private accounts of thirteen past bailiffs. It is worth while to note their names: Augustine Clark, John Cock, Thomas Scott, John Dowsing, Thomas Michel, Joceus Battings, Thomas Dennis, Eustace Battings, Richard Fitz-John, Michael FitzJohn, Robert Culling, Walter Calf and John Arnold.

One feature which interests me about that list, like that of the 'conspirators' given above, is that, FitzJohn apart, all the names are 'English'. That, I think, rules out any suggestion of racial prejudice, which ought to have disappeared by this date anyway. We have no record of the results of the inquiry – apart from Richard FitzJohn's hasty departure overseas – but it may reasonably be assumed that the delinquent officials were made to pay up. They may not all have been guilty of embezzlement, but they were all guilty of not having rendered to the Exchequer an account during their term of office. Having mentioned racial prejudice, it might be apposite to mention here that, as from 1290, there were no more Jews in Dunwich. All the Jews in England were banished from the realm. This no doubt restricted the scope for financial speculation; but I would not care to say that it diminished the amount of peculation that went on, or greatly raised the standard of the coinage. However, for the time being Dunwich finances were healthier. The reformers had won one of their points.

With money available, the achievement of the second aim

could be undertaken. A plan was put forward – nothing original, just the same remedy as before – and the traditional rulers came back into office over the next five years to put it into effect. Looking back now over the centuries, it seems a rather senseless plan, inspired by jealousy, greed, hate and self-interest. In the circumstances, though, had we been Dunwich people, I suppose we would have done what they did.

The channel formed by the break-in of the sea and the break-out of the river, just below Southwold, had to be blocked. 'For ever', the Dunwich men would have said, and meant. I should think it was about a hundred and fifty yards long and thirty yards wide in the centre opening out to more than that at each end; its depth would vary with the state of the tide, between three feet and eighteen feet or so. It *was* blocked. How many thousand tons of gravel, sand and clay were used I cannot even guess. How many man-hours of labour, how many carts, horses, oxen; how many women carrying baskets, I do not know. I do know that it was a colossal task. Men were called in from a wide area to supplement the Dunwich labour force.

Work would only be possible for a limited period of time each day, and quite impossible for weeks at a time when weather and tide were contrary. One exceptionally high tide, or a sudden downpour five miles inland, could have undone in half an hour the work of a whole week. They persisted nevertheless, and seemingly luck was on their side. Since this was 'the king's work' – it had his sanction and the support of the sheriff – it is more than likely that the king's barge was put to use in carrying material and dumping it in the gap. The most difficult part of the operation would be the construction of a solid barrier at each end, using hundreds of large wooden piles. A barge with a pile-driver rigged on it would have been essential for this. The whole operation would have to be carried out under constant harassment and opposition from the Walberswick and Southwold sides. Showers of stones and insults would be a common occurrence, and the work would have to be guarded night and day. One night of neglect on the part of Dunwich would have cost them dear, if Walberswick men were vigilant, as assuredly they were.

The work, for all its urgency, once begun, can hardly have been finished in under a year; perhaps two or three. What it cost, I doubt whether anybody ever knew. We only get an inkling from records of ten years later. Here is part (the rest will be quoted later) of the entry in the Patent Roll of April 1300:

> Commission to William Carleton and William Howard to hear and settle a complaint by the burgesses of Dunwich that, previously they, in conjunction with men of the adjoining parts, stopped up a port at Southwold by the order of King Henry III [this was the 1250 operation] and afterwards that port was in great part reopened by an inundation of the sea, whereby merchants preferred to put in and take their goods there rather than to Dunwich, and traded and paid toll there, to the loss of the said burgesses of Dunwich, and on their complaint the king [Edward I] commanded the sheriff of Suffolk to inquire into the matter and *to close the port again* by distraint of the adjoining tenants, and whereas the said burgesses have by the king's command applied £2000 to the closing thereof—

It hardly seems possible. Two thousand pounds then was the equivalent of nearly half a million now. Where *could* they have got that much money for a project of that nature? I think that perhaps Messrs William Bedell and William Austin, honourable members for Dunwich, were nearer the truth with the petition which they presented to Parliament in 1304:

> Petition of the men of Dunwich asking that the king should order restitution of part of the expenses and dues paid out by them *to the amount of £500* on the stopping-up of a certain haven which was opened by a storm of the sea near to Dunwich and deteriorated the haven of the said town, of which expenses certain men of Southwold and Walberswick ought to be sharers, and to which in like cases they used to contribute, which they are *now unwilling to do.*

And even that was a huge sum of money. That last phrase must be the understatement of the century. What a pity, what a loss to vernacular literature, that history does not record what the men of Southwold and Walberswick actually said when told that they were expected to pay half the cost of the deliberate destruction of their own haven!

Whatever the size of the bill, since the money was largely paid out in wages to Dunwich men – and some outsiders, including no doubt some from Walberswick and Southwold, a real 'job-creation' scheme, if ever there was one – it did not really cost the town of Dunwich all that much; simply moved the money round a bit; what was paid out in wages would find its way back eventually, via the shops and taverns, to the pockets of those who had paid it out. A lot of the timber used would be salvaged from damaged ships and houses, which had to be cleared up in any case.

The river-course from Walberswick down to Dunwich was cleared, as was also the haven-mouth at Dunwich; a work which would be performed to a great extent by the river itself and the normal tidal scour. The tidal scour was not nearly so effective at Dunwich haven as it would have been at Southwold, as Dunwich men were to have demonstrated to them all too soon. But that was in the future. Thus the fishermen and merchants of the three towns up-river were compelled to use the Dunwich channel and to pay tolls and customs as before. To prevent any impudent evasion of tolls, a new guard-house was built on the shore of King's Holme, at a point where boats going up-river were obliged to pass within hailing distance. One of the bailiffs was given special responsibility for this, with men on permanent duty, others on permanent call, and a boat specially designed for swift pursuit.

The reaction of the Walberswick and Southwold men – more particularly that of the lord of Blythburgh – hardly needs to be explained. The fact that their heaven-sent haven had been destroyed by order of the king, his sheriff and justices can have made little difference to them. They had been cheated of their rights. Where there had always been resentment, there was now bitter hatred. The war between England and France, like that between England and Scotland, took second place on this bit of coast to the war between Walberswick and Dunwich. That was the only war which interested them.

GREYFRIARS GATEWAY.   R. PARKER. 77

Fig 10 Grey Friars Gateway

They should have known, those men of Walberswick, that one day they would win. They had an ally more powerful than all the kings, sheriffs, justices and all the men of Dunwich put together. The sea was on their side. The sea would once again, one day, give back what they had lost. But did they know that, having given them back their haven, the sea would on another day, in its own good time, destroy it? That too was in the future. For the present they did all they could to spoil what Dunwich men and Dunwich money had done.

26 Grey Friars

If you have ever gazed upon the forlorn ruins – forlorn for all the carefully tended grass and neatly-painted notices – of a medieval monastery, then glanced at the dull phrases in the fifteen-penny guide: 'was built at such and such a date by abbot so and so' – 'destroyed at the Dissolution by King Henry the Eighth' – 'the building on your right was where the monks' – 'all that remains today is' –; if you have then motored on to savour some more exhilarating experience such as a bath or a supper of freshly-caught fish which has erased all memory of monks from your mind, you will understand why I am now taking 'poetic licence' for granted.

The sorry plight in which the forty inmates of the Franciscan house of Grey Friars found themselves was alleviated to a considerable extent by the widespread sympathy which their pitiful condition evoked. Having no worldly possessions, they did not feel impoverished by the destruction of their house, distressing though it must have been to see the labour of years demolished overnight. They were simply thrown back into the position in which they or their predecessors had found themselves on first coming to Dunwich thirty years before; with the difference that they were not the only ones in a similar plight. Upwards of a hundred houses had been destroyed or rendered uninhabitable, and there were many families now dependent on charity; the very kind of charity which the friars would gladly have shown if they had not themselves been reduced to beggary.

Despite the frequent charges of idleness and uselessness levelled against them, the friars were acknowledged by a great many people to have at least one immeasurable asset, to perform at least one function which was then, by many people, held to be of real service to society. In renouncing the cares and vanities, the possessions and aspirations of this world, the friars held the key to happiness in the next. Because they, more patently than many if not most of the long-established orders, practised what they preached, their intercession was believed to be one of the most potent agencies known of securing entry into Paradise for the human soul. Whether in fact that was so or not, matters little. Whether or not we believe today that it was so, matters not at all. What does matter is that people believed then, in the thirteenth and fourteenth centuries, that it was so. To perform acts of charity towards the friars, or through them, was to accumulate credit in the account-book of the celestial banker at whose door the naked soul would one day have to knock. To leave in one's will a few shillings to the friars that they should sing twenty, thirty or fifty masses for one's soul was a simple and sensible form of insurance against eternal damnation.

But it would be uncharitable to attribute all the many acts of kindness arising out of the disaster of that New Year's Day at Dunwich to this kind of spiritual materialism. There were those who performed acts of charity out of disinterested compassion; because they were decent, good-hearted people. William FitzRichard was one. He had suffered as much material loss as any of the merchants and property-owners. He blamed it on no one, not even on the Devil, certainly not on himself. Hearing of the plight of the friars, he said: 'I know not whether I shall go to heaven or to hell, but I will not see these unfortunate creatures homeless and hungry.' He sought out the general minister of the vanished friary and told him to send two or three brethren straight away to his own house, where they would be lodged and fed. Accommodation was limited, even in a house like that of the FitzRichards, but two of the friars were lodged in the barn and took their meals in the house.

Several other burgesses followed his lead, and about a quarter of the friars were accommodated in that way. Some were lodged with the Knights Templars, where the affluence of the establishment and the arrogance of the warden made them so uncomfortable that they left as soon as they could. Some found refuge in the Maison Dieu, and were content to be there, for it gave them an opportunity to help people in greater misfortune than themselves. The offer made by the master of the leper hospital of St James was declined with thanks, though the use of his ancient church for worship was much appreciated. The Dominican house of the Black Friars, built at the same time as their own, maintained the attitude of rivalry which had always existed between them, and probably hoped that the Grey Friars would depart and thereby lessen the competition in a dwindling market. Some of the friars did in fact leave to join houses of their order in St Edmundsbury, Ipswich, Yarmouth, Norwich and elsewhere. All found a home.

The real dilemma confronting the friars lay in deciding whether to set about re-establishing themselves on a permanent basis in Dunwich, and if so, how. Their resources in terms of money and influence were negligible. They were called 'mendicant' – beggars. They had no large manorial estates to serve as a continuous reservoir of wealth, as had the long-established Benedictine monasteries such as the Priory of Eye. They received not one penny from the tolls of the market, the tithes of the churches, or St Leonard's fair. Without a large measure of public support – of a purely spontaneous nature, not imposed by statute and custom – there was little hope of ever seeing their house rebuilt in the town. Merely to stand in the market-place and beg would produce no more than was needed to keep them alive and clothed; and in any case the rules of their order forbade the acceptance of money other than for the relief of the poor – if they could find any poorer than themselves. Likewise they were forbidden to work for payment, except in the form of food. How, then, could they enlist the support they needed?

Preaching was obviously one way. In this the friars had a real advantage, though it was their rivals of the Black Friars who had been given the title of 'Friars Preachers'. Some of the Grey Friars were men initially of rank, breeding and education. Unlike many of the secular clergy and the monks, they had not embraced religion to escape from the hardships and obligations of the world, to seek a privileged position; but rather, as philosophers, had deliberately renounced all worldly comforts in order to lead a life of poverty, humility and chastity.

This was manifested more effectively in deeds than in words. But words were the tools which they used to move others to perform acts of kindness, so that they had the means to perform still more. They had the freedom of the market-cross, the street-corner, the village green; speaking to the people in the language of the people. Their sermons had to be brief, avoiding scholarly wrangles, contention and too much verbal flagellation. It would have been foolish to tell the people of Dunwich that the recent disaster was the visitation of divine wrath upon their own wickedness. Equally foolish to attribute it to the machinations of the Devil, for then the wickedness of the friars themselves might have been adduced. The theme of the sermon had to be one of general good and evil, with the emphasis on good; of punishment and reward, with the accent on reward; not here and now – anybody could see with half an eye that the wicked prospered here just as much as, if not more than, the good – but hereafter.

There must have been some preachers amongst them who were particularly adept at getting the message across. The climate of opinion must have been singularly favourable to the growth of such seeds as were sown. Perhaps civic pride had something to do with it. Perhaps the unpopularity of the Priors of Eye and Leiston gave rise to a determination on the part of Dunwich folk that their salvation should be achieved by mediators nearer at hand. Some may have felt the need to propitiate God lest, in the event of another like disaster, they might all be victims. Whatever the reasons, the results were soon to be seen, and are still to be seen today.

Talk of re-building Grey Friars had begun in earnest within a year of the disaster. The problem was, where? There was very little room in the town. About half the old site was left, but it would have been folly to build on it; folly to build a house intended to last 'for ever' on a bit of ground unlikely to last for another twenty years – though, as it turned out, that bit of ground did last for another forty years. There was no possibility of the whole town acting as a corporate body and giving to the friars a piece of land, for the only land thus owned was the Common at the southern end of Sea Field. Apart from the emotive and legal implications of interfering with 'common' land, and the difficulty of deciding whose soul was to benefit from a donation made by a collection of individuals, such a site would have been too remote. The problem was solved by three of the leading families – De la Falaise, Valeins and Cuddon – getting together to make available to the friars a seven-acre plot of ground immediately outside the ramparts, between Middle Gate and Bridge Gate.

This provided an excellent opportunity to resolve another problem which had been under discussion by successive town councils for years – what to do about the Pales Dyke. It was in a bad state of neglect; the ditch silted up and overgrown; the timber revetment decayed; the palisade and platform broken down. It was really not of much use as a defensive work; indeed it afforded an excellent means of getting into and out of the town without being seen, as numerous small boys had discovered, though a knight in armour might have found entry more difficult. To have made the dyke effective would have been a very costly matter; as also would its maintenance in a state of effectiveness. Those burgesses who had money to spend on material things could find more profitable investments than a defensive earthwork which was never likely to be used again. Those burgesses with money to invest in spiritual things saw little likelihood of a restored Pales Dyke earning any entries on the credit side of the heavenly account-book.

But what would the king say if 'his' town were allowed to be deprived of its defences?

The petition which was sent to the king did not, apparently put the case as bluntly as that. It is doubtful whether it made any mention at all of the dyke. If it did, then the king must have been caught in a benevolent mood; or he was singularly indifferent to the supposed defence of 'his' town; or he might have been thinking solely about the sixty-five pounds which the burgesses paid him annually – owed him annually – in rent; or he could have been motivated by the desire to notch up a few credit-points for himself in the book, as his father had done by giving seven oaks from the royal forests to the Black Friars. His reply made no mention of the dyke, either. It merely stated that 'there would be no harm in his granting to the burgesses of the Town of Dunwich permission to give to the Friars Minor a site, between the King's highway on the south and the house of Richard Kilbeck on the north, where-on they might build and dwell—'

The burgesses went ahead with their plan. The Pales Dyke was thrown down to fill in the ditch along a frontage of about two hundred yards. A road was made along it; another along the north-western side of the triangular plot. Then the long task of construction began. The most arduous part of the work was the collection and transport of the material; it was on this that hundreds of the townsmen were employed part-time for many months. Their quarry was mainly the sea-shore, in par-ticular that part of it where the first Grey Friars monastery had stood. The sea had not yet had time to bury or remove the piles of stones and rubble which it had left there. At low tide it was possible to recover the fabric of earlier buildings also, such as the churches of St Michael and St Bartholomew; a circumstance which gave no small satisfaction to those who had a sense of history. There could well have been, among those stones and flints, many which had once formed part of the fabric of a Roman fort, though that would have been beyond the understanding of even the most historically minded.

Load after load was salvaged and carted up the hill to be

added to the growing piles all round the site and in its centre. Sand was dug from the heath, sifted and dumped by the cart-load alongside the stones. Gangs of men were employed in carting lime from beyond St Edmundsbury, slaking it and mixing it to make the mortar. The building-stone – it was still called 'Norman' stone – for the facing of doors and windows had to be brought from further afield still, necessitating a sea-voyage to Lynn, where the stones arrived after a long journey through the Fens from Northamptonshire. This was William FitzRichard's contribution to the work, though he did not live to see it completed. Yet more men were engaged in preparing and erecting scaffolding, carting and sawing timbers. There was no lack of men or materials; and no lack of the will to work. The actual work of construction was done by two master masons and the friars working under their supervision; but the whole project represented a sustained communal effort of very special significance in which cost was subordinated to considerations of a higher order. What gives it a special significance is that this work of construction was going on at the same time as the futile, negative work of filling in the Southwold haven; a significance which cannot have been wholly lost on many of those taking part in both projects.

Once the friars had been provided with dormitory, refectory and kitchen in the form of the 'house', a large building in the centre of the site, and sufficient material assembled for the completion of the whole plan, the labour contribution of the townspeople gradually eased off, and the friars were left to continue the work in their own time at their own pace. Contributions of money were still needed, and continued to come in steadily. A church within the precincts was high on the list of priorities, for this was to be the main source of revenue, now and for many years to come. It was adopted by some of the leading families in the town as their burial-place, the more eagerly in that there seemed a fair certainty that their bones would rest undisturbed there until the Day of Judgment. Unlike those unfortunate ones who in the past had been buried in the graveyards of St Michael's, St Anthony's chapel, and the like. Their bones had been strewn about the beach or washed away entirely by the sea; some could be seen sticking out of the face of the cliff which the sea had made, and they too would soon fall. True, as many of the bones as were found had been gathered up and re-interred in hallowed ground; but who was to know whose bones were buried where? And how were they to be sorted out on the dreadful day of doom? Augustine De la Falaise had no intention of presenting himself at the final roll-call wearing John Gonomanaway's left leg – which was a good six inches shorter than his own – or his own wife's head, which he asserted had been cracked ever since he had known her.

Unfortunately for Augustine he, like many others who had initiated and aided the project, died before its completion. But their descendants maintained their patronage and privileges, paying for masses, dirges and obits; thus being assured of undisturbed repose, prepared to wait for centuries if need be.

Ultimately the whole precinct was surrounded by a wall of flint and stone, involving more labour and material than all the other buildings put together, and conferring on the monastery something of the air of a fortress. In the centre of the east side a gateway gave access to Scot's Lane which led straight down into the town. In the west side was erected a handsome gatehouse incorporating two gates, the larger of which gave access to the house, the smaller to the church. These gates looked out upon the countryside; the other looked across the town to the sea with its boundless horizon. A practical arrangement, no doubt, but one which came to have symbolic significance for the small band of brethren enclosed within. They were not bound to country, town or sea; but saw themselves as constituting a spiritual link, not only between the elements composing this world, but also between this world and the next.

27 Fun of the Fair

'Fair' is another of those evocative words, so much so that this might well seem an appropriate occasion for requesting poetic licence and giving a lively description of St Leonard's Fair at Dunwich while it still existed. Despite a search lasting many years, I have so far failed to discover any contemporary account of a medieval fair; the earliest accounts seem to date from the seventeenth century and depict scenes so remote from those with which we are familiar today that they appear wholly medieval in character. But I cannot be sure, so I shall content myself with telling what I know, and leave your imagination to tackle the task which mine has shirked.

What I know about the St James's fair at Dunwich is what Gardner tells me, namely that it was there in 1750 and was held in the street of that name on July 25th and 26th. I assume that it did not exist in the thirteenth century, for there is no mention of it between 1200 and 1350, unless the vague reference in 1324 to fairs and markets granted to 'the religious' is a hint of St James's fair having been started. I think it more likely that it began as a replacement for the vanished St Leonard's fair, perhaps in the mid-fourteenth century.

More is known about St Leonard's fair. It was founded – if that is the right word – about 1075. Robert Malet's gift to the Priory of Eye included *unam feriam ad festum Sancti Leonardi per tres dies* – a three-day fair at the festival of St Leonard. That makes it one of the earliest ever set up in England. It was held on Nov. 5th, 6th and 7th. The Prior of Eye paid five shillings a year towards the town rent in respect of the fair, and collected all the tolls paid by stall-holders and traders at the fair. There is no way of knowing how much that amounted to; my estimate is that it could have been £20 at the peak of prosperity. The Prior still paid 5s. in 1334. Peter FitzJohn wrecked the fair in 1270, and, according to Gardner, Augustine FitzJohn did the same thing, or tried to, in 1285. Nothing is known about the fair after 1334.

In view of such lack of knowledge, I think we are entitled to pose a few questions, and have a shot at answering them. My answers are not necessarily correct.

Why is there this lack of knowledge about fairs, since they were such a common feature of medieval life? Question and answer all in one. They were such a commonplace thing that they did not call for comment or description. Everybody knew what a fair was. By the middle of the fourteenth century there was one in practically every town and village in the land, two or three in some towns. 'The fair' was a landmark in the yearly calendar, the same as Christmas, Easter, Michaelmas and so on. It was a highlight in life, a time of reunion, merry-making, bargain-hunting, brawling, fornication and every-thing else that imparted colour to an otherwise drab exis-tence; something to look forward to, look back on, remember. But nobody thought of *writing* about it; not even those who could write; they were too busy writing about wars and miracles.

Why did fairs come into being? *Not* because they provided the populace with an opportunity to add colour to life. They started out as a source of income for lords of manors and re-ligious foundations. A fair could only be established if a lord or abbot was granted a licence by the king, on payment usually of a small fee; some fairs, like St Leonard's, were part of the endowment of a religious house. The right to hold a fair was much sought after, and jealously guarded when granted, solely because of its cash value. The licensee took the tolls from those offering goods for sale, and had the duty of 'protecting' them, that is, protecting his own interests. That is why we hear of thousands of disputes about the ownership and conduct of fairs. The late thirteenth and early fourteenth centuries saw more fairs established than any other period; and more arguments about them, naturally.

How did a fair differ from a market? In many respects, it did not. The basic element of both was buying and selling. But whereas the market was a regular daily, or weekly, event, a predictable, regulated, workaday thing, the fair was some-thing special. I think I might launch out a bit here, not on a flight of fancy, but generalisation based on widely gathered impressions.

One never knew for certain what one was going to see or do at the fair. The only certainty was that, whatever else it was, it would not be dull. To begin with, there were the people; not one's own people; 'fair folk' from far afield. Some of them were solidly-established merchants or their agents; like Robert de Dunewic, burgess of Norwich, who went regularly to the fair of St Ives (Cambridgeshire, not Cornwall). Others were wanderers, living rough, staying three days here, a week there, then moving on to the next fair perhaps thirty miles away, and back again next year if this year's departure had not been precipitated by angry officials spurred on by injured clients. There was a great deal of swindling. It was taken for granted. But for every unhappy victim there would be a dozen spectators delighted to see a neighbour made a fool of.

The vast majority of fair-folk were fair traders. They dealt in the self-same commodities which were to be found in the market. Here, to illustrate that, is a list of goods mentioned in the court-rolls of the Abbot of Ramsey's fair at St Ives in 1275: three ells of vert (yards approx. of green cloth); a coffer; 'a ring of pure gold for 5½d.' (not *quite* fair!); fleeces of wool; ham; bread – wastel and simnel; tanned hides of horses and oxen; canvas; a pinnock of cloth; a horse for 24s.; eleven score sheep-skins at 8d. each; wines; spices; charcoal. That is obviously not an exhaustive list, but those are the very things which might have been bought in Dunwich market. Some of them probably were!

Why bother to have a fair, then, if the markets could have supplied the same things? Not *all* markets could have supplied them. Dunwich was exceptional. Remember, Dunwich merchants were in contact with the whole of Europe. Not only that, there were many articles – jewellery, ornaments, weapons, fine leather goods, special fabrics, fine pottery, medicines, regional foodstuffs, and so on – for which the demand was restricted, and of which the supply also was limited. Fairs were a good way of distributing such commodities.

Moreover, the prices at the market tended to be rigidly ꞏ⁓ᵈ. Fair prices could fluctuate considerably, except for bread and ale. A prospective customer might find it well worth his while to travel twenty miles for a day's shopping around at the fair. Particularly as there was yet another difference. Half the fun of buying at a fair was in the haggling which accompanied nearly every purchase. It could take as long as two hours and six pints to sell a dicker of sheep-fells. One never paid the price first asked, and a lot of good-humoured – well, mostly good-humoured – banter was exchanged before a bargain was struck or, in the case of an important sale of animals, hides and suchlike, the 'God's penny' was handed over in front of witnesses. This was a pledge of a bargain made in good faith, the handing-over of the goods being made perhaps at a later date in another place. One transaction of which fairs had a virtual monopoly was the buying and selling of horses. In fact it later became of such importance that 'horse-fairs' were staged separately, and a horse-dealer who frequented them was known as a 'higgler.'

How, why and when did the fair change from being a purely commercial event to being the motley affair of round-abouts, coconut-shies, cheap crockery, candy-floss and cacophony that we know today? The biggest change took place about a hundred years ago. But it must have begun very early. In fact the entertainment element was probably there right from the start. To be a commercial success, from both owner's and stall-holder's point of view, the fair had to attract a lot of people. Some really big fairs, such as the Sturbridge Fair near Cambridge, would draw thousands of visitors from large distances. Even a small village fair might have been attended by five or six hundred people at a time. What brought them there, as much as the bargain-hunting, was the amusement. There were wrestling-matches, jugglers, tumblers, greasy-pole climbing, greasy-pig catching, etc. One could let the imagination go riot here, but caution is called for; much of what is popularly ascribed to the Middle Ages in fact dates from no earlier than the sixteenth century, or later. But there were certainly miracle plays in the thirteenth century, and there was every reason why such entertainment should have been combined with the fair. As time went on, the entertainment aspect equalled and eventually surpassed the commercial. Entertainment *is* commerce anyway; it always was.

Enough of generalisation; now for some specific fact. Sir Guy Ferre, lord of the manor of Benhall, got licence for a fair on his manor in 1292. The word passed round quickly. The fair was well attended in its first year. In its second year it was *too* well attended (Patent Roll, Aug. 1294):

> Commission to John de Berewyk, etc. to hear and settle a complaint by Guy Ferre, junior, who is going to Gascony in the king's service with those first crossing over, and under the king's special protection, that (sixteen men of Framlingham, Blaxhall, Saxmundham and Orford) with these men of Dunwich – William Scolding, Thomas Wennawston, Walerand le Pestur, Robert Stil, Thomas le Pestur, Roger Steward, Hugh le Pestur, Roger Primerole, Geoffrey le Talghmonger, Roger Hugon, Roger Brond and John Kelton – *entered his free fair* at Benhale, which he holds by charter of the king, *assaulted* Robert Swan, William de Haselbecke and Roger Dernford, his bailiffs deputed to collect the tolls and customs at the fair, *broke his houses* in the town and *carried away* some goods which had been taken by the bailiffs by way of distraint for toll and other customs belonging to the said fair.

I call it 'fair-bashing.' There were two categories. At the higher level a lord of a manor, baron, abbot or social upstart such as a FitzJohn, would employ a gang of ruffians – at the cost of a barrel of beer – to go and wreck a fair in order to discourage attendance and deprive the owner of his dues. It was a malicious, premeditated act of brigandage. At the lower level there was more to it than that, though the culprits obviously took their cue from their social betters. I do not think that the affair reported above – one of numerous such incidents, few so detailed as this – comes into category one. The perpetrators of the outrage came from different localities; there was no local lord whose fair would have benefited from the ruin of that of Sir Guy, or who was likely to have borne him a special grudge.

Fair-bashing was a popular pastime. An excess of ale, exceptional circumstances in a location away from home, a crowd to give illusory anonymity, the company of a number of other high-spirited youths, and you had a perfect recipe for hooliganism. If Sir Guy had been at home it would not have happened. The first young hoodlums to start trouble would have been escorted to the manor-boundary, pikes to the rear, and flung out on their ears. Perhaps minus an ear or two. As it was, an adequate fair-ward was lacking, Sir Guy having taken his men to France with him. The deputy bailiffs were local men who knew the culprits, but were powerless to stop them, once the beer had taken command. Those youths – it is certain that they were all young – were not the riff-raff of Dunwich; not when they left home; three of them were the sons and nephews of Dunwich bailiffs. No doubt they told their fathers that it was the others who started it.

Obviously they went too far. Assault was inevitable in a drunken free-for-all, but house-breaking was not normally a part of the game. The youths must have had encouragement from some of the fair-people, and I imagine that the dis-trained goods were not the only goods to be 'taken away' from the bailiff's houses. I regret that I cannot tell you what was the sequel to the affair. I doubt whether there was a sequel, apart from twenty-eight hangovers. Within less than two years many of those young men were on their way to the wars in Gascony. I wonder, as they clung to the rail of a rocking ship, did they talk of the fun they had had at the fair?

28 War

There had been rumours of war for several years. Not the Dunwich-Walberswick war; that was now part of life; going on steadily all the time, and not worth starting a rumour about. The war in question was that between King Edward I of England and King Philip of France. The political basis of it, an argument about who was vassal to whom and who owed allegiance for what, was too complicated and academic, I imagine, for Dunwich men even to try to understand. The practical implications, on the other hand, were delightfully simple. If French and Flemish ships were officially 'enemies,' then they were fair game, to be legally and loyally attacked, provided it could be done without loss. The same principle applied to Dunwich ships in foreign ports, unfortunately, as the Dunwich merchants knew to their cost. Many of them still remembered the twenty-three Dunwich ships caught napping in the last political brawl nearly thirty years before. Vigilance and caution were called for.

Better still, perhaps, was intelligent anticipation. That is no doubt what inspired them to take care of – 'carried away his goods out of his ship' was the official description – the cargo of Henry Scoft of Malines when his ship put into Dunwich in Jan. 1291. A stern rebuke followed, plus an order 'not to molest any people of the King of France, whether of Flanders or elsewhere under his dominion.' In the following year a total embargo was placed on the export of wool from England, a sure indication that diplomacy was floundering. Kings seemed to have a way of cutting off merchants' noses to spite royal faces. Dunwich had enough troubles without the intervention of inter-dominion strife. Trade was badly affected. A little light relief was afforded in 1293 by the capture – or theft, according to which side one was on – of consignments of wine and other goods destined for the Knights Templars, who did not rank as subjects of the King of France. The King of England made the diplomatic gesture of granting safe-conduct to the foreign merchants sent to look for the missing goods 'taken at sea as they assert by mariners of the realm,' but it is most unlikely that they found them. In 1294 trade with France, Holland and Flanders was virtually at a standstill. How the king managed to keep his wine-cellars stocked I cannot imagine. He does not appear to have had the same kind of thirst as his father, who ran up a bill of £1000 with his wine-buyer twenty years earlier. Perhaps Richard FitzJohn was helping him out.

In the spring of 1295, Gascony having already been occupied by the French, it was clear that war was inevitable. Gascony, it may be as well to explain, was a geographical region, a province in the south-west corner of France, part of the large duchy of Aquitaine, which was part of the kingdom of England in the sense that the King of England was its overlord, or thought he ought to be. To speak of Gascony being 'occupied by the French' may sound like stating the obvious. It always had been occupied by the French people who lived there. What happened in 1295 was that most of the towns and castles there were seized in the name of the French king by French knights and their supporters owing allegiance to the King of France. The difference which that made to the French people living there must have been minimal, since the 'English' knights who previously occupied the towns and castles spoke French, looked French and in most cases were French in origin. But, as I implied earlier, the war-game was a peculiar game, and a trifling detail like that did not prevent England from being at war with France, or vice-versa.

Dunwich, then, prepared for war. The idle merchant ships were overhauled and refitted for a new role. All through the summer the ship-yards throbbed with activity of an intensity not seen for many years; not since the barge and galley were built. Whether any new ships were built I do not know, but if they were it is certain that they would be built to a new design which was then being generally adopted. It incorporated two very significant improvements on the design which had been in vogue for centuries. One was the steering-gear. In place of the steering-oar attached on the starboard beam, a rudder was fixed centrally in the modified stern, pivoting on hinges set in a vertical stern-post and operated by a horizontal bar fixed to the top of the rudder. This made for greater speed and manoeuvrability and placed the ship less at the mercy of both waves and attackers, for the steersman – or men – were now protected from both. The other innovation was the rigging of lateen sails by means of an extra mast forward, and a bowsprit projecting forward of the prow. This enabled a ship to be sailed into the wind; not directly into it, but to within a couple of spans or three. One would like to be able to give much fuller information about these important developments as well as giving credit to the genius responsible for them. But records simply do not exist. It is probable that they evolved gradually over a long period, and that hundreds of mariners and shipwrights were involved in the creation of this new design.

Not only ships, a large amount of equipment — spare sails, masts, anchors, oars and dozens of items of smaller gear — would have to be prepared, along with armour and weapons for the men. Their 'armour' consisted mainly of a stout leather sur-coat, so that the trade in hides 'of horses and of oxen' enjoyed a boom. Peter de Dunewic was in overall charge of the naval prepartions. William de Neyreford detailed to defend the coast of Dunwich with 'horses and arms and all in his power'.

There was no difficulty in finding men to man the ships. Dunwich was swarming with men, some of them in enforced idleness, some no doubt ready for a change of employment from shovelling stones and sand. Service at sea in the king's name was in many ways preferable to service on land for some manorial lord. The king had the legal right to impress them into his service, but there is little evidence of enforcement being applied. Conditions were hard – conditions were hard in any walk of life for that class – but the pay was good; sixpence a day for officers and threepence a day for the men, as against one penny a day for normal work. There was one snag; they often had to wait a long time before being fully paid. Usually the merchant in whose ship they served advanced them or their families a part of their wages, then sent the bill in to the bailiffs, who passed it on to the Exchequer, which paid it eventually, or offset it against the amount due from the town for various reasons, fee-farm rent mostly. It is perhaps not generally appreciated what a tremendous amount of accountancy, and what a relatively small amount of currency in circulation, there was at that date.

As to the danger involved in a naval expedition, it was not usually any greater than that involved in any normal trading voyage or fishing trip, which was part of life for these men. What aided recruitment more than anything else however was the prospect of loot. Theoretically it had to be accounted for and offset against wages, but in practice it was quite impossible to keep check on every individual 'capture,' or to place a value on it in the unlikely event of it being declared. War, in effect, was licenced piracy on a grand scale.

Throughout the time the Dunwich flotilla was being prepared it was not known whether the war would be against Scotland or against France – such was the vagueness of politics – but it mattered little to Dunwich which it was. No orders had been received as to the place or date of assembly. There was talk of two fleets being required, one to go north, the other south; a crazy idea, if ever there was one. But no one knew for certain, not even Peter de Dunewic. In August the situation was suddenly clarified, and assumed an air of urgency. France was to be the target. The only question was whether there would be a French invasion of England before the English invasion of France got under way. This caused William de Neyreford to realize the importance of his job; and the impossibility of performing it. The horses and men which he needed were all busy with the harvest. The king might say that harvest was no excuse for ignoring the call to arms – kings had a habit of saying that kind of thing – but his subjects knew better, and the harvest-work went on. All that William de Neyreford could do was to see that the beacons were re-furbished and supplied with fresh barrels of tar, and men appointed to light them when the invasion fleet was sighted. If it were sighted.

Excitement and enthusiasm waned as summer gave way to autumn and no invading fleet appeared on the constantly-scanned horizon. Harvest was completed as usual. The fair came and went, with no attendant incident. Christmas was getting very near. And then, just when everybody was settling down for the winter, having given up all idea of a military adventure for the present, came the order to embark and set sail. There was an air of excitement about the departure, for scarcely any of the four hundred men leaving Dunwich that day had ever been on a military venture before.

Eleven ships sailed from the port to join flotillas from Lynn and Yarmouth. As they sailed along the coast their numbers were increased by more ships from Orford, Goseford, Harwich, Ipswich, then more from the Cinque Ports, until an armada of some eighty ships was moving westward down the Channel. To have launched such an expedition in winter was not quite the crazy idea it must have seemed to many of the men, for the wind blew steadily from north and east, and progress was rapid. Those same winds cooled the martial ardour of the younger men, chilled hands and faces compelled by overcrowding to be exposed, and doubtless turned the thoughts of many to those at home huddled round log fires and listening to the fat goose sizzling on the spit.

In early January 1296 they reached Plymouth, where crews and soldiers had a welcome break ashore whilst the military elite of the expedition was embarked. This consisted of the king's brother, Edmund Earl of Lancaster, Henry de Lacy Earl of Lincoln, and about two hundred knights with their horses and accoutrements, squires and retainers. Two days were spent on the embarkation of knights and stores, and a general re-allocation of space, then the whole fleet moved off. If accommodation had seemed cramped before, it was now unbelievably so. But that is something which the modern mind can scarcely comprehend. When one thinks of the Saxon invasions, the Viking voyages, the Norman Conquest and these numerous military excursions into the Bay of Biscay, then of the ships in which they were made, one begins to ask oneself: how could they do it? Was there something comforting, attractive even, about a situation wherein men and animals were in constant contact with each other? Did danger seem less real with a horse breathing in one's ear all day, or a fellow-traveller's knees in the middle of one's back all night? Possibly. It would nevertheless be a great relief, I am sure, when favourable weather brought the fleet to anchor in the estuary of the Gironde, some thirty miles below Bordeaux, on Jan. 18th, St Anthony's Day.

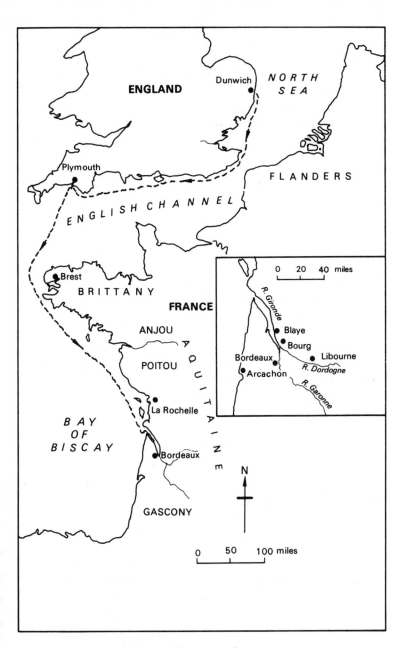

Fig. 11 Voyage to Gascony

Knights and foot-soldiers disembarked, linked up with the two contingents which had preceded them, now occupying the towns of Blaye and Bourg, and planned the capture of Bordeaux. The details of the next four months are shrouded in characteristic obscurity. Even the broad outline of the campaign is difficult to determine. Here is the only light thrown upon the Dunwich contribution, and that came thirty years after the event.

> Our men of Dunwich have revealed to us by their petition – that as they, in the twenty-fourth year of our grandfather, Edward former King of England, were in his war in the parts of Gascony with eleven of their ships and stayed there at their own cost for a long time in his service; and lost four of the eleven ships with all their goods and equipment; and did later ask the king our grandfather to have regard to their losses and expenses – he sent John de Botetourt the then admiral of the fleet – who found that their costs and damages amounted to £1420 10s.—

This preamble, for it is only a preamble, goes on and on, now in Latin, now in French; ultimately the facts are established. The men of Dunwich and 'other faithful subjects' went from Plymouth to Gascony; stayed there from St Andrew's Day (the roll says, but I think it is a mistake for St Anthony's) to Whitsun, thirteen weeks 'and more' at their own costs and charges; lost four ships with all their gear, valued at £200; wages of the mariners (names given on a separate roll which, alas, has vanished!) amounted to £1220 10s. Total debt to Dunwich: £1420 10s. Let it be paid? No, let it be credited to them to offset the town-rent and other debts. *Thirty years* after the money had been earned! What a way to wage a war!

What a war! Most wars, in retrospect, have an element of madness about them. This one seems to have been farcical. Filling in the gaps of official 'history,' it would appear to me that the English fleet spent much of the time ferrying men and equipment up and down and across the wide river, or blockading the mouths of the Garonne and Dordogne, and even more time just sitting there waiting for orders which never came or were countermanded soon after arrival. I do not suppose that the Dunwich men altogether wasted their time. The ship-masters and some of the mariners were as familiar with that estuary as they were with their own Suffolk coast. They knew and were known by the local merchants. Both sides were equally ignorant as to the progress of the war, and equally indifferent as to its outcome. Whether the King of England was vassal to the King of France, or vice-versa, trade was still trade; and trade they did, I'll be bound.

There was, apparently, a half-hearted attempt to take Bordeaux. The fleet was certainly involved, and it would be in this operation that the four Dunwich ships were lost; probably victims of an attack by galleys. Without wishing to rob the affair of any heroic quality it might have had – and which a chronicler of the day, if one had been there, would certainly have given it – I would not rule out the possibility that the Dunwich ships, finding themselves in a tight spot, calmly surrendered. After all, there was no reason why they should *all* be lunatics.

Bordeaux was not taken. The dejected knights, depleted in numbers, were re-embarked, and the fleet set sail for England. The voyage home across the Bay and round the rocky coast of Brittany in the teeth of April gales can have been no picnic. Let your imagination deal with that. Grant me poetic licence, please, to deal with the Dunwich flotilla nearing home on that fine Whit Sunday morning.

The ships had been sighted from the beacon-towers when still some ten miles out. The news spread round the town like wildfire, and soon a dense, excited crowd was gathering on the quay to await the arrival of the ships. Only when the Lynn and Yarmouth flotillas had continued on their course was it possible to be sure how many ships were heading in for Dunwich, and even then the outcome of the venture was a matter for conjecture. The seven vessels, two barges and five cogs, came slowly in, oars manned and sails half-furled. To the anxious watchers on the quay it seemed that ships had never moved more slowly. One by one they came into the narrow haven-mouth. Tension mounted in the swelling crowd, relief in some offset by anguish in the rest. There was little jubilation heard, no cheering either from the ships or those on shore. Eyes scanned the names of ships as each came into view – *Godbefore, Goodyear, Sainte Marie, Isabel, Margaret, Welfare,* lastly *Katerina.* Eyes searched for faces so well known, so hard to recognise with certainty until one broke into a smile beneath a waving hand. On many lips, in many eyes, the unspoken question hovered: where was *Burmayden,* where *Leonard, Rose* and *Mariote?*

The crowd upon the quay grew denser still as men filed off the ships, but even then the sound of voices hardly rose above a murmur, heightened only by a joyful squeal as little boy or girl was raised aloft by strong brown hands, held momentarily at arm's length for an admiring gaze, then stifled in a moist embrace which mingled silked locks and shaggy beard. The womenfolk said little. What was there to be said, other than 'Thank God'? And those who had no man to greet, nothing to thank God for, what could they say? What could they do? What would they do tomorrow, and the morrow after that?

The merchants reckoned up their loss, and more than one vowed openly that never again would his ships, his men or his money be put to the service of the king.

29 And More War

For the next thirty-five years of its history, as Fate moved in relentlessly on this doomed town, happenings followed one upon the other with such dramatic and complicated effect that one must abandon all hope of maintaining a strict chronological sequence in the narration of them. Though all these happenings were to some extent inter-related, the only way to keep the picture clear is to deal with one thing at a time. With war still fresh in our minds, and because the aftermath of war was the most immediate of the cares besetting Dunwich, let us deal first with what in effect were to be the last

rounds of the war-game for this most unenthusiastic partici-
pant.

Dunwich, in common with a host of others, was still a 'king's
town'; still hopefully expected to provide the king with ships
and men for waging war, and still in duty bound to pay £65
a year in fee-farm rent for that dubious privilege. Neither
duty nor privilege were likely to be rated very high so long
as the bitter memory of that 1296 fiasco remained. The king's
attitude did not help; he seemed to show more consideration
towards his 'enemy' than to his own supporters. Early in 1297
an order was sent to all ports that no one should leave the
realm without a special licence. The order was relaxed in
favour of a flotilla sent specially to Gascony with a shipment
of corn, returning with a supply of salt. Those same ships
were immediately ordered to stand by for an expedition to
Flanders. Dunwich, with other ports, was reminded of the
treaty now in force with France, and warned that there was
to be no plundering of French ships trading with England.
The order was repeated a few months later – a sure sign that
it had been ignored – then followed a year later by an order
that goods seized from Frenchmen before the late war, and
not consumed, were to be kept for restitution to their owners
in accordance with the Pope's deed of arbitration. That, at
least, would raise a laugh on Dunwich faces.

In Feb. 1298 commissioners were appointed to take *all* the
ships in Norfolk and Suffolk capable of carrying men, horses
and other necessaries, and to prepare them with decks and
hurdles, so as to be ready manned at Sluys in Flanders on the
first Sunday in Lent. How many ships turned up I do not
know. The expedition was an utter failure, and the king was
back in England within the year.

Then away he went to Scotland. A fleet also went, reduced
to fifty-eight ships. They, and he, accomplished nothing. Just
another fiasco; followed by another meaningless truce. Dunwich men were not there; they found more occupation nearer
home, as is told in the next chapter. Not surprisingly, the king
was short of cash. He tried to remedy that by a total ban on
the export of money and silver. How could merchants carry

on trading if they were not allowed to take money with them? Quite easily; by hiding it 'secretly in sacks of wool, hides and bales,' as the king soon discovered. The bailiffs were ordered several times to search all ships leaving port.

In February 1301, in anticipation of the expiry of the truce, orders were sent to all ports for ships to be with the king at Berwick at Midsummer. Of a total of eighty, Dunwich was only asked for *one* ship. With John de Thorpe and Peter de Dunewic in charge of requisitioning, Dunwich could hardly refuse, and one ship was sent; probably one of Peter's own ships. (As a matter of interest and for comparison, that fleet included six ships from Yarmouth, three from Lynn, two from Blakeney, and one each from Hull, Grimsby, Wainfleet and Saltfleet.) The order to send merchants to Berwick with provisions, under promise of 'good payment,' met with a similar response. Walter Bacon of Dunwich sent a ship carrying victuals (herrings?) 'of the king to Scotland and there served the king in his Scottish war for seventeen weeks.' For this he received the 'good' payment of £1 14s., which the bailiffs recovered from the Exchequer four years later. Assuming a master and a crew of five, those men of Walter's earned two shillings a week shared between them; less than a penny a day. Perhaps Walter, and they, made a profit on the sale of the victuals. Walter seems to have made something out of it, for two years later he enlarged his house in Dunwich, paying a fee for the enclosure of an adjacent lane.

The Parliamentary Rolls – always a few years behind the events to which they relate – in 1304 reveal an attempt by the Dunwich men, through their members of Parliament, to have the total number of requisitioned ships reduced by ten, no doubt hoping thereby that Dunwich would be omitted altogether from the list. Their excuse was that they had already incurred expenses of £1000 on the king's behalf. The king was not impressed. On Jan. 5th, 1307 the king addressed a stern letter from Lanercost Priory (near Carlisle) to the mayor and bailiffs of Dunwich, Yarmouth, etc. ordering them:

under pain of forfeiture of life and limb, lands, goods, chattels, etc. not to export corn, beasts, victuals, horses, armour, money, silver or gold vessels, silver in money, without the licence of the king.'

Corn and victuals could be sent to Gascony, but all the rest the king needed 'to prosecute his war in Scotland.' He also needed one ship from Dunwich, which Dunwich was to supply at its own cost. The king need not have bothered. By the time his letters had reached Suffolk, and had been digested and forgotten, King Edward I had gone to a land where no war-games are played, and where no one challenges overlordship.

His successor left the mayor and bailiffs in comparative peace for over fourteen years, as regards demands for shipping; during that time there was a lot of action on the Suffolk coast which the king knew little about; though he did know something about similar action on the Channel coast. Then in 1322 the Scottish War flared up again. The bailiffs, said the king, had agreed to provide a ship armed and equipped at their own costs for eight weeks. They thought differently, and it was agreed that one strong ship, with arms, victuals, etc. and double-manned should be supplied at the king's expense and sent at once with the rest of the fleet to the Humber. A month later the bailiffs and six men were summoned to Colchester to talk about a subsidy for the Scots War. Talking cost nothing, so they went. Then the ships were to be at Tynemouth by Trinity Sunday. If any were sent, they escaped the records. The best of them apparently escaped the requisitioning orders as well, thanks to the timely and skilful use of bribery. Rather than see their land occupied by Scots, the northern barons made a truce without the king's help and another period of peace broke out. With Scotland, that is. War with France followed almost immediately; or rather, war with a group of dissidents led by Roger Mortimer and, later Queen Isabella.

Mortimer fled to France. His expected return, with a French army, led to a watch on the ports, the appointment of spies, and the order to take him 'dead or alive' in 1323. This had repercussions in Dunwich totally unconnected with the war-game. In May 1324 the usual orders, when invasion was contemplated, reached the mayor and bailiffs: 'All ships capable of carrying 40 tuns of wine or more to be prepared at once'. to be ready at three days notice. Two ships of Dunwich were to assemble with the fleet at Plymouth. They did not, nor did the fleet. The wine-trade was resumed in June; somebody had some common sense. Queen Isabella and Prince Edward left for France in March 1325. A year later it was known that, when she and the prince returned, it would be to oust the king from his throne and place Roger Mortimer in the position of power held at present by the Despensers.

All through that summer Dunwich lived through an invasion scare yet again. So the history books might say. Actually Dunwich men, like those of Yarmouth, Ipswich, Orford, etc. – but with better reason than those other ports – had ceased to care a rap about a political situation which made no sense at all. When in September 1326 the fleet was ordered 'on pain of imprisonment and loss of goods, etc.' to be equipped for one month, double-manned, and assemble in the Orwell, *not one single ship* obeyed the order. The Queen of England and the heir apparent invaded their own country with a force of Hainaulters, landing completely unopposed in the Orwell on September 24th. Those whose business it was to fight, including Thomas Earl of Norfolk, joined them. The rest of Suffolk watched the cavalcade pass by, then got on with the harvest.

The war-game, for Dunwich, was nearly over. The harbour that had once sent thirty ships at a time to fight for the king would not send many more.

30 Piracy

I ought perhaps to have given this topic fuller treatment earlier, for it must have been a feature of Dunwich life since the early days of the Saxon invasions; perhaps even earlier than that. The word 'pirate' is of Greek origin; it seems to have meant 'one who tries it on'. Its earliest use in English occurs in the ninth century, when it meant 'sailor'. The word itself is relatively rare in the period with which I am dealing, but the deed is all too common; more common, I would say, than highway robbery. Like most other scourges of humanity – plague, pestilence, famine, war – it had periodic phases of extra intensity. One of them seems to have developed late in the thirteenth century and reached its peak in the early decades of the fourteenth.

There were as yet, in 1290 or thereabouts, no full-time professional pirates, no Barbarossas of the North Sea, so far as I can tell. There were however a lot of opportunists, normally engaged in lawful commerce, who were willing to 'try it on' if conditions were favourable. On some routes and in certain ports piracy was as big a risk as the weather. In time of war – that is, most of the time – piracy took the form of privateering; in effect the same thing under a different name. Any shipowner could arm his ship and legally plunder the ships of the 'enemy'. It was one of the long-established rules of the war-game. Much of what I call piracy undoubtedly occurred as a direct result of conditions favourable for privateering; and much of it was perpetrated, not on the 'high seas', but by men operating from the shore. One thinks of ports and harbours as being 'havens of safety' for ships having braved the perils of the deep. In fact the cargo was often at greatest risk when the ship was moored or anchored, especially in less frequented spots like the Deben or Orwell rivers. I can find little indication as to specific security measures adopted in busy ports, but plenty as to their total absence or failure on occasion. The presence of bodies of men-at-arms was not necessarily a security measure; rather an additional risk sometimes.

It might be supposed that piracy and privateering would at times have resulted in a total cessation of sea-borne commerce. That rarely appears to have been the case, and one can only offer a few tentative suggestions as to the reasons why. One is that successful trading ventures – as distinct from mere 'carrying' – when ships came safely home and cargoes reached their intended destination, were very profitable. There is an instance on record of a single cargo being worth more than £16,000 – on record, incidentally, only because it was stolen – but the circumstances suggest that it must have consisted partly of coin. A normal cargo could be worth anywhere between a hundred pounds and four thousand, which was a large sum of money in those days. It needs to be borne in mind that the value of stolen cargoes was nearly always exaggerated by the aggrieved owners.

Even the carrying trade, which throughout the Middle Ages seems to have constituted a major element of Dunwich's commerce, was a fairly lucrative business. An average-sized ship cost about £100, and the sum earned by one ship carrying one freighted cargo could vary between ten pounds and fifty. The cost of a voyage, say, from Dunwich to Dunkirk and back, in terms of wages and provisions might be as little as two pounds. Harbour dues, tolls and customs, for all the animosity they aroused, were not excessive; they were reckoned in pence. The winnings, therefore, when one won, made the gamble a tempting one. Several successful ventures, or a few years of successful carrying, could set a man up for life. The fact that all might be lost on the next gamble did not deter men from taking the risk. As we have seen, the risk was spread out among a number of small investors, and nearly all merchants operated in partnership with others.

Allied with the gambling element was what I would call the 'sporting' element. The odds were by no means all in favour of an unlawful aggressor at sea, which is no doubt why many of them preferred to stay on land and let the intended victim come to them. An experienced master who knew his ship and his seas could often out-manoeuvre an assailant and escape his clutches by half a cable's length, leaving him stranded on a sand-bar until the next high tide. A cunning master with a resolute crew could present the appearance of a sitting duck which at the last moment transformed itself into a fighting-cock capable of giving as good as it got, even reversing the roles of victim and aggressor. The skill and bravery of his men were a merchant's greatest assets. If they were not to be relied upon it was, as like as not, because the merchant failed to assess them at their true worth, paying his men a miserable wage, taking the minimum of trouble over their comfort and safety, and sending out his ships grossly undermanned. Many a cargo must have been lost, when a few more pounds invested in men would have saved it. Instances of robbery in which crews were killed or injured are surprisingly rare, suggesting that they rarely put up a fight. The greatest asset on the side of the pirates was probably the parsimony of many merchants, and the knowledge that a man was not likely to risk life and limb for the sake of a mean man's money.

Why should there have been such an alarming increase in piracy in the last decade of the reign of Edward I and throughout the reign of Edward II, particularly on the East Anglian coast? And particularly in the vicinity of Dunwich! Had it anything to do with what was happening to Dunwich? I think it had. Dunwich, the once thriving port, was decaying through circumstances beyond its control. In their frustration and anger, many Dunwich men decided to hit back at Fate by resorting to robbery. Some had the justification that they might as well risk hanging as slowly starve; others saw no reason why, failing to get rich by fair means, they should not do so by foul. Did the political situation favour an outbreak of lawlessness? Undoubtedly. Despite the increase in law-making, the vastly improved administration and a genuine desire on the part of the king and the majority of the barons to see stable government and justice done to all, pre-occupation with war depleted the resources needed for law-enforcement, and encouraged an attitude of contempt for law.

But there is another aspect of the situation, particularly in so far as it affected Norfolk and Suffolk, which calls for comment. A very high proportion of the cases of piracy reported between 1299 and 1318 concern Flemings. There seems to me to be something about this which goes much deeper than the political situation of the moment; much further back into the past; the survival, perhaps, of inter-racial or inter-tribal rivalry with roots many centuries deep. The Flemings had come over 'only for the plunder' in 1173. The Flemings were the victims of the most brutal attacks in the Peasants' Revolt of 1381. Who were these 'Flemings'? They were the inhabitants of what we now call Holland and Belgium and part of north-eastern France and was then called loosely 'Flanders', the very territory from which the ancestors of most Norfolk and Suffolk men had emigrated six or seven centuries earlier. There had been close links between Flanders and East Anglia for a long time, links which, one would have thought, ought to have bound them together in amity.

Similarity of racial origin, similarity of language, common interests ought surely to have made for friendship. Sometimes, I am sure, they did. Dunwich mariners were as much at home in Dunkirk or Stavoren as Antwerpers were in Dunwich or Yarmouth. Dunwich housewives could have gone shopping in the market of Bruges – if their husbands had let them – without noticing any marked difference between it and that of their home town. Anyone entering a quayside tavern anywhere between Calais and Bremen on the one side or between Dover and Grimsby on the other would have heard the same talk, seen the same faces, drunk the same beer and paid for it in the same currency in each of them. Wool and hides from Lincolnshire, Norfolk and Suffolk were as vital to the well-being of Flanders as were cloth and leather from Flanders to the well-being of the English counties. Why, then, should the men of either side make war on the other? Was it their way of hitting back at politics which they could neither control nor understand? There is material for a thesis here, beyond the scope of my story and my ability.

Let us come down to cases; what happened, when and where. These are all from the Patent Rolls and Close Rolls. They represent only a fraction of the incidents which occurred; those cases where the merchant concerned was wealthy or powerful enough to set the machinery of the law in motion.

1299. Inquiry re persons who invaded a ship of Richard and Peter FitzJohn, laden with wines, salt, men's armour and other goods *near Dunwich*, plundered the ship of those goods and took the ship to Gillingham, where they sold, scattered and consumed them.

1300. Some persons attacked and plundered a ship of Ralph de Monte Hermeri, Earl of Gloucester and Hertford, which put in *at Southwold* while the earl was on the king's service in Scotland; *broke up and sank* the ships of his men in that port, and prevent merchants from putting in at that port as they used to do.

That is an interesting example of the inter-relation of different aspects of the situation which I mentioned earlier. It was a mixture of land-based piracy, waging war in a homely fashion, and the long-standing Dunwich–Walberswick feud. I do not claim to know who the 'some persons' were, but I am quite certain where they came from.

Those responsible for the safe-keeping of the seas were fully alive to the problem, and came up with a sensible and practical solution, as witness this order to the Warden of the Cinque Ports in 1301 :

Masters of ships sailing to Gascony to fetch wine or ply other merchandise shall keep their ships continually in the form of a fleet, and in such depth of the sea or river and so gathered together they cannot be taken, arrested or aggrieved – when they put in to buy victuals or trade, they shall proceed prudently and wisely, and depart speedily—'

There was safety in numbers. There were other advantages too, as any wolf-pack knew; as a group of English ship-masters demonstrated two years later. They were on the way home from Gascony, a convoy of eight ships of Bristol, Yarmouth and elsewhere, including *La Pleyntie* of Dunwich, master William Clark. At the same time a ship worth £4200, was on its way to England.

—the said ships and sailors and others in them came to the said ship of Seville off the port of St Matieu in Brittany – entered her and took the said goods, along with the ropes, anchors and other gear, and brought her to England, and took the goods to several places in Norfolk, Suffolk, Sussex and Somerset—

Juries were to be summoned in those counties, and restitution made 'according to merchant law'. There was a complicated code of law, based partly on the Law of Oléron of 1266 and partly on codified custom, relating to international commerce. There was no effective way of stopping piracy, apart from having numerical superiority and catching the culprits red-handed. Even the time-honoured practice of reprisal – 'if men of your country steal from men of mine, men of my country will steal from men of yours' – was of little practical use as a deterrent.

In 1300 or thereabouts (it was first reported in the Close Roll of 1305) three ships belonging to Richard FitzJohn of Dunwich and James Le Reve of London, laden with cargoes worth well over £4000, went to trade in Holland and Zeeland, 'Malefactors plundered the ships in the port of Merland in Zeeland', led and instigated by Katherine, Lady of Vorne. The king requested the Count of Flanders to see that justice was done. The count made one evasive reply after another. Reprisals were ordered. Bailiffs in English ports were instructed to seize the goods of Flemish merchants — any Flemish merchants — to make up the value of the stolen goods. In 1306 inquiry showed that Yarmouth had managed to recoup £10, London £100 and Harwich £13. No Flemish ships, apparently, had put in at Dunwich. Then King Edward I died, and fresh orders were necessary. Reprisals were ordered on a specific basis: £1000 was to be collected at Yarmouth, London and Harwich; £1600 at Berwick 'and the rest of Scotland'; £640 in Northumberland; £600 in Yorkshire and £640 in Norfolk. Dunwich was not on the list. And either somebody was hoping to make a profit, or the extra was intended to cover expenses.

The only known haul resulting from the order was made at a spot which would be extremely difficult to identify today – the port of Ravenser, now lying on the sea-bed a mile or two south-east of Withernsea in Yorkshire. The bailiffs there had managed to seize three Flemish ships which had evidently been forced to seek shelter in a storm. They dutifully handed them over to the sheriff. Then, in August 1309, the king having made a treaty with the Count of Holland and Zeeland by the terms of which all Flemish ships and cargoes were to be restored, the Ravenser haul was handed back to the owners. At least, I assume that it was.

Meanwhile, a bit of unusual Anglo-Flemish collaboration had been going on:

1308. Complaint of Walter le Fleming, citizen and merchant of York, that William FitzJohn and Bodekin le Bawer and other malefactors of Holland and Zeeland took and carried away by armed force goods of his to the value of £44 from a ship *near Dunwich* – the late king said he would cause justice to be done, but—

The Count of Flanders said that none of his men were involved. He could have been telling the truth; knowing what William FitzJohn was capable of getting up to. The sea off Dunwich was fast becoming a place for honest merchants to avoid.

1311. Complaint from Geoffrey Attechurch of Yarmouth that John Starcolf and John Munk of Dunkirk in Flanders, together with other malefactors of those parts, entered by force the said Geoffrey's ship called *La Grace de Magna Gernemutha* on the *sea coast near Dunwich* and, having expelled the mariners, carried off £20 in money, and goods to the value of £40, and *chopped the said ship with axes,* damaging it to the extent of £40.

Said the king to the count: kindly do justice and certify by the bearer that you have done so. Eighteen months later, nothing had been done. The count had a lot of correspondence to deal with; and somebody may have suggested to him that 'Flemings' were being accused of crimes which they had not in fact committed.

1311. Robert Assheman of Great Yarmouth complains that Lemmekin and Hannekyn Gilessone of Blankenbergh, Clays Corn of Yzre, Noydekyn of Newhithe and others, entered his ship called *La Margarete* laden with goods to the value of £200 on the Eve of St Laurence last on the sea coast of England, took all the goods, *scuttled and sank* the ship and her tackle worth £80—

One begins to suspect that there was a *gang* of pirates operating from Dunwich, or somewhere near. It becomes a certainty when one learns that, as a consequence of robberies at Yarmouth and attacks upon Stephen Drayton, John de Belton and *nine* Flemish merchants, the following men were in Ipswich gaol awaiting trial:

> Simon Porter, Thomas Godknape, Alan Whyte, John Pope, Walter Thurston, William Hawys, Geoffrey Morebread, Robert Mustard, William Payne and Edmund Payne, all of Dunwich, along with a score of others.

None of those men are traceable in the rent-roll of 1334, though the relatives of some of them are, including Alice Morebread, widow. It may be safely assumed, I think, that they lost their heads, or dangled from the gallows. Richard Sparrow of Dunwich was more fortunate. He had been involved in the plundering of a Flemish ship at Orford, but was pardoned in 1312, and retired from the sea to take up the respectable occupation of baker, with a large house in St Leonard's parish.

That ought to have put a stop to piracy for a time. It no doubt put a stop to the activities of one particular gang, but piracy went on. In 1315 there were no less than eleven commissions of inquiry into piratical episodes along the coast between Lynn and Harwich. It is clear that, in some instances, the crews of the ships sent to patrol the coast themselves indulged in plundering. And there was no answer to that.

It seems clear also that there was collusion between the Flemish pirates and the English. In January 1317 the sheriff of Lincolnshire was informed that:

> Ten merchants of Lincolnshire freighted a ship of Baldwin Skynner at Boston with wool to go overseas. Certain malefactors of Sluys in Flanders attacked the ship on its voyage *by the coast between Dunwich and Orford,* stole the wool and other goods to the value of £1100 and took it away to Flanders—

The king wrote to the Count of Flanders, who made 'frivolous excuses', passed on by the Mayor of Antwerp. So, said the king, arrest all the goods of the men of Sluys and elsewhere in Flanders *except* corn, meat, wines, spicery, etc and guard them well. Of course it did not work, but it had a slightly better chance of success than the proposed method of settling in 1318 the claim for losses arising from piracy at Yarmouth seven years before. The stolen amount, several hundred pounds, was to be collected from merchants, mariners and fishermen in *all* ports!

There does appear to have been a lull in piratical activity then for about twenty years, except for one outstanding episode of a very special kind which will be described later. Now, before we leave the topic, there is one aspect of it so far unmentioned which interests me more than any other, namely the *technique* of piracy. How was it done?

We read about 'entering', 'breaking', 'taking away'; in one case they 'expelled' the sailors from the ship; in a few they 'assaulted' the merchants. There is no mention of killing or wounding, and the victims, in those cases we know about, seem all to have lived to tell the tale and supply the names and addresses of their assailants. There cannot have been much secrecy about the business. Did the pirates simply crowd into a ship, or a number of small boats, row out to intercept a becalmed merchant-ship and scare the life out of all on board by threats, oaths, wild yells and brandished weapons? If so, would they not have met with a volley of arrows or crossbow bolts, at least on some occasions; enough to make the game too hazardous? All encounters, remember, were at close quarters. There was no cannon-shot across the bows; no Jolly Roger suddenly replacing the ensign at the mast-head; none of the traditional Boys Own Paper stuff. To fill in what would otherwise be a complete blank, let me tell you how I would have done it.

I would have recruited a band of twenty-five strong young men and one experienced master who knew the coast like the back of his hand. I would have hired from a merchant, for a small down-payment and the promise of more to come, a ship of the latest type, with rudder, lateen sails, slender prow and lots of space between decks. I would have established a base in the river Deben, or the Alde, from which to steal out under cover of darkness so as to be positioned at first light to windward of a heavily-laden ship which my craft would overhaul in less than half an hour. With grappling-irons all prepared, and all but a normal crew carefully concealed, I would make as if to pass by my victim, then at the crucial moment swing the helm hard over and come alongside, at which moment my hidden gang would suddenly emerge with crossbows loaded and poised. No mariner crew, outnumbered four to one, would risk three bolts in each of their hides for the sake of someone else's wool. Not that I should bother much with wool and suchlike stuff. There would always be money, jewels, plate and similarly attractive trash on board.

No, I would not harm the master or the crew; or the merchant, unless his rings were too tight on his fingers. I would let them all go. They would not identify me or my ship. I would carry in the hold an assortment of more than twenty different name-boards, so that every attack would be made by a different ship, not one of which actually existed in the port to which it was assigned. The sheriff? There were ways of keeping sheriffs quiet. The patrol? My ship would be the patrol. Disposal of the loot? There was the lonely chapel at Minsmere, two half-ruined churches at Dunwich, barns everywhere – But why should I give away all my secrets? You might prefer to plan your own campaign.

31 Of Little Faith

On March 21st 1305 the king at Westminster wrote a letter to the mayor, bailiffs and community of Dunwich, instructing them that:

> the Friars Minor of Dunwich shall have the king's galley of that town with all its tackle and appurtenances in whose hands soever they may be, as the king has given it to them.

That must surely be an incident unique in monastic history. Monasteries had been given money, land, privileges and rights, oak-trees, 'wreck', etc, but never before, or since, a fully-equipped galley. Did the king hope that they might put to sea in it – they had the necessary strength, numerically at least – and sweep the pirates from the sea with psalms and alleluyas? Or was it intended as a jest? Or a scornful comment on the lack of support supplied by Dunwich for the king's wars?

It was none of these things, I think. Someone – the men who represented Dunwich in the Parliament, most probably – had told the king that the galley would never sail again, even if it were wanted. For twenty years it had sat idle and helpless, half in meadow, half in mud, where the last great flood had left it. The tackle and 'appurtenances' had all been put to other uses long ago. The timbers of the hull by now must have been warped and many of them rotting, so that the galley could not be hauled to the ship-yard for repair. And if that were possible, it could not have put to sea, for the simple reason that the haven-mouth of Dunwich was not wide enough to enable a vessel of that size to be taken out. The galley would have to stay at Dunwich. It might as well therefore be given to the friars. In that way, what was lost to the king in the sphere of war might constitute a gain for his soul in a higher sphere.

But what could the friars *do* with an unfloatable galley? Did they regard the gesture as a joke? You may be sure they did not. To them it was a godsend. They needed timber urgently for the completion of their houses and the permanent roofing of their church. They might have asked for oak-trees, and got them. Here was something better; well-seasoned timber already sawn and shaped; it only needed cutting to the proper lengths and carrying up the hill. I have often heard people say, when speaking of a timbered house, that 'in olden days they used ship's timbers to build their houses'. Except in very rare instances indeed, the statement is wholly untrue. Grey Friars at Dunwich was one of those exceptions; and yet another bit of symbolism was incorporated in its fabric by the agency of king – and Fate. Three years later, that contribution to the spiritual wealth of Dunwich was offset by another royal gesture of a different kind, in a setting less than a quarter-mile from the Grey Friars boundary-wall.

The Knights Templars, so called because their first house,

founded in 1117, was near the Temple in Jerusalem, established a 'Temple' in Dunwich in 1185 on an eight-acre site granted to them by King Henry II, in the west part of the town, just inside the rampart. The professed objective of this religious order was to encourage and finance crusades in defence of Christendom against the 'infidel' Saracens. Crusading was not everyone's idea of enjoyment, or hope of salvation; but to be able to stay at home whilst taking part vicariously in a crusade by paying for someone else to go to the Holy Land was quite an attractive idea to many. The Temple soon amassed considerable wealth, much of it in the form of property, both in the town and in the surrounding countryside. The bailiffs, under compulsion, made a contribution of ten shillings a year, but got it back with interest by levying rents of 16s. 8d. on the property which the Templars held, and for which *they* charged their tenants rents of £1 13s. 5d. Some of the tenants paid their rents in 'white herrings' valued at fivepence per hundred.

A lot of the income accruing to the Templars was undoubtedly expended on crusading in the early days, for their premises at Dunwich – said to be the most important of their houses in Suffolk – were never very impressive. They included a church or chapel, inevitably. Gardner, quoting Weever (1631), says that the church was 'vaulted over, and Isles all leaded'. But it was not there in 1310, only a chapel which was 're-covered with reeds' at a cost of 2s. 6d. This was said to have been a round building, as most Temple churches were, modelled on the Church of the Holy Sepulchre at Jerusalem, and was 'reputed to have been a Place of great Privileges for Pardons'. By that, Gardner was probably referring to its frequent use by criminals claiming sanctuary. No less than four thieves took refuge there in the year 1287. All churches afforded this privilege, and it was more used, and abused, in Dunwich than in most places. A pretty problem must have been posed when John de Oyntus, having stolen the lead from the church of St Nicholas, took refuge in the church of St John.

The Templars were for a long time 'held in great Esteem

for their Sanctity; but Riches made them proud and vicious, which rendered them odious'. I know nothing about any vices they may have had. As for their riches, I doubt whether that would have rendered them odious, but it would make others envious. King Philip the Fair of France, accusing the Templars of the 'grossest Crimes of Irreligion and Infidelity' (another way of saying they were too rich?), caused fifty-seven of them to be burnt and abolished the order in his own realm. The Pope, having no jurisdiction over the order, approved, and exhorted King Edward II of England to do likewise. King Edward saw no reason for burning them, but every reason for appropriating their property.

Accordingly he sent the sheriff of Norfolk and Suffolk to Dunwich in 1308 to take over the Temple in his name and make out a detailed inventory of what he had won. If this kind of thing had not happened we should never have known very much about the Temple. As it is, we can know a great deal. The sheriff accounted for the rents; £3 11s. 9d. received in oblations and tithes; 8s. for two quarters of malt sold; and £4 0s. 6d. from the sale of two horses, one ox, four pigs, one last of herrings, twenty cheeses, a piece of wax, an old cart and a tunic. Not a lot of 'riches' in that lot, but a bargain or two for somebody at the sale. He noted that the carter was paid 1½d. a day; the Warden 9d. a week; and the chaplain 2d. a day plus 3d. a day for his food; whereas the chaplain's clerk, who helped in the task of 'celebrating in the chapel', was paid 2d. a week, out of which presumably he had to feed himself.

Then he listed the contents of the chapel, house, yard and outhouses, a list which I find interesting enough to quote in full, for it is the earliest inventory I have ever seen:

one gold cup 20s.
one mazer 5s. 4d. (wooden drinking-bowl, with silver rim)
three feet silver cups 6s. 8d. (cups with feet of silver? feet detached from silver cups?)
35 gold florins value £4 7s. 6d., price of a florin 2s 6d.
7 gold rings 7s.
2 gold clasps 5s.
17 clasps of silver 15s.

money found in 4 pouches £111 14s. 6¼d. which Robert de Suf-
field parson of Brampton Church *says he was able to take
care of.* (To be sure he was! Robert de Sefeld was the man
sacked from the mastership of *Domus Dei* in 1306 for embezzlement and misappropriation of funds.)

1 pair of plates   2s.

1 pair of mustelers (wine-jars)   3s.

1 shilling in silver   12d.

1 mattress   6d.

4 score and 19 lambs   £2 9s. 6d.

1 great chest and 1 small chest with 8 bulls. (No, not papal
bulls, and not livestock; lead discs stamped with religious
symbols, usually with the name of St Nicholas, sold as
'charms' to protect sailors in particular; several have been
found at Dunwich)

and 1 pix with the King's protection not valued (meaning that
he had permission from the king to exclude certain 'sacred'
items from valuation)

1 pair of organs   12d.

4 vestments whole   £1 9s. 8d.

1 cross plated with silver   18d.

1 chalice of gold   16s.

1 old chalice   3s.

1 new missal for use   12d. (service-book)

1 portiforium   13s. 4d. (portable breviary or prayer-book)

1 gradual   18d. (book of anthems)

2 legenda   3s. (books of legends, lives of saints)

2 antiphonariums, new   12d. (books of chants)

1 small chest with *relics of saints* and another small chest with
other relics.

1 pix with Eucharist (box containing consecrated bread)

1 piece of wax   12d.

2 last and 1000 herrings   £4 4s. od.

Timber   13s. 4d.

Norman stone from the quarry   13s. 4d. (to build a new
church?)

2 old carts with gears for 3 horses   10s.

20 cheeses   2s. 6d.

1 *crossbow*   8d.

1 pelin (?) and 1 basin   20d.

2 jars, 1 plate, 1 posnet   7s.

1 lead (tub) and other utensils for brewing, 1 tub, 10 boards
   1od. (must be 1os.)

1 small pig   1od.

1 quarter of an ox   12d. (it might have been tough, but what
   a price!)

1 lamb received from a certain stranger as an oblation.

That last item was evidently brought to the house just as the
sheriff had completed his survey, and would, one hopes, be
added to the ninety and nine already in the fold. Some of those
valuations are worth a closer scrutiny; they tell us a little
about the nature and intentions of those who made them.

The list as a whole, I believe, tells us more about religious
houses – some religious houses – than do many pages of many
books written over many years. It helps to dispel what I call
the 'monastic myth'; the idea that all religious houses were
abodes of piety, poverty, good works and prayer, affording
comfort and sustenance to the poor and setting an example
to the world. The Temple at Dunwich was a hoarding-house,
to which rich and poor alike contributed, often in their wills,
their money, gold and silver ornaments, piglets, lambs – especially their lambs – for what? To pay the wages of the
Warden, chaplain and carter; to feed them and the two
'knights' Templars – yes, *two*; that is all there were – to have
religious offices celebrated. It was no fault of the Templars
that they had not spent anything on sending anybody to
Jerusalem; there had not been a crusade for thirty-six years.
Perhaps they thought that there would be another crusade,
one day. Meanwhile they were simply hoarding what they got.
Neither can one accuse them of living in luxury; only one
mattress between the six of them; and their diet seems to have
been mainly roast lamb, herrings, cheese and beer. One could,
of course, do worse.

The king kept the Temple and its lands in his hands for
four years before granting it to the Knights Hospitallers of
the Order of St John of Jerusalem, on whom then fell the
burden of responsibility for the defence of Christendom, and
it became known as 'the hospital'. (Nothing to do with healing

the sick, and nothing to do with providing hospitality; not in this case, though it had in many others.) The Warden, John de Medfield, resigned. His successor left after two years; *his* successor left after one year. It was not a very attractive job, now that the sheriff was prying into everything, insisting on a new roof for the chapel, repairs to the houses of the tenants, new shoes for the men who collected the tithes from Dingle, and so on. Old Richard Osmond, the chaplain, had had the best job; a new robe, costing 20s. every Christmas, and five-pence a day for doing nothing until the day he died. The two Templar brethren, Robert de Spaunton and John Coffyn, were not condemned to beggary. They were employed by the Bishop of Norwich, at fourpence a day each, to be sent to certain monasteries to do penances for monks who were too busy to do their own penance. Not an ideal job – lying on a cold stone floor all night saying endless *Aves* and *Paternosters* to atone for someone else's sins – but well paid.

When the house was handed over to the Knights Hospitallers, another inventory was made. It differed very markedly indeed from that made four years earlier. I will only quote one item from it:

> I feretrum for relics of no value and for the relics in the said feretrum, value unknown.

Was that an indication of the 'Infidelity' for which the Templars were condemned? Another two hundred years were to elapse before 'relics' in general were discarded as deceitful trumpery. The new inventory, made by the Warden, put totally different values on some of the articles which were left, doubling most of them. All that was left in fact were the contents of the chapel, and by no means all of them. All the gold, silver and money had vanished. Where had it gone? Perhaps thieves had 'entered in' and 'carried it away'. Or pirates.

Were there some in Dunwich who saw that act of royal piracy in 1310 as sacrilege? Did anyone protest? I think not. By now the Age of Faith was unashamedly the Age of Plunder. Churchmen and laymen alike contended for the spoils, and spiritual ministration was for many but a form of words devoid of any meaning. I may be guilty of romancing when I voice the suspicion that some at least of Dunwich's churches were being used as store-houses of loot acquired on piratical ventures. I am merely being realistic when I say they might as well have been so used. St Leonard's was unfit for sacred use; stripped of timber, lead and bells, it only wanted one more mighty tide to wipe it off the map. St Martin's was still used; its parishioners still paid their tithes. How many went to church I do not know; but those who did got rather inadequate service; from 1308 there was no priest; sub-deacons followed one another in a quick succession, ending up in 1333 with an acolyte, a man (or boy?) who could not celebrate mass, hear confession, grant absolution or solemnise matrimony. By that time it probably no longer mattered. St Nicholas's was in the charge of an acolyte from 1301 to 1317, when he was removed from office. St Peter's likewise was looked after by an acolyte, put there in 1315 by influence of his father who was Master of *Domus Dei*, and there until he was murdered in 1323. The hospitals of St James and *Domus Dei* were both, thanks to dishonest wardens, reduced to beggary by 1315, and both 'fallen into debt' by 1323.

The saints were having a thin time in Dunwich.

32 Murder at St Peter's

If you like murder mysteries, try this one. It is quite different from all those others. The story begins, not with the discovery of the body, but with the release of all the suspects. I quote in full from the Patent Roll of March 30th 1324:

Commission to Edmund de Hengrave, Thomas de Bavent and Peter Gernegan (justices) *to free from the gaol of Dunwich* John son of Warin de Blythburgh, John Fyket, Adam Toogood, John le Latoner, John son of Alexander Beccles, William de St Feyth, Richard Dennis, Richard Leveson, Roger Totelyne, Adam Curlur, Augustine Ille, Henry Kingshawe, Roger Battis-

ford and Simon Hamondys in custody there *for the death of*
William de Brom, late parson of the church of St Peter in
Dunwich.

I will tell you all I know; there is enough mystery about it
without my trying to add any. First a word about that gaol at
Dunwich. It was just off the market-place, quite near to the
Guildhall, for obvious reasons. It was not a 'dungeon'; just an
ordinary building of timber frame with flint and mortar infilling and thatched roof. Dangerous or important prisoners
were not incarcerated there, but sent to Orford Castle, Norwich or Ipswich. Very few imprisonments in Dunwich gaol are
recorded; only four in fact. The FitzJohn brothers were there
for a time in 1272. Gilbert de Birlingham was detained there
in 1262 for murder, and executed. In 1290 John de Kelshall,
crime unspecified, escaped from the gaol, and the keeper of
the town was fined £5 for allowing him to do so. In the same
year William Miller of Hoxne also escaped, and the town was
fined £5. Dunwich gaol, then, was not a very secure prison.
How does it come about that *fourteen* men could be detained
there? They could all have escaped, surely, by knocking a hole
in the wall or pushing their way through the thatch of the
roof. They might have been chained and manacled, but it is
most unlikely that the town possessed the necessary equipment
for that number. Did they stay there of their own free will?
Did they *insist* on staying there, for their own safety or con-
venience? Why did it need an order to three justices to release
them? The sheriff could have done it; or the bailiffs; but they
did not.

When did the crime take place? It must have been in the
summer of 1323, for a priest, Adam de Blofield, was appointed
late in that year to replace the dead 'parson of St Peter's'. The
prisoners had apparently spent the whole winter in gaol. At
the town's expense? Certainly not. Prisoners supplied their
own sustenance, through the agency of wives, families, servants
and friends; if any. If not, they had to rely on charity, very
largely. These prisoners, as will be shown presently, were in
a position to ensure that they would be well supplied with
victuals and all that was needed for their (relative) comfort.

Who was William de Brom, the murdered man? He was the son of Adam de Brom, former king's clerk, who was appointed master of *Domus Dei* in 1306, and remained in office until his death in 1319. A fairly well-to-do man, as all king's clerks were, Adam de Brom had further enriched himself by misappropriating the funds of the hospital and re-letting at revised rents the properties which it owned. Throughout his term of office he sought and obtained royal protection and a licence to beg alms because of the 'poverty' of the hospital. I have no definite proof, but it seems almost certain that it was due to his influence that the priest of St Peter's – William de Ponte Audemero, appointed by the Prior of Eye in 1314 – was dismissed after only one year and replaced by Adam's son William. William was an acolyte – wholly unqualified to perform any priestly office – yet he held the post of 'parson' for nine years before he was killed. His age at death would be about thirty.

How was he killed? I do not know for certain. If he had been stabbed, bludgeoned, shot with an arrow, strangled or drowned, it is difficult to see how fourteen men could have been accused of his murder. There cannot have been any witnesses to the deed. If there were, surely *one* assassin, or at most two or three, would have been named.

Where was he killed? I do not know. In the church of St Peter's, perhaps; but the possibilities are endless. We are deprived of one of the most vital clues.

Why was he killed? Not because he was an inefficient parson, we may be sure of that. There were a great many inefficient parsons. Some people might have been scandalised by his inefficiency, but they would be the last people to contemplate murder. His death might, however, have been due indirectly to the fact that he was a parson. There was at least one man living in Dunwich who had good reason to resent William de Brom's appointment. That was Alexander Beccles. He, too, was an acolyte, who had been parson of St Nicholas's from 1301 to 1317, when he was sacked and replaced by a priest, one John Gleyberd. He, Alexander, had been sacked by the Prior of Eye; whether at the instigation of William de

Brom's father or not, I cannot say. It is a possibility. It is more than a possibility that Alexander resented William de Brom's holding an office for which he was unqualified when Alexander was debarred from holding a similar office with the same disqualification. But Alexander Beccles was not among the accused. No, *but his son John was.*

I know of no one else who had cause to hate, resent or be jealous of William de Brom. I do not know whether he had any family or relatives in Dunwich. He, like his father, was an 'outsider'.

Could it not have been a simple case of robbery with violence? No. Fourteen men – certainly not these men – did not attack and rob one man, an ignorant parson. He was better off than some of the accused, but not nearly so wealthy as some of them. He was certainly not murdered for his money.

What do we know about the accused?

John son of Warin de Blythburgh: nothing.

John Fyket: He lived in Dunwich – all the accused did – had been bailiff in 1307, 1314 and 1318; came of a family prominent in civic affairs for more than a century; was a merchant; owned a house in St John's parish and a tenement in St Leonard's.

Adam Toogood: nothing.

John le Latoner: nothing.

John Beccles: He was the son of Alexander Beccles, one-time parson of St Nicholas's; had a shop in the market-place, rent 12d., between the shop of John de Hoxne and that of Thomas Austin. His father, and probably he also, lived in a house in St Leonard's, to which he had lately moved.

William de St Feyth: nothing.

Richard Dennis: He lived in a house in St Peter's, a fairly good house, rent 9d. He was married, with one son.

Richard Leveson: Lived in a house in St John's, rent 6d.; married; had a son who kept a stall on the market.

Roger Totelyne: nothing.

Adam Curlur: Lived in St Peter's parish in a good house, rent 9d.; owned another house in St Peter's; owned a shop in the market-place, between those of Nicholas Dyonis and John Bolur; rented another shop in the market-place, owned by *Domus Dei*.

Augustine Ille: A very substantial merchant, one of a line of civic dignitaries, all merchants. His father was bailiff in 1311 and 1317. He himself was bailiff in 1324, again in 1330, 1331 and 1338, and mayor in 1333. He was one of the men to be implicated in a shocking mass-murder and brutal act of piracy in 1330. He was, for some of the time, a business associate of John del Cliff, a very eminent merchant.

Henry Kingshawe: nothing.

Roger Battisford: A merchant, son and grandson of merchants. His father was bailiff in 1301. He himself was bailiff in 1307, 1319, 1320, 1321 and 1332, and mayor in 1328. He owned a shop in St John's in the market-place, between that of William King and Richard Gerard, whose son had recently been murdered at Chatham.

Simon Hamondeys: He occupied a house in All Saints, called 'Half Mark', which he rented from *Domus Dei* for 4d; married, with a son.

So, six of the accused were 'nobodies'; nothing is known about them except that they lived in Dunwich. Three of them were very eminent citizens; the rest men of some substance. Two of them occupied premises owned by *Domus Dei*, and had therefore had dealings with the father of the murdered man. Three of them lived in St Peter's parish, and were therefore well known to the murdered man; and familiar with the church of St Peter's, of which they would almost certainly have been churchwardens at some time or other.

How does one account for such a strange association of three different social classes, high, middle and low? It could be that they were associated in some enterprise needing capital and ships, shops for the disposal of (stolen?) goods, and unscrupulous and relatively unknown characters to do the dirty work. Such as piracy. There had been a great deal of piracy in the previous twenty years, but only one case had been reported near Dunwich since a gang was executed at Ipswich ten years previously. Had the pirates been better organised since then, better equipped, and operating further afield?

Why, having been arrested and imprisoned, were the accused all released? Because none of them were guilty, and it could be demonstrated that they were not guilty – of the murder of William de Brom.

Then why were they arrested in the first instance? Because they were found all together in the place, or near the place, where the body was found.

Why did they not establish their innocence there and then? To have done so would have been to reveal their implication in some other crime.

How was it that such a large group of men, including three very eminent men, was able to be arrested? The sheriff, or his nominee, was in the town with a strong force of men-at-arms on the look-out for Roger Mortimer and his supporters suspected of trying to enter the country. Spies were everywhere, and vigilance was stricter than it had been for many years.

There is one other interesting – and perhaps significant – fact to be considered, concerning Roger Battisford in particular. Let us look at the list of bailiffs for certain years:

1307 G. Dowsing, John Fyket, Stephen Michberd, Walter Calf. William Austin, *Roger Battisford*, John Ode, Roger Fyket.

1319 Will Helmeth, Augustine FitzWilliam, Henry FitzJohn, John Callow, John de la Falaise, Walter Barnard, *Roger Battisford*, John Cocks, John Shipmeadow.

1320 George Joycers, Robert Cocks, Roger Croude, William Terry. William Austin, Richard Gerard, *Roger Battisford*, Walter Barnard.

1321 John Shipmeadow, John Payne, John Cocks, William Helmeth. William Austin, Richard Gerard, *Roger Battisford*, Water Barnard.

Each time that Roger Battisford was elected, it was as a result of a second election during the year. Four times he was elected in association with William Austin, future mayor and MP. Three times he was elected in association with Walter Barnard, who became mayor in the following year. Twice he was elected in association with Richard Gerard, who kept the shop next door to his, and whose son had been murdered two years earlier. What was it that caused a re-election during those four years, and on four other occasions between 1307 and 1321? It had only happened five times previously in a hundred years; and was only to happen once again, when Walter Barnard was mayor again. Was there corruption in high places? There was corruption in all places, high and low, at all times; but it does seem that this particular period saw more of it than usual, and it did coincide with the phase of intensive piratical activity. Was Roger Battisford the evil genius at the head of some nefarious undertaking of an elaborate nature? Would William Austin have been arrested, but for the fact that he was at York on parliamentary business?

One more fact which might have a bearing on the case. St Peter's church was the church nearest to the harbour. Like that of St Nicholas, it was cruciform, i.e. it had north and south transepts. It was very old, and would be constantly in need of repair at this date. One, or both transepts could be shut off from the nave of the church by being boarded up, under pretext of repairs if no repairs were actually in progress, thus forming a convenient hiding-place for those who had something to hide. William de Brom could well have been allowing the use of part of his church as a cache for pirated loot. Did he reveal the whole set-up to the sheriff? Not very likely; he would not deliberately deprive himself of a steady income.

Well, who *did* murder William de Brom, how and why?

It is too late now to secure a conviction, and anyway no jury would convict on this evidence, but my candidate for the gallows would have been *Alexander Beccles*. You may ask why he was not arrested. If I had been the sheriff, and had netted a gang of fourteen men known to be up to no good, I would not have looked for a fifteenth. I would not have examined too closely the source of information leading to the capture. I would not have thought of trying to determine the exact cause of death, knowing it to be impossible. Alexander Beccles was perfectly safe; so long as his son John did not talk too much about the frequent gifts of mulled wine which his father had been in the habit of sending to his dear friend the late William de Brom, whom he hated like poison.

33 Trouble All Round

It would be absurd to use the word 'happiness' in connection with the Dunwich of the early fourteenth century. No doubt there were some individuals who were happy for a time. Like the unnamed fisherman, for instance, who, fearing a nocturnal visit by thieves, draped his nets all round the interior of his little cottage and sat up all night praying to St Edmund. Thereby demonstrating not so much the strength of his faith or the power of the saint as the strength of his nets. For the thieves did come, entering by the simple expedient of kicking a hole in the wall, but got so entangled in the nets that they were obliged to leave empty-handed. Then there were those who made a prodigious collection of eggs on King's Holme and caught the market just right; or made a haul of herrings which nearly broke the net, but not quite; those who won the favour of a pretty wench or quaffed a flagon of old but not too mild. They were happy, I should think. But none could escape for very long the general air of anxiety which pervaded the place.

If, knowing what the ultimate fate of the town was to be, you have conjured up a vision of a disaster such as that which overwhelmed Pompeii, put it from your mind. Dunwich might have been 'happier' if it had been another Pompeii. Life might have gone on merrily as though it would last for ever, before being obliterated for ever. As it was, Dunwich was condemned to a lingering death, conscious all the time of an inevitable end which ever seemed deferred, postponed from one life-time to the next, thus keeping hope alive and yet compelling to despair. Fate did not aim at taking lives before their time – only men did that – but seemed determined that the lives she spared should be made ever more difficult to live.

Fate had numerous allies, none more willing than those men of Walberswick. Their persistent efforts to reopen the haven at Southwold which the Dunwich men had blocked at such great cost succeeded in the end. The document of 1300, quoted earlier, continued thus:

> — yet some persons have come by night and reopened that port, and have broken down certain causeways put within that port to strengthen the obstruction thereof, whereby the watercourse leading to Dunwich is impeded, so that merchants cannot come up to Dunwich as they were wont to do.

Not only was the Southwold haven open, but its connection with the town of Dunwich was deliberately blocked. At the same time, without any assistance from the men of Walberswick, the main outlet of Dunwich to the sea was being blocked by the sea, not once, but time and time again:

> The sea then overtook a third part of the town, and so enfeebled the haven by storm and tempest that it closes up once or twice every year.

It *had* to be kept open, whatever the cost.

'The people of the said town incur grievous charges each year in opening the said haven.' They could not supply the king with ships for his wars. They had recently spent more than £1000 'in his service' – meaning in their own service – and they were impoverished. The king ought to see to it that the men of Walberswick and Southwold were made to bear their share of the cost of keeping Dunwich as a port, the same as his predecessors had done, they said. They petitioned Parliament in 1304:

> '—whereas the men of Southwold and Walberswick are bound to clear the haven of Dunwich on one side at their own costs, and the men of Dunwich on the other side likewise as often as the said haven shall happen to be blocked by storms – the said men of Southwold and Walberswick have totally withdrawn that service, so that the men of Dunwich have incurred the expense of £300 of their money in opening the haven.'

The Dunwich men cannot seriously have thought that they could force their enemies to spend money on keeping their haven cleared. All the money in the world would not have prevented King's Holme from creeping in until it linked up again with the town side, as the geographical department of Fate intended that it should. There may have been an understanding in days gone by that Walberswick was responsible for the north side of the harbour – when it was Walberswick's harbour as well as that of Dunwich. There was no legal backing for it, then or now, as Parliament would have discovered if the charters had been examined. The Chancellor was instructed to send a letter to the treasurer and barons of the Exchequer that 'the parties being called and heard before them, they do what rightly is to be done'.

There was only one thing rightly to be done. That was for all concerned to get together, accept the inevitable, and make the best of it by concerted action. But that was the one thing they could not, or would not do. Deep-rooted hatred, jealousy and rivalry prevented them. The chief concern of all of them was money, money, money. The ruin of the port of Dunwich was the salvation of other places. Another enemy appeared on the commercial horizon:

—the men of Westleton in a village near to the town of Dunwich buy, sell and forestall all kinds of commodities coming to that same town, whereby the farm of the king of that town is deteriorated each year to the extent of £10, as they say—

So the market of Dunwich was threatened, as well as its port. The king *must* do something about it, they said. It was really his fault, and it would be his misfortune:

And the present king (Edward II) and his father, because the men of the said town had it at farm, have granted several *markets and fairs* to the religious and others at two of the entrances to the town, to the great damage and loss of the town, and the fee-farm, whereby the town is so impoverished by those sales that they cannot raise half of the said farm-rent. So they beg the king to take the town into his own hands, and put a keeper in at his own will, to inquire into the grievances. They ask that he shall reduce the farm rent, otherwise he will lose his town and the rent.

218

What price 'liberties' now? They still vociferously defended their liberties nevertheless.

> —the sheriff|of Suffolk has sued them at law before the justices for lands which they hold outside their fee, where they do not dwell, contrary to the liberties granted and confirmed by the king and his forbears, whereby they incur expense, etc, etc.

'Liberties' meant money to them. They were right, in a sense it *was* the king's fault. He had granted to Augustine de la Falaise the manor of Westleton, and Augustine, despite the fact that his family had profited from – and contributed to – the prosperity of Dunwich for more than two centuries, now saw the advisability of transferring his interests elsewhere. Instead of suppressing the Westleton market which was so obnoxious to Dunwich, he obtained a renewed grant for it. This was one of the markets 'at the entrance to' Dunwich. The other was Blythburgh, the manor of which in 1309, on the death of Robert FitzRoger, came into the hands of his son John; who was a man of a different stamp from his father, as we shall see presently.

Interrupting the thread of my narrative for a moment, the petition of 1324, quoted above, spoke of fairs and markets granted to 'the religious'. Is this, I wonder, a reference to the fair of St James? If so, it would date that fair to about 1315. It would also add one more to the already long list of grievances aggravating the situation. There must have been a dozen different groups within a few miles of Dunwich Guildhall, all with conflicting interests, all hating each other like mad. It is a wonder that there were not a lot more murders committed.

John, son of Robert FitzRoger, was evidently determined to do what his father had tried and failed to do. His father had been obliged to remain content with what the Blythburgh manor brought in, in addition to the rents, namely, a fair and market, view of frankpledge, assize of bread and ale, a worthless right of wreck, two pence for every wheeled cart shod with iron and loaded with corn or fish passing through Blythburgh or Walberswick, and for every horse carrying the same a halfpenny, etc. Not a bad income, actually, though a mere trifle compared with what he had been getting from his other estates. John FitzRoger changed his name to John de Clavering, and decided that, when the time was ripe, he would live up to it, and have a bit more cash with which to do so.

The time was not yet ripe. There was every indication that the men of Southwold and Walberswick were coping with the situation, and that Dunwich would go down petitioning, protesting, pleading – anything but fighting.

Dunwich must have been more than a little discouraged when they learnt – if they ever did learn – the response to their petition of 1324. The 'good men of chancery' were to inquire into the extent of the evils in the town, find out how much it was deteriorated, what lands and tenements were destroyed by the sea, and – this must have caused either derision or apoplexy — *find out whose fault it was*. They got some belated consolation, however, in March 1327, when the loss of £1420 10s. incurred in the war in Gascony in 1296 – thirty-one years earlier! – was credited to their account 'having regard to the state of the town and the men thereof'. They must also have derived some amusement from a letter which they received at the same time as that welcome news, to the effect that the king had made a present to Thomas Earl of Norfolk, as a reward for his loyal support, of ten thousand marks. The king did not however intend to *pay* the earl £6600, any more than he intended to *pay* the men of Dunwich £1420 10s. The gift was to come from the revenues of various estates and towns, *one of which was Dunwich*, whose annual contribution was to be £25 7s. 11d. from the fee-farm. It is to be hoped, for the earl's sake, that the rest of the princely gift was better secured. He never received one penny from Dunwich.

The Walberswick men became impatient. Every year, it seemed to them, ought to have been Dunwich's last. Yet still ships managed somehow to put in there. So they took action in the summer of 1327. Nothing violent; there was no need for violence; just a little firm persuasion, applied quite openly. A number of them, including William Peacock and William Butt – the other names are not of any consequence, but those two are—

—have prevented them [the men of Dunwich] from receiving the said tolls and customs and from levying the profits of the ferry, and have gone to meet merchants coming in, and restrained them from exposing goods for sale, so that many of them have withdrawn, to the impoverishment of the town and diminution of the said farm-rent.

It appears that Dunwich took the insult lying down. They made official complaint, of course; hence the entry on the Patent Roll a year later. On reflection, they had taken no action, apart from petitions and plaints, for more than twenty-five years; not since that time they made an attack on Southwold and sank the ships of the Earl of Gloucester. Perhaps they were planning a similar attack during that autumn of 1327. It must have been for most people in Dunwich the most depressing time they had ever known. There was little spontaneous merriment, I wager, at St Leonard's fair that year. Yet some of them, perhaps, looked forward with the same fond hopes to better times when spring should come again. After all, things could not get any worse.

34 *Per Impetu Maris*

Chroniclers have always had a knack of missing the most dramatic events of history, thus having to make do with second-hand accounts long after the event, or substituting fantasy for truth. The only historical record of the event which I am going to describe is this, written twenty-seven years later:

On Jan. 14th in the first year of the present king (1328) there was a certain port – by the force of the sea (*per impetu maris*) it was completely blocked.

Hence the need for, not fantasy, but a fair measure of imagination; not as a substitute for truth; a reinforcement of it.

The unwonted calm of those autumn days of 1327 should have warned the Dunwich folk. There may have been – there would have been, were I a medieval chronicler – dire portents of impending doom. The sea at sunrise one December morn would have been as a sea of blood. The swirling clouds in the western sky would have taken on the shapes of apocalyptic riders waving swords of flame. The rooks, blacker still against the winter sky, would have spiralled heavenwards in joyous flight, then fallen wildly down from tremendous height like damned souls hurtling to their doom. Strange lamentations would have been heard out on the lonely wastes of King's Holme at dead of night. The cross on the top of St Peter's church, leaning drunkenly ever since the night the parson was murdered, would have crashed to the ground on a day of calm. It did, twenty years later.

The weather changed for the worse soon after Christmas Day. For a week in early January blustery winds blew in from north and east. The sea got steadily rougher; squalls of sleet or snow kept folk indoors, huddled round fires and braziers, seeking comfort, little though there was. On the afternoon of January 14th the wind freshened to a gale coinciding, as Fate decreed it should at intervals of thirty years or so, with the high tide of the month. As darkness fell, the fury of the wind increased. While it was yet light the dwellers in the lower town had piled all their belongings upon carts, barrows, horses, shoulders, making a mass exodus, as they had done before, towards the upper town, and there sought refuge in the churches, monasteries, barns, the gaol, and yards and houses of those more fortunately placed. It was at times like this – and only, so it seemed, at times like this – that a truly Christian spirit stirred the town. No one was left to shiver in the cold and darkness of that night.

Few slept. Some prayed who had not prayed in years, whilst doubting what their prayers could do. All converse was in vain, for no voice could be heard above the howling of the wind and the crashing of the waves. To venture out of doors was to risk injury by being hurled against a wall or struck by flying debris. When, despite the heavy stones and ropes put there to hold it down, a thatch was ripped away, all one could do was douse the fire, cower underneath such cover as was left and hope that that, too, would not go. There was nothing to be done about anything. Nothing to be seen. Just one continuous overpowering surge of sound throughout that never-ending night.

When long-awaited daylight came at last, then red-eyed men and women leaned against the wind and slowly made their way downhill towards the edge of devastation. What they saw was even more appalling than the mental pictures which had tormented them all night. Houses dissolved into sodden piles of rubble before their fascinated gaze. The waves would smash the timber framework of a house, then use the beams as battering-rams to smash the next in line. The sea was like a monster-vandal gone berserk, like some obscene leviathan intent on gorging itself with more than its jaws could hold, then spewing it out to wallow in the dark spongy mess that soiled its foaming beard.

The shore-line – there was no shore-line – the zone that was neither sea nor land was everywhere piled high with unrecognisable debris in heaps which, having created, the monster just as nonchalantly destroyed. A thousand people watched from vantage-points beyond the furthest reach of the waves; but being well within the range of spray, salt tears streamed down the cheeks even of those too shocked to weep. Few spoke. Lips moved, but whether in prayer or imprecation none could tell. Some families in tight-knit groups looked long in blank despair upon the spot, perhaps two hundred yards from where they stood, where swirling waters hid the site of what had been their home for generations; then turned abruptly, trudged back up the hill, collected their belongings and left Dunwich, never to return.

Both wind and sea abated their fury as the day progressed, though all through that next night the roar of breakers went on. The next day it was possible to take stock of the situation, to substitute facts and figures for hysterical hyperbole. It was not the end of the world. It was not even the end of Dunwich. It was nevertheless disaster on a scale hitherto unknown in Dunwich, as mayor and bailiffs soon discovered when they made their survey, starting at the southern end of the town.

The parish of St Nicholas had once contained three hundred houses, which the erosions of the past forty years had reduced to less than two hundred. There were now no more than thirty houses left standing, some of them so near the low cliff-edge that no one would dare to live there (though rents would still be charged, on the book at least); one barn, one windmill ruined, two others having gone, and perhaps a dozen acres of land. The ecclesiastical value (mostly tithes) even after the diminution wrought by the last great storm, had been £4 6s. 8d. a year; at the next assessment it was valued at 4s. 2d. The church still stood; the east end of the chancel only a few feet from the cliff. Incredibly, a priest was found to take the 'living'; several priests, each staying for about two years, were to keep up the pretence of a parish of St Nicholas for a further thirty years almost.

St Martin's parish had had about a hundred houses in it. Twenty-five remained. A lot of empty sites, vacated by the sea, were never again likely to be occupied by man. The church still stood; or most of it. The chancel was already leaning to the east, with daylight showing between it and the nave. Another six or seven years at most would see the last of St Martin's. The churchwardens even now were preparing to take down the bells. No sense in leaving them up there to fall on someone's head – or form the basis of an idiotic legend about bells heard beneath the waves.

St Leonard's, already the most devastated parish still existing as such before the storm, was reduced to twelve houses and a windmill lying on its back. Much of the area had previously reverted to open space which was used for cultivation, stabling, storage and various other purposes, including the fair. The church had still been standing before the storm, stripped of timber, bells and furnishings. There was no sign of it now, unless that pile of masonry out there, beneath a bigger pile of debris, was it. The fair continued to be held for a further six years, until the Prior of Eye discovered that the five shillings which he paid for the privilege of collecting tolls was somewhat in excess of the tolls collected.

St Peter's, never a very large parish, now had just over

twenty houses, cottages and shops clustered round its church, which, some far-distant and far-sighted founder having chosen for it a site twenty feet above the harbour, was undamaged. The greatest devastation here was in the area adjacent to the harbour, now an indescribable tangle of timber and jetsam which had once been ships, houses, warehouses and wharves. Only the parishes of St John's and All Saints remained relatively undamaged, though even they could not be said to be unaffected. All Saints in particular, though never very populous – it had only about twenty houses excluding monasteries – had suffered from the gale, and an even greater proportion of its area was henceforth 'land', not 'messuage'. Those figures quoted above, by the way, are not the product of my imagination; they are taken from the bailiffs' rental of 1334 which Gardner quotes in full.

All that was heart-breaking enough. But when the mayor, William Helmeth, and his four fellow administrators picked their way cautiously across the heaps of debris to where they knew – or thought they knew – the haven-mouth should have been, their first reaction was one of bewilderment, then despair. There was no haven-mouth.

It had been blocked before, a dozen times in the last twenty years. But one had always been able to see exactly where it was, and had been able, with tremendous labour at tremendous cost, to succeed in clearing it again sufficiently to allow the passage of fishing-boats and fair-sized ships at high tide. They would never try to clear it again. A million tons – it might have been two millions, three millions, what of it? – of sand and shingle now not only blocked the haven-mouth but hid completely where it should have been. King's Holme, impelled by that almighty tide, had reached at last the goal it had been aiming at for all those years, and no one would dislodge it now.

It was ironical that William Helmeth should have been one of those to witness that colossal mocking gesture. He, more than most, would sense the finality of it, the futility of seeking to amend, for much of that expanse of sand and shingle was technically 'his'. He owned the land through which the haven had been cut by his grandfather's men, and others, eighty years before. He 'owned' it still, whatever that might mean. There was no question now of putting men and money – assuming they had had the money, or the men – to the making of another haven-mouth. Dunwich as a port was no more. What the sea had created, the sea had destroyed.

The despair which had settled upon the populace after the previous disaster was a hundred times greater now. Out of despair on that previous occasion had arisen anger in many, piety in some, determination in most to do what could be done. Now, in the aftermath of that overwhelming disaster of January 1328, the dominant mood was one of surrender. About a hundred families left the town at once, followed by many more in the next few months, and yet more in ensuing years. These were for the most part the poorer families, those who possessed little and who had lost all; all but the few portable belongings which they had been able to salvage. They migrated to other towns and villages to swell the numbers of the poor already there, many of them facing a bitter opposition by comparison with which the elements seemed kind. Some of the wealthier class left also. Some, like the De la Falaises, had already gone. Names which had figured in the annals of the town, not always honourably, for two hundred years – FitzJohn, Fyket, Bedell, Ode – would figure there no more. And yet amazingly, very many stayed. Perhaps not so amazingly, upon reflection. Those whose names had studded the records for a century and more, and were to do so for a century to come, were those who had lived in the upper town. The sea had not destroyed their homes, though it had removed the source of their livelihood.

There was no need to get a boat to go and see what had happened at the other end of King's Holme. There had already been a gap before the storm. It was bound to be wider and deeper now, they thought. As a matter of fact, it was not. That same document which I quoted at the beginning of this chapter goes on:

—and another port at that time was made, which port is almost two leagues (a mistake for 'miles') distant from the said town, and it is very narrow and not deep, and in that port there is very little putting-in of ships.

However narrow it might be, any 'putting-in' of Dunwich ships would from now on have to be through that haven-mouth. They would have to make peace with Walberswick and Southwold, for they were going to have the greatest difficulty in collecting tolls from ships which did not come nearer to Dunwich than two miles away and in ensuring that their cargoes reached Dunwich market.

That famous charter of theirs – reluctant though they might be to admit it – was henceforth of little practical validity, for all its frequent renewals and confirmations. It might state specifically that goods brought into the port of Dunwich must first be offered for sale in Dunwich market. It might be backed by the authority of king and parliament. It must have been somewhat tattered from the frequent pounding of self-righteous and indignant fists driving home a legal point; for legal it undoubtedly was, as the saints themselves would have affirmed. Unfortunately, however, the newly-created geographical situation took no account of legality, but made a mockery of it. Dunwich market could only be reached by sea-borne cargoes entering via Southwold and Walberswick, and the men of those two towns, I do not doubt, told the burgesses of Dunwich just what they could do with their charter, seal and all.

Commercial activity in the port, which Dunwich men still obstinately called 'the port of Dunwich', was resumed to some extent, though almost negligible. The fishermen were able to operate from the beach, making their labour doubly arduous and increasing the risk to their boats a hundredfold, so that some of them deserted to Walberswick. Some of the burgesses made the best of a bad job by turning from the sea to the land as an investment. Old Augustine Batting, before he died, acquired a fair slice of land and no less than thirteen houses, in one of which *six families* lived. Thomas Dilbeg owned six houses. John Edwyne, a baker, snapped up seven houses and a shop in All Saints, where property was safe – for the time being. Peter Helmeth now owned the greater part of St

Leonard's; not, one hopes, with a view to building on it. Several others followed their lead; whether from faith or greed is not for me to say.

Fate played a rather mean trick on the Grey Friars. For years they had been seeking licence to enclose and hold the vacant plot of ground on which their first house had stood; more precisely, the burial ground of that first house. They had no use for it, but many of the brethren were buried there, and it was considered

> 'that it would be indecent that a plot of ground for some time dedicated to divine worship where Christian bodies are buried, should be converted to human uses'

even though it was worth two shillings a year. They got their licence, ten months after the sea had swallowed three quarters of the said plot of land.

The Black Friars still felt secure on their particular patch of ground; their turn was to come. The Prior of Eye, Robert Morpayn, tried hard to get compensation for the loss suffered by his house – his financial loss, that is; his house was all of twenty miles from the sea – and succeeded in persuading the Bishop of Norwich to let him impropriate the church of Laxfield. His own son Peter, another acolyte, was appointed to the living there after just one year's pretence of being in charge of St Martin's. The wave of piety on which the new Grey Friars had come into elevated existence after the last disaster was not much in evidence this time. Though it did, somewhat belatedly, manifest itself in a re-building of All Saints, high up on the hill, next to the Grey Friars. Well out of reach of the devouring waves. They thought.

35 Time to Strike

Dunwich was on its knees, gasping for breath and still dazed from the shock. A lifetime of experience in the war-game told

Sir John de Clavering and his brother Edmund that now was the time to strike. No question of a ransom; no nonsense about chivalry and honour, mercy, sparing the wounded and so on. That was for romantic chronicles. This was a matter of hard cash. A firm stroke now, and the Dunwich-Walberswick war was over. Sir Edmund had the resources and the technical know-how. The procedure, as Parliament heard it, was this:

'Sir Edmund and his men of Walberswick, at the entrance to the said haven, have erected a *britask* big and strong, and guard it with a great number of armed men and others, so that no boat dares or can go to the town of Dunwich to unload or sell anything, but unloads at Walberswick and sells there—'

Sir John had already, in 1324, obtained royal sanction for his market at Blythburgh every Monday, and for two annual fairs. Now he set up, without royal licence, a market at Walberswick, and made plans to ensure that there would be plenty of customers. The 'britask' was a stout palisade of timber, the nearest thing to a medieval fortress that could be contrived in such an unlikely spot as the north-west corner of King's Holme, which is where it must have been sited; or possibly on the Walberswick side of the entrance, so that any ship heading for Dunwich would have to pass within range of a small army of bowmen stationed on the rampart.

Most ship-masters would take the hint, and put in at Walberswick instead of trying to reach Dunwich. Those who insisted on proceeding down the harbour, even if they escaped damage to the ship and injury to the crew, would risk further molestation on the way back. Added to the danger, there was the economic factor. A resolute master might insist on going to Dunwich because the ship and cargo belonged there. In that case he would find himself compelled – by the irresistible argument of twenty cross-bows loaded and levelled at a distance of only twenty yards — to pay harbour dues and customs to Sir Edmund's bailiff. Having paid, he would go down-harbour for a mile and a half to find himself being asked to pay again at the Dunwich guard-house, which was there to collect the fourpences and various other dues. It may not have been fair, but it was legal.

Sir Edmund had no great regard for legality, but he was quick to see the unfairness of having to pay twice for what one only had once. Having established what he considered the only proper point of toll-collection, he arranged for the elimination of the rival establishment down-water. He had men at his disposal well-versed in the art of elimination; one of them was Thomas Peacock, brother of the William who had taken an active part in the persuasion campaign of the previous year. He chose his companions, a late hour on a dark night, and:

> Then came Thomas Peacock, Geoffrey Ridel and others unknown, under the orders of that Sir Edmund, in time of peace, and by force of arms they maliciously *burnt the guard-house* and feloniously *killed* William Scott, bailiff of Dunwich assigned to collect tolls and customs, and beat his companion William de Radenhale, and *broke his arms*; and took three boats which they were guarding, and took away horses and oxen to the manor of Blythburgh, so that the bailiffs cannot keep guard nor collect tolls.

It sounds rather flat when read in cold print, and the obvious preoccupation with the financial implications robs the incident of much of its colour. It was in fact a savagely brutal attack, the drama of which would be heightened by the lurid glare of the flames, the crackling of the burning timbers and the agonised cries of the wounded man. It would be all over in minutes. By the time the Dunwich men arrived on the scene they would be able to do nothing but let the building burn itself out while they carried home old William Scott's body and his injured companion on improvised stretchers.

Sir Edmund had achieved his objective. The harbour of Dunwich was put out of action as a toll-collecting station. The town of Dunwich was further impoverished; not so much by the failure to collect tolls – which by now cannot have amounted to more than one pound a year, if that – as by the fact that merchants were frightened away by threats of further violence, and Dunwich market rendered almost useless. The Clavering set-up was strengthened and enriched, not merely to the extent of three stolen boats, the horses and oxen, but also by the prospect of a steady stream of customers in their own market. Sir John, undoubtedly the instigator of the whole scheme, had a further card to play. At the session of parliament before which all the details just quoted were presented by the members for Dunwich, Sir John de Clavering, member for Blythburgh – or one of his many other possessions – brought forward a bill designed to withdraw from Dunwich *all the liberties* which it had enjoyed for the past hundred and twenty years. He evidently thought that the proper thing to do was to legalise the situation. That was what parliament was for; to legalise things.

I must permit myself a judgement here. Sir John was undoubtedly a 'valiant knight,' a fighting man. Whether he was a brave fighter or not, I do not know. His conduct in setting on armed men to commit cold-blooded murder on two defenceless elderly men may have been simply a characteristic of the times, not to be judged by modern standards. It would probably have been detrimental to his 'honour' to have engaged in armed combat personally with men of low rank, common burgesses and fishermen; so he must not be dubbed a coward. Taking what one wanted by armed force or threat was likewise in accord with an accepted principle amongst many of the knightly class – it had been so for centuries. I would call him an arrogant knave nevertheless, and so, I believe, would a good many of his peers. But what dominates my assessment of him is the impression that he was an ignorant knave.

Surely he *knew* that the town of Dunwich belonged to the king, legally? The liberties which he was seeking to annul had not been given away by the various kings in succession, but handed over in trust, on payment, to be exercised *for* the king. It so happened that King Edward III had confirmed the Dunwich charter at Canterbury only a few weeks previously. Did Sir John really believe that it would be annulled? Or that parliament would support his bill? Parliament consisted mainly of men who held lands and rights by virtue of charters. If a charter could be erased as easily as Sir John hoped to erase this, what security was there for all those holders of lands and privileges who made the laws? And did Sir John not know that Dunwich was represented by *two* voices in Parliament, those of John de la Falaise and Thomas Fitz-William? Those two members earned their two shillings a day expenses on that occasion at least. The bill was rejected.

Sir Edmund had achieved all his objectives, and more. The outstanding result of his actions was one which, I warrant, he least expected, and makes me wonder whether he, too, was an ignorant fool. Perhaps not. Perhaps he had every reason to suppose that a pack of dispirited merchants and fishermen would knuckle under to his threats, especially having suffered such misfortunes as those of Dunwich. Be that as it may, he completely underestimated a number of factors; the bitter hatred which some at least of the Dunwich men felt towards their rivals, their determination to cling to the only source of livelihood they knew, their burning desire for revenge, and their ability to achieve it. It almost seems as though they needed some such spur as the guard-house episode to shake them out of their lethargic despair, for when their answer came it was deliberate, dramatic and devastatingly effective.

It not only shook Sir Edmund, Walberswick and Southwold; it shook the whole county, and caused something like a state of minor panic in administrative circles. I have to rely entirely on the official records in my attempt to discover the nature and sequence of events, and it is evident that the men who inscribed those records did not know exactly what had happened. They were still trying to piece together all the alarming reports a year after the event, by which time rumour probably far outstripped truth. Late in 1330 one of the clerks began a letter from the king to the sheriff of Suffolk:

> The king understands that the men of Dunwich have inflicted damages upon each other by reason of disputes, and that they with arms—

That is all. The letter was never finished. A few weeks later, Jan. 13th 1331, three justices of the shire, Sir Richard de Willoughby, Simon de Hethersett and John Claver (not to be confused with John de Clavering),|were|commissioned|to

hear and settle a complaint by Anastasia late the wife of John
Butt of 'Walberdeswyk' that:

> John Payne, Constantine Paston, Augustine FitzWilliam and
> Augustine Ille of Dunwich, and others, took away a ship of hers
> on the coast by Southwold with the goods therein, *broke up
> and sank the ship*, and *assaulted* her men and servants.

It sounds like just another case of piracy. Though a rather
special kind of piracy, for John Payne was mayor of Dunwich;
Augustine FitzWilliam and Augustine Ille were bailiffs, and
Constantine Paston was a well-to-do merchant.

Before those letters had reached the knights to whom they
were addressed, more letters were on their way to the same
men, ordering them to deal with the same matter, plus a
detail:

> —concerning the persons who *entered a ship* of the said Ana-
> stasia, by Southwold, carried away her goods and *murdered
> sixteen men who were in the ship*.

Something more than piracy! Anastasia Butt, by the way, was
the mother of the William Butt who with William Peacock
was involved in the enticement of merchants away from Dunwich in 1327. He may or may not have been involved in the
attack on the guard-house, along with Thomas Peacock. John
Butt, his father, was dead; his death may have been wholly
unconnected with this episode.

On March 29th 1331 a further commission was appointed
to make inquiry. This time it included John de Radenhale,
brother of the William who had been wounded in the attack
on the guardhouse. The order for the new commission named
the same four men as culprits, and stated the charge that they

> *took away a ship* and cargo by Southwold, *sank the ship at sea*
> and *assaulted* her servants that were on board.

In July, four months later, the Bishop of Norwich and Sir
Constantine de Mortimer were instructed to

> 'settle all disputes between John de Clavering, who claims to
> have a right to a port or hythe at Walberswick and to take
> anchorage and other dues there, and the burgesses of Dunwich,
> who assert that such ships should unload at the port of their
> town.'

The order was repeated in November. If the inquiry ever

took place, it produced no result, and revealed no further facts. Meanwhile, in October, the king had written to the mayor and bailiffs of Dunwich as follows:

> The king learns from the reports of *many men* that the men of Dunwich on the one part, and John de Clavering and Edmund his brother on the other, have made divers assemblies of men-at-arms and do daily make such assemblies, by reason of certain disputes there, committing *invasions, burnings, homicides,* robberies, etc.

As is only to be expected, rumour by this time had magnified the affair to the scale of a minor war. The men of Dunwich were strictly ordered to put a stop to it at once, or suffer dire consequences; and they were to send someone to inform the king as to what was happening. Sir John and his brother Edmund were to appear before him in council before Martinmas. Edmund may have done. Sir John did not. He was dead.

That is all the evidence available for the reconstruction of an episode, or series of episodes, which must have been the talk of Dunwich and district for many years. What *did* really happen? The motives of the crime were undoubtedly hatred and revenge. The master-minds behind what seems to have been an elaborate plan were, I think, John Payne and Augustine Ille. The latter was one of the leading characters involved in the affair of William de Brom's murder seven years before. John Payne had had two of his sons executed for piracy eighteen years before. The equipment and technical skill were, I think, supplied by Paston and FitzWilliam. Both were shipowners. Fitzwilliam had a ship called *La James.* Paston one called *La Goste;* both were still active ten years later.

Two ships at least must have been involved. The attack must have been carried out under the guise of normal trading activities, otherwise they would not have got past the 'britask' and its garrison without arousing suspicion and alerting the Walberswick merchants of the danger. Evidently some such attack was feared, for John Butt's ship was manned by an unusually large number of men, more than double the normal complement. *Goste* and *James* – assuming that those were the ships used – must have carried at least twenty men each at the time of the attack to provide a sufficiently overwhelming force to ensure surrender without a fight. It does not seem likely that there was a fight. If there had been one resulting in the deaths of sixteen of the 'enemy,' there would surely have been casualties on the attacking side as well, and wounded on both sides. None of the documents mentions injury or wounding; only killing, murder and homicide.

The incident occurred at sea, by Southwold, If Butt's ship were attacked and sunk in the normal way – and it was no easy task to sink a large ship fully laden, I imagine – surely some of the crew ought to have managed to get ashore, and give precise evidence. It is fairly certain that none did so. Lack of evidence is the only explanation I can offer for the fact that no one was even brought to trial, let alone convicted. If this had been a standard act of piracy – on a somewhat larger scale – it would surely have provoked reprisals against Dunwich ships. We hear of no reprisals; no aftermath of any kind. The ships and men involved were all well and active for years afterwards. It looks as though the incident was so utterly shocking that it silenced, as it was probably intended to do, all opposition and made reprisal unthinkable.

How then were those sixteen men murdered and their ship sunk, all at one fell stroke? There is only one possible answer for me – gunpowder.

It is not known for certain when, where or by whom gunpowder – 'black powder' – was invented, but Roger Bacon is traditionally credited with the rather dubious honour. It was a mixture of 74.6% saltpetre (nitre), 13.5% charcoal and 11.9% sulphur. All three ingredients would be easily obtainable in Dunwich. The knowledge of how to use and mix them was also available in Dunwich, from a source least open to suspicion. Roger Bacon had been a member of the order of Friars Minor at Oxford some forty years previously. He obviously passed on the knowledge of his invention to a number of people, amongst whom would be some of his fellow friars. At least one of the brethren of Grey Friars must have known about it. I hesitate to implicate that godly man in this atrocious crime; he could have imparted the vital secret in all innocence; or had his conscience quietened by a handsome financial reward to be spent on some adornment for the monastery. John de la Falaise is the man whom I see as an important link, perhaps unwittingly, in a complex network of intrigue and communication. He was a close friend and associate of Thomas FitzWilliam; they were both members of parliament; their sons were associated later in a not very creditable affair. He was also closely associated with Grey Friars; one of its chief benefactors.

But – what is the use? All we can say is that, if gunpowder was the instrument used then this was probably the earliest use of it in this way. We cannot hope to solve the mystery. It is too late now to bring any of them to trial. When the huge cloud of dense white smoke which enveloped the unfortunate ship and her crew had cleared, there would be little left in the way of accessible truth. I only hope that some of those hate-inspired men were capable of feeling remorse. They evidently did what they intended to do. Walberswick, South-wold and Blythburgh seem to have been shocked into sub-mission for a long time. Sixty years would elapse before the 'war' was resumed; so, as a peace-keeping measure, there was something to be said for violence.

36 *Margarete* of Dunewic

I have always had a fondness for ships. I think most people have, even though like me they may not know much about them, and I am glad to be able to narrate something about one ship of Dunwich at this particular point in my story. *Margarete* was not quite the 'lady' I would have liked her to be. Her story is not the glorious epic I would have had it be, yet it is perhaps appropriate in that the ship symbolises to some extent the town to which she belonged and whose fate she shared. She was in all probability the last ship to be built at Dunwich.

Peter del Cliff, her owner, came of a long line of merchants and ship-owners, all of whom had played an active part in the civic administration of the town. His grandfather Augustine had been a member of parliament for fifteen years; his father John was at Westminster in 1326 when the keel of *Margarete* was laid down. His cousin Robert was bailiff in that same year. He himself had not yet taken office, being too occupied with business affairs. His father and his younger brother Augustine, who was a parson, still kept the name of De la Falaise; it was more suited to parliamentary and clerical circles. Peter called himself what everybody on the quay and in the town called him – Peter Cliff; though he admitted the 'del' in the middle as a concession to officialdom.

I think the *Margarete* was built in 1326 or early 1327; there is no record of her before that date. She was certainly not built later, for the shipyards at Dunwich were put out of action by the disaster of 1328, and no Dunwich merchant would have considered having a ship built at Walberswick during those tense years of strife culminating in the mass murder, nor for some years afterwards. She was, I know, a cog of about fifty tons, built to the latest design, with main-mast, fore-mast, bowsprit and stern-rudder; smaller than John de la Falaise's *Godbefore,* larger than the *Katerine* which Peter owned jointly with John Paston. Most ships were now jointly owned, to minimise the risks. His father was in partnership with Augustine Ille. *Margarete* might therefore have been involved in that disgraceful episode of the murder off Southwold. Like all her predecessors, she was designed and built primarily to carry cargoes of grain, wool, hides and suchlike; but she was also made adaptable for service as a floating castle, with elevated prow and stern, for she was liable to be commandeered for royal service at any time.

With Andrew Lister as master, and a crew of six, she made numerous trips with cargoes of corn from Dunwich to London and back in all weathers. In February 1336 she was lying in the Pool of London when the dreaded eventuality occurred.

She was seized by the sheriff's officers and detained for royal service. John de la Falaise had influence at court, which he used to good effect. *Margarete* was 'de-arrested' and allowed to go, on condition that Peter gave pledges before the king in chancery that she would be at Dunwich within three weeks after Easter ready to go on the king's service. Not military service; Peter undertook 'to send the ship to Gascony to buy wines for the support of the king and his lieges.'

It was a kind of 'military service' in a way. The age-old dispute about the overlordship of Gascony had broken out again, and French privateers were already anticipating the outcome by plundering English ships whenever possible. Andrew Lister and his men had the king's special protection for the voyage, but that would be of little use if the small convoy of English ships encountered a large convoy of Frenchmen. However, the trip was safely accomplished, and *Margarete* resumed her corn-carrying.

In May 1337 a state of war – which was to last for a hundred years – was brought about by King Philip VI of France confiscating Gascony 'on account of the disobedience and rebellious acts of Edward, King of England and Duke of Aquitaine.' The young English king retaliated by securing the alliance of the German emperor and of his own brother-in-law the Count of Hainault, who, to complicate matters, was the nephew of the French king. Later he went a step further and assumed the title of 'King of France,' a claim which his successors were to uphold, in title at least, for five hundred years. In October 1337 the king, with his queen and children, crossed over to Antwerp, which was to be his headquarters for two years.

The fleet which assembled at Goseford (as the mouth of the Deben river was called) included nine Dunwich ships, one of which was *Margarete* with Stephen Batman as master. Andrew Lister on that occasion was in charge of the *Godbefore,* John Frese of the *Welfare,* Stephen Frese of the *Plentye* and Roger Ode skippered his own *Redcog.* It was a memorable occasion for a number of reasons: so many Dunwich ships had not operated together for years, escorting the royal family on such a mission was safe, honourable and enjoyable; and they were all promptly paid. That is to say, they got their money a year later: standard rate of pay, sixpence a day for the master, threepence a day for the men. For twenty-seven days service the *Margarete's* complement of twenty-three were paid £8 12s. 1½d., which included an extra 8s. 1½d. for some unknown reason. Then *Margarete* returned to the more profitable business of coastal freighting.

In the next two years the situation worsened. The king was desperately short of cash. His alliance with the emperor had cost him 300,000 florins; and supplies were difficult on account of French privateers being in control of the Channel. The Flemish alliance was firmly cemented with some money and the promise of more, and in Sept. 1339 the king was preparing to return. The fleet sent over to escort him back consisted of sixty-four ships of Yarmouth, Dunwich and Bawdsey (Goseford). There were at least six Dunwich ships; probably more, but only six are named: *James* of Augustine FitzWilliam, *Redcog* owned jointly by Roger Ode, FitzWilliam, and Edmund Kerrick; Paston's *Goste*, Richard Codun's *Plentye*, *Katerine* of Cliff and Paston, and *Margarete*. Half-way across to Antwerp, they came up with the *Taret,* a large Flemish ship heavily laden with supplies and money, heading for Antwerp under the king's protection. It could be that the Suffolk men thought she was French. Perhaps they wanted their wages in advance. Or perhaps they simply could not resist the temptation. They plundered the *Taret* of her cargo worth £16,527 17s. 1d., divided it amongst themselves, and said not a word to the king or his admiral.

The owners of the *Taret* said a great deal. The king, honouring his obligations, paid compensation, and made arrangements to get his money back. Before that could be done, there was a more urgent task on hand. Back in London, plans were made for a large-scale attack on the French fleet, which had made serious raids on the south coast. In June 1340 it was anchored in the Scheldt, off Sluys. On June 24th the English fleet set sail. As it entered the broad estuary the enemy fleet came into view, over 140 large ships, and many

supply-boats, manned by 40,000 French and Genoese. 'King
Edward saw such a number of masts in front of him that it
looked like a wood,' wrote Froissart. John Frese saw them too,
for he was there in the *Margarete*, as was Roger Ode in the
Redcog, and many, many more. The king

—drew up his ships in line so that there was one shipload of
men-at-arms between every two of archers, with a number of
additional vessels full of archers kept in reserve – A fierce battle
broke out, each side opening fire with cross-bows and long-bows
– The soldiers used grappling-irons on chains in order to come
to grips with the enemy boats – The battle that followed was
cruel and horrible – it lasted from early in the morning till
noon, and in that time the English were hard pressed, for they
were outnumbered four to one—

But they won. We need not believe that 'their enemies were
all killed or drowned, and not one escaped.' We need not believe everything that Froissart or any other chronicler says.
But it was a great victory, and *Margarete* was there. She may
only have been carrying supplies; but no matter.

She did not get a mention. The *Redcog* did. After the battle
an inquiry was held into the *Taret* affair. The sixty-four culprits were named, and given the alternative of paying up the
value of the loot, or standing trial. They chose the latter,
for some of them, it seems, were innocent. Roger Ode got off
lightly; he was pardoned three years later, 'having stood in
the king's service upon the sea – at his own charges for two
months and more.' Peter Cliff was also pardoned, on condition
that the *Margarete* was sent to serve in the fleet.

This undoubtedly was done, for she was soon in the records
again. In the autumn of 1342 the king took an army to
Brittany in the hope of creating an alliance there against
King Philip. A fleet of eight ships was anchored off Brest. The
weather was bad for fighting on land. It was even worse for
ships sitting off a rocky coast lashed by westerly gales. As soon
as the weather eased up a bit, William Swatine with *Welfare,*
William Counterpain with *Sainte Marie* and John Frese with
Margarete, along with every other man jack of the fleet, upped
with their anchors and headed for home. The king and his

officials called it 'desertion' and 'rebellion,' as would no doubt rightly the Board of Admiralty today. John Frese and his colleagues, I am pretty sure, called it plain common-sense.

I do not know what penalty, if any, was imposed on Peter Cliff. He was alive and well when in May 1344 his father died, and he inherited part of the manor of Hernetherne in Westleton (held in fee of the Prior of Ely by service of one clove gillyflower yearly), and he continued to live in his house in St John's parish in Dunwich, and run his two shops, until business, and he, declined.

As for *Margarete,* she was one of the last ships of Dunwich to sail in the king's service. She never appears in the records again. I should imagine she carried many more loads of corn to London, and perhaps some 'corn and oats' to Calais in 1355. I like to think that, after fifty years or so of honest toil, her transgressions pardoned, she was left to settle at last in some quiet creek beside the Dingle marshes, and that what remains of her lies buried there today beneath the lush green grass.

37 Decline

My story might well have ended there. It has not so far been a particularly happy story, and there is no joy to come. But like the spectators of a Greek tragedy, knowing at the beginning what the end would be, let us sit steadily on through the depressing course of events and hope that here and there a little light relief may shine, a little may be learnt from contemplating the misfortunes of others; and bearing in mind that, for anybody to have gone on living there at all, there must have been some courage, some kindness born of adversity, some joy in some of Dunwich hearts.

The dominant element in their lives continued to be what it always had been – the sea. It continued to do what it always had done. There was still something left of the lower town; this was eroded year by year until a continuous cliff was formed, more or less in a straight line running north-south. The face of sand and gravel crumbled as the wind and rain broke off the top edge and the waves undermined the bottom, so that time and tide competed for the steadily receding yards, and the cliff became higher as it retreated. There was nothing that man could do about it. They did try. When, more than a hundred years later, the great church of St John's was threatened, they tried to save it by 'building the Pere ageyn St John's Cherche,' and people left money in their wills for that purpose. But it was no use. They resigned themselves eventually to watching it go, bit by bit, and speculating: this year? Next year? Sometimes, no doubt, recalling what once had been. The old haven-mouth was closed for ever; for as long, that is, as there was a haven.

King's Holme, its target reached, could go no further south. The sea began to eat away more quickly now its eastern edge, and it too might have disappeared as the town was disappearing, but instead it was pushed gradually westward in upon the harbour. This was perhaps the hardest task the sea had tackled yet, and progress was so slow that men did succeed more than once in cutting a channel through the mass of shingle; not very wide, and not for long. The harbour slowly became choked with mud brought down by the rivers Blyth and Dunwich and pushed there by the tides, so that here at least a little land was gained. Large boats could still put into and sail out of 'Dunwich.' The 'port of Dunwich' figures in the records for many years yet, and not a word appears about the 'ports' of Walberswick and Southwold. The explanation is that 'Dunwich' for the next half-century or so means 'Dunwich-Southwold-Walberswick.' They had not amalgamated – nothing so miraculous as that – they never would amalgamate, not even if the Almighty himself had ordered it. But the water available for anchorage was shared by all three, and the way in and out was similarly shared; only Dunwich still took the tolls and dues. When there were any to take.

Gardner was right to make his history *'An Historical*

Account of Dunwich, Blythburgh and Southwold.' I might have done the same, but for the fact that what fascinated me most when I started my task was the absence of any future for Dunwich. There can be no discussion, when I reach the end of my story, not far distant now, of the question: what next? Whatever Dunwich was intended by Fate to have, it has had.

The size of the town in 1334, in terms of people, is fairly easy to estimate, thanks to Thomas Gardner getting hold of a rental and recording it in detail. There were then 68 houses, 54 shops, 13 cottages, 4 bakeries and 3 pubs. I reckon that would mean about 150 families; say 600 people. Perhaps 700. There would be a certain amount of what we call 'overcrowding.' I find it rather frustrating, knowing the names of those families, not to be able to say anything about them as individuals. There must have been some interesting characters among them. All I can do is speculate. Was Adam le Pycher the same man as Adam le Thrower? How did Adam Horseleg get his name, and where had he gone? What was Matilda Bolur's bakehouse like, and Celicia Raysoun's alehouse? Who gave his name to 'Kytewyteaker'? How did Ada Ringulf, *'le Lecher,'* manage to live in a house of which the rent was only one penny? I think I know.

A surprising number of the once wealthy families were still there, though perhaps fewer than the rental suggests, for many had moved out but still retained their property in the town. Orders applicable to all ports continued to be sent as a matter of routine – bureaucracy was already well established in its ways – to the 'bailiffs of Dunwich.' They heard of the ban on the export of wool and corn, the prohibition on men-at-arms and pilgrims passing overseas, the exhortation to send oats to Calais. But they played no part in the campaigns that produced the 'famous' victories of Edward and the Black Prince. With *one* exception. Henry Lodden of Dunwich won a mention at the battle of Crecy in 1346. He had abandoned his stall in Dunwich market-place and joined the army; and you could hardly wish for a more eloquent testimony than that to the state of commerce in Dunwich.

The king's butler, who was responsible for collecting the excise duty on exported cloth (2s. 4d. on every cloth of scarlet, 5d. for a single bed-blanket, half as much again for aliens) and the duty on imported wines (2s. on a tun 12d. on a pipe), sent his deputy to Dunwich, but he did not have much to collect. The bailiffs were reduced to two in 1346, and the office of mayor abolished. Augustine FitzWilliam was the last. But letters were still being addressed to 'the mayor' thirty years later.

Whilst the French wars were in progress, the perquisites of some religious houses were taken into the king's hands, which meant that he, and not the Prior of Eye, appointed to the livings of the Dunwich churches when they fell vacant. John Snork of Monewden, parson of the parish of Pennington in Hampshire, wanted to return to his native Suffolk, and successfully applied for the vacant 'living' of St Nicholas at Dunwich in 1343. I would love to know what he said when he arrived and found that the church was not there.

In 1348 the bailiffs in desperation applied once more for a reduction in the town rent, giving as their reasons:

—the port is obstructed by sand and by jetsam – divers of their lands are submerged and overflowed – their shipping in these times of war has been destroyed by the enemy – very many men have left the town to dwell elsewhere and those remaining there are not sufficient for the payment of the farm.

Inquiry was ordered, and as a result the fee-farm rent was reduced, after some delay, from £65 to £14 10s. 9d. Even that was beyond their means. There could not, surely, be any further disaster lying in wait for them? There was.

In the summer of 1349 the Black Death, that creeping deadly pestilence which carried off a third of England's population, reached Dunwich, having apparently come in from the landward side, not from the sea as might have been expected. The evidence everywhere for its effects is slight and circumstantial. Only three hints are found at Dunwich. Robert de Malton was appointed parson of St John's in 1349; the living was vacant again within a few months. Appointments to the wardenship of *Domus Dei,* the traditional sinecure reward for former king's clerks, were made as follows:

1349 John de Brampton.
1349 William de Sonde.
1349 John de Tamworth, said to have 'resigned.'
1353 Richard de Boule.
1353 John de Hale.
1354 Roger de Elyngton.

Twenty-two years later John Woodcock was appointed to replace Roger de Elyngton, who was 'dead.' Two years after that, Roger was found to be alive, and Woodcock disappeared. It was that kind of a place. Roger 'lived' for another eight years; by which time he must have been so old that even he did not know whether he was dead or alive.

But the really significant clue occurs in a petition made in 1352 for deferment of payment of the town rent, which was granted—

as they have shown the king that although the said town which before these times was almost entirely inhabited by fishermen is now *so wasted and diminished by the late mortal pestilence* and by the king's enemies plundering and killing the fishermen of the same at sea that the men there cannot pay—

The casualties among the fishermen caught by the French would not be many. The 'pestilence' probably wiped out a hundred or so of the population.

But it was not this that caused the urgent appeal of the Dunwich men, It was the fact that the Prior of Ely was suing them for arrears of £25 in respect of their obligatory payment to him of £5 a year. Apparently the 24,000 herrings had by this time been converted to a cash payment. Both this and the town rent was deferred. I do not think that the monks of Eye received any more money from Dunwich, but the monks of Ely forty years later managed to squeeze about £10 out of the reluctant bailiffs.

No more merchants came from overseas to Dunwich. No Dunwich merchants sent their ships abroad. Trade was wholly of the coastal carrying type between the East Coast and London. John Moress in particular was frequently en route from Boston or Lynn with cargoes of grain. There was corn in

Suffolk still, and many hungry mouths in London; desperately hungry, by the look of it, in 1375 and 1376. In March the 'mayor and bailiffs of the town of Donewych' and the bailiffs of 'Leystoft' (now appearing for the first time as a port) were informed that William Newport, citizen and fishmonger of London, had a permit to load 300 quarters of wheat, beans and peas to take to London. William de Kelleshull, another citizen and fishmonger of London, was authorised to ship 200 qrs. of the same commodities. Things had come to a pretty pass when London merchants were coming to Dunwich to *fetch* corn, and presumably fish. In May, Richard Wodehewer of St Osyth had licence to load 20 qrs. of wheat, 100 qrs. of malt and 60 qrs. of flour in the port of Dunwich 'and bring them to London for the sustenance of the king's lieges there.' The following February Nicholas Crymelford, citizen and merchant of London, had licence to ship in the port 200 qrs. of wheat and bring them to London, 'not elsewhere,' 'for the munition of that city.'

The Peasants' Revolt in 1381 does not seem to have affected Dunwich; or any event went wholly unrecorded. Foreigners, Flemings in particular, in many parts of East Anglia were attacked, robbed and murdered, but there were no such atrocities at Dunwich, where some were certainly living.

Two incidents occurred in 1382 which show that something of the old piratical spirit still persisted. Two merchants of Lombardy had chartered 'a small ship of Seland' at Antwerp to carry 'six bales, one pipe and three fardels of merceries' to London. On the voyage the ship was attacked by French privateers and chased to Dunwich, where the goods were put ashore to be carried to London by the safer overland route. The bailiffs promptly seized and detained them, demanding customs duty and the subsidy of 6d. in the £ levied on all imported goods offered for sale. The merchants had no intention of offering such goods for sale in Dunwich market. The bailiffs no doubt hoped they would; but they had to release them, and the merceries went on to London.

John de Vautort loaded a 'crayer' at Lowestoft with wheat to be taken to London. On the voyage the crayer was 'so hard driven' by the French off Dunwich that 'the seamen and servants abandoned the same and fled ashore in a boat.' Their arrival galvanised the sleepy harbour into activity such as had not been seen for years. Those men 'with other seamen in divers vessels of Dunwich and neighbouring towns' sallied out in force and rescued the captured crayer, driving off the pirates. The crayer was taken to Lowestoft, but not before it had been taken to Dunwich and the cargo unloaded and detained there, on the grounds that 'it belonged to Dunwich by reason of the rescue.' They were stretching the right of 'wreck' to its utmost limits. Of course they failed in their claim, but it was worth trying.

The bailiffs must have been desperate to keep their market alive somehow. A legitimate wreck every now and then would have helped, but the only wreck for years had been that of 1367 when:

> A certain ship of Prussia with a cargo of flax, bowstaves and barrels of wax of Osmund Ferro was cast by a storm upon the soil of the king at Dunwich, between the present port of Dunwich and the former one called Old Haven.

Nothing seemed to come their way. They had not even had a whale on their territory for the last fifty years.

How were things faring with the religious? Not much better than with the profane; in fact rather worse. In 1384 the Black Friars

> whose mansion-house is in peril by incursion of the sea, which has destroyed the greater part of Dunwich

appealed for and were granted licence for Sir Robert Swelyngton to give them ten acres of land and four acres of marsh in Blythburgh

> for building thereon a new mansion-house in place of that at Dunwich, and licence for the said Friars to transfer their buildings thither, and in aid of the new erection to sell the old site to any person who will buy it.

There is an intriguing element in that. If the friars really contemplated moving their buildings, they must have been constructed of timber; the removal of such buildings was quite common. They could not possibly have intended to move buildings of stones and mortar; the labour and cost would have been vastly greater than that involved in the original construction; the sale of the old site would barely have paid for the cartage. Anyway, who in his right mind would want to buy a site in Dunwich? Apparently the Black Friars stayed put; at least, Gardner, quoting Blomfield, says 'they continued here to the Dissolution.' In 1349 they had been granted an extra five acres in Dunwich, given by John de Wengefield, 'for the enlargement of their dwelling-place.' It is possible that they moved to the Blythburgh site and retained the old site in their possession; more likely, that they moved their buildings westward on to another part of their enlarged site at Dunwich. The friars had by this time completely ousted the monks as objects of lordly patronage. Competition to be buried in their precincts was very keen, and a most aristocratic collection of bones lay in the graveyard of Black Friars. I am surprised that they ever contemplated selling it. They may of course have intended to take the bones with them.

The hospitals and churches were certainly having a lean time, judging by the hasty resignation of those appointed to take charge of them. It is possible that there was another outbreak of the plague. Something unusual was happening:

1386 John Hereford appointed warden of *Domus Dei*, lately held by John de Elyngton (replacing his father Roger?). Order to the brethren and *sisters* to be obedient to him.

1389 Dec. William Cotterel, king's servant, made warden of Dunwich and Orford.

1390 June. Adam de Elyngton (John's son?) made warden of *Domus Dei*.

1390 July. John Lucas made warden of *Domus Dei* on resignation of Adam de Elyngton.

1392 July. John Peyntneye made warden of St James hospital.

1393 July. Hugh Blythe, king's clerk, warden of *Domus Dei and St James*.

Nothing more was recorded about the hospitals for more than sixty years. How the monks of Eye were managing to live I cannot imagine; their revenues were still in the king's hands in 1384.

38 Scrap of Parchment

The truce between Dunwich and her neighbours had never been a happy one. It had nevertheless lasted for nearly sixty years, maintained, I suspect, by uncertainty as to where the sea would break through next, and hope on the part of Dunwich men that it might yet create another haven-mouth under their sole control. If that was their hope, it was never to be realized. The sea-front remained unbroken and moved steadily westward. The river – it can no longer be called a 'harbour' – became narrower and narrower as King's Holme encroached upon it and the mud and silt built up. The bailiffs of Dunwich still insisted on their ancient right to levy tolls and customs. The same men now held office year after year, some of them on and off for twenty years, and the old names were still occurring: Cuddon, Bagg, Helmeth, Morris. If ever a group of men could justifiably be called 'die-hards,' it was these Dunwich bailiffs.

Opposition was mounting. The men of Walberswick, Southwold and Blythburgh, smarting under the injustice of paying tolls to 'that place' for the use of their own haven, rebelled. The bailiffs, backed by their two members of parliament – not surprisingly, since bailiffs and MPs were the same persons as often as not – invoked their charter yet again, confirmed in 1379 for the seventh time. Their charter *did* say that they had the sole right to collect tolls, etc. in the 'port of Dunwich.' The trouble was that the men of Walberswick etc. did not believe that there was any such place any longer as 'the port of Dunwich,' and so they began collecting tolls once more in *their* port.

Reaction was swift. The Dunwich burgesses, as always, petitioned the king. He in 1390 ordered the sheriff of Suffolk, under pain of a £40 penalty, to make proclamation that

—although by stress of weather the port of Dunwich has many times changed [as regards,] the mid-stream and course of the river in divers places between Dunwich and Southwold, no man of Blythburgh, Southwold and Walberswick of whatsoever

249

estate or condition henceforth coming there with ships, vessels and boats laden with fish or other merchandise shall, under pain of forfeiture and imprisonment, hinder the Burgesses of Dunwich from levying tolls and customs.

So there!

That might have been that, if the Swillingtons, lords of the manor of Blythburgh, had not come upon the scene. Men of Dunwich in their day had done battle with Cressy, FitzRoger, Clavering, Neville, and emerged victorious. Swillington was to be their Waterloo.

Sir Robert had opened the campaign in 1381 by seizing King's Holme — not that there was much that he could *do* with it –and then trying to entice the Black Friars away from Dunwich, and so deprive the enemy of some moral support. Sir Roger Swillington, his son, adopted firmer tactics. In 1398 he induced his tenants to withold customs and tolls from Dunwich, the threat of imprisonment notwithstanding, and laid further claim to King's Holme and any wreck which might be cast upon it. Moreover, he took possession of 'certain tenements' – almost certainly lands which had been created by the silting of the marshes – which he asserted were in Walberswick, and which the burgesses said were part of Dunwich and had been 'time out of mind.' Sir Roger backed his claim by going to law, accusing by name William Morris, John Bagge, Nicholas Dennis, Edmund Swatinge, etc. and not mentioning the mayor and bailiffs and commonalty of that town. Here was a novel point of law which had not arisen before. No one had ever *ignored* the corporate state of Dunwich. The king was too busy to deal with the matter anyway; he told the justices to hear the case and postpone any decision until he came back from Ireland. In July 1400 the escheator of Suffolk, Sir Richard Bavet, was ordered to take into his hands the port of Dunwich, 'a place called Oldehaven and a marsh called Kyngesholme,' which Sir Robert Swillington and his son Roger had wrongly seized.

Victory for Dunwich! Sir Robert died. Sir Roger, instead of building a 'britask' and leading an army in the Clavering manner, decided to fight the Dunwich men with their own weapons. First, in 1404, he obtained formal ratification of his own charter, which stated specifically that he owned 'the coast and wreck of the sea from the south part of Eyecliff by South-wold to the port of Dunwich.' So far so good. Then he did a bit of brilliant historical research. Perhaps he did not do it, but employed a clever attorney to do it; no matter, it was done.

There must have been, hidden amongst bundles of dusty rolls of parchment in a chest in the manor-house at Blyth-burgh – or in the archives at Westminster, or somewhere – a particular document, a copy of which must have been in the town-chest in the Guildhall of Dunwich. But Sir Roger knew the futility of asking to see *that* copy; if it still existed. Neither had been unrolled for perhaps a hundred and fifty years. The document at Blythburgh manor-house – or wherever it was – was discovered in 1407. Its contents were as much of a joyful discovery to me recently as they must have been, for a totally different reason, to Sir Roger Swillington five hundred and seventy years ago. (I discovered it in the Cambridge Univer-sity Library, printed in the Calendar of Patent Rolls for all the world to see; so it certainly existed at Westminster.) It was the document which I have quoted in full on p. 76.

In June 1409 it, and the various writs leading up to it, was 'exemplified,' i.e. copied, attested and certified under official seal, 'at the request of the tenants of the town of Southwold.' It thus became 'law' once more. (It had never ceased to be 'law'; but a law which is hidden for a hundred and fifty years is not very effective.)

Sir Roger held the ace of trumps. He first played a few other cards with caution and discretion. John Trusse of Dun-wich had trespassed against him, been found guilty, and then outlawed for failing to comply with the sentence of the courts; he was pardoned. Thomas de Beaufort, the king's brother, chancellor and admiral of England, had been granted the town of Dunwich for a period of twenty years from 1407. There was nothing to be gained by upsetting the king's brother. There were several past indiscretions to be smoothed over, such as the fact that the Swillingtons, father and son, had

'illegally occupied the marsh of Kyngesholme' from 1381 onwards. There were certain truths, long hidden, distorted or
ignored, to be brought to light and legalised. The document
which reveals all this is an order dated July 13th 1408, to the
escheator in Suffolk to 'meddle no further with the port of
Dunwich, a place called Oldhavene and a marsh called
Kyngesholme,' because there has been an inquiry.

It is one of the lengthiest entries in the whole of the Calendar of Close Rolls. It contains one of the longest sentences I
have ever seen, possibly one of the longest ever written – one
thousand and thirty-seven words without a full-stop! Except
the one at the end. The only punctuation-marks are the semi-
colons and commas which the translator put in. I am grateful
to him that he spared me the task. The word 'and' occurs
fifty-six times in the sentence. Obviously I cannot quote it.
Below, in brief, are the findings emerging from the inquiry
which had preceded the order; they carry the authority of the
Archbishop of Canterbury, the Bishop of Winchester, the
Bishop of Bath and Wells, the whole of the king's council, and
King Henry IV himself.

(a) The men of Dunwich had *no right* to take tolls of Walberswick and Blythburgh.

(b) They never had had such right, except once, when it was
given by agreement between them and Dame Margery
Cressy, at which time the haven was 'below the town of
Dunwich and not silted up.'

(c) The marsh in dispute was *not* part of Dunwich, but part
of Blythburgh.

(d) 'It ought *not* to be called Kyngesholme; that name is
newly put upon it by the men of Dunwich; one part is
and ought to be called *Lenaldesmershe*, another *Middel-
mersshe,* and a third *Cherchemersshe.*'

(e) Sir Roger *did* own the said marsh.

(f) He *did* have the right to collect 4d. for every ship anchor-
ing on it.

(g) He did own the ferry over the harbour.

(h) Sir Roger and his father had *not* encroached upon the
rights of the king at Dunwich.

Complete victory for Sir Roger!

Heaven only knows what it had cost him. But he had not finished yet. This remarkable man still had to demonstrate that he was truly a 'chivaler,' a gentleman in a sense more appropriate to modern times than to those in which he lived. He held discussions with Thomas Duke of Beaufort and with the burgesses of Dunwich. An arrangement was agreed upon which the Dunwich men could hardly have refused to accept, even if it had been less fair. This agreement was ratified on June 20th 1410. Sir Roger *granted* to the men of Dunwich:

—a marshe called Churchmarsh, alias Lenaldesmarsh, lying between Dunwich and Walberswick, i.e. along the sea-coast on the east and along the great river running from the port of Dunwich to the town of Dunwich on the west, with one end abutting on the said port, and the water between the said marsh and hamlet on the north, and to the old port of Dunwich on the south—

This he granted them, according to the form of certain indentures, along with 'stones, sand, wreck of sea and all other profits and commodities,' in return for the payment to him, his heirs and assigns annually at Christmas of *one root of ginger!* One could hardly be fairer than that. For that was just about what King's Holme – I cannot abandon the name I have used all along – was worth at that time.

The king, Thomas de Beaufort and the burgesses of Dunwich granted to Sir Roger, his heirs and assigns and the tenants of Blythburgh and Walberswick that they

—may come when they please with any victuals, goods, etc. of their own in their own ships and boats within the said port of Dunwich *wherever it may be changed or diverted* and anchor there both in the port and on land in any part, and load and unload the goods, etc. And they shall have a *ferry*, and all profits from the same, in the new port between the north and south sides—

The men of Dunwich were to be allowed to cross the harbour in their own boats without payment, and Sir Roger and his heirs, etc. were to pay £1 a year for the ferry to the king or to whoever held the farm of Dunwich. Sir Roger further granted these concessions to the men of Dunwich:

Freedom from toll, tronage (charge for use of weighbridge) and all customs in his fairs and markets of Blythburgh (one weekly market, three annual fairs); permission to anchor, dry their nets and take lastage (stones for ballast) on the land of Walberswick on the north of the port. Permission to take any wreck of the sea which 'they may prove to be their own'.

The king further granted that the tenants of Sir Roger might anchor, dry their nets and take lastage on the land of the south of the port. The boundary between the two places was to be

> the mouth of the said port and *the thread of the water* of the said port, wherever it may be diverted or changed by heaping of sand or otherwise.

Forty shillings was 'paid into the hamper' for that agreement, and the whole affair was settled at last. Or was it?

It was a striking testimony to the character of Sir Roger Swillington. It was a wonderful confirmation for me of many things wherein I would have been obliged to rely on speculation otherwise. It shows in unmistakable manner the improvements which had taken place in the machinery of law and administration since the day when Margery de Cressy was swindled out of her rights at Ipswich by the astute burgesses of Dunwich. But it only settled *some* of the problems of Dunwich.

39 Dying Hard

Firstly, there was the £5 yearly which they owed to Ely. They tried their hardest to dodge, but in vain. The Prior, who was also the Bishop, knew the ropes too well. They got away with it for as long as ten years at a time, then the king was forced to make them pay. Well, not actually *pay*, but admit that they owed it; so I suppose they did sometimes pay.

Then there was the business of the charters. They had to be kept up-to-date by confirmation. Sir Roger Swillington had demonstrated how necessary it was to know what charters you possessed and what was in them. There was panic one day in the Guildhall in 1420. When they went to look for the charter of King John, dated June 29th 1199 (they knew the date all right) it was not there! It had been 'accidentally lost'. How could one lose such a thing? Perhaps it had got mixed up with some other documents when all that Swillington business was going on. Perhaps somebody had burnt it, mistaking it for that incriminating document of 1231 which he had been told to destroy – or perhaps I am being too suspicious. Anyway, it was lost, and William Barber, bailiff — and 'husbandman' — had to go and take his personal oath before the king in chancery that he would surrender it when found. What a study in trepidation that would have made – a Suffolk farmer confronting the law in all its majesty! The missing charter was not there when the next inspection and confirmation took place in 1424. But William survived.

He was in trouble again a few years later. The Prior of Ely sued the burgesses for a debt of £17; that 'charitable' payment which they had to make was in arrears again. The burgesses ought to have insisted on fulfilling the bargain they had originally made, more than three hundred years before, and landed the Prior with 24,000 herrings; though that might not have been very easy at this date. William did not appear before the justices I wish he had, and I wish someone had recorded what he said. However, he was pardoned. A lot of people at this time were pardoned for offences which they could not help but commit, such as getting into debt. Leniency was becoming much more common than it used to be; justice more tempered with mercy. John Randessone, 'shipman' of Dunwich, was let off in respect of trespass against John Page of Thorp in 1432. John Baxter, merchant of Boston, was pardoned for not appearing before the justices in respect of £23 which he owed John Morris of Dunwich; but that was because he was already inside the Fleet prison.

Then there were those foreigners. One can understand foreigners wanting to live in England, but why choose Dunwich, of all places? In 1436 thousands of aliens had to be registered and given permits to stay. They included Hugh Coupere, Herman Taillour, Richard Shomaker, Richard Mason, Peter Skynner and Adrian Coupere, all of Holland or Brabant; all, be it noted from their names, artisans and craftsmen. One hears so much about 'weavers' who settled in East Anglia; evidently many other trades were represented too, and it is interesting to note that they all adopted English names. However, they did not give any trouble in Dunwich.

When the Earl of Beaufort had 'enjoyed' the profits of the town of Dunwich for his term of twenty years, that privilege was conferred for life upon the Earl of Surrey. Dunwich, like the 'Measondieu' hospital, had become a trifle to be bestowed at the king's pleasure. The farm rent was slightly reduced to £11 18s. 11¾d. (One of the Exchequer clerks must have been a draper by training.) Giving the farm away was probably cheaper, and certainly easier, than trying to collect the money.

You may have noticed, although I did not draw attention to it, that there was no reference to Southwold in the documents relating to the Dunwich–Blythburgh settlement of 1410. There was however a separate writ, at that same date, exempting Southwold fishermen from paying tolls for boats using the haven-mouth. The town was expanding steadily. If it had not been for contention on the part of claimants for its overlordship, it might have achieved much sooner the status which was its due. Perpetual quarrelling with Dunwich over rights and tolls went on all through the fifteenth century. Dunwich men, it seems, had learnt little from the lesson and example set by Sir Roger. Southwold men had no Sir Roger to back them. From time to time – 1440, 1449, 1458 – the dispute was 'adjusted'. Eventually, on Feb 28th 1490, the long drawn-out affair was settled.

Dunwich would no longer receive 6s. 8d. annually for every Southwold ship using the haven, nor 4d. every time one anchored, nor 4s. a year for every twelve-oared boat, nor 2s. for every two-oared boat. Not that Dunwich had in fact been receiving such sums for years, but the Dunwich bailiffs had persisted in voicing their right to claim them. Now, they would not even try. Moreover

'The bailiffs and commonalty of Dunwich shall have no power to arrest any person at a place within the haven of Dunwich called the Key, otherwise called the Wodeishend, nor from thence to the town of Southwold.'

Dunwich harbour, as a source of revenue for Dunwich, was dead. Southwold was promoted to the dignity of 'a town corporate by name of the two bailies and commonalty of the town of Southwold'. The history of Southwold from then on is a fascinating story, but no part of my self-appointed brief. It would be quite untrue to say that Southwold in any way contributed to the decline of Dunwich. You might as well blame one end of a see-saw for going up when the other end goes down.

40 Make-Believe

It would be unfair to blame Southwold. I do not know that the men of Dunwich did; but I do know that some of them bitterly resented the usurpation of Dunwich's position by this upstart newcomer, ignoring the fact that Southwold had been a 'town' and a 'port' for as long as Dunwich. They had long since been reconciled to the fact that Yarmouth and Ipswich had far outstripped their own town in importance, and could accept the rise of Lowestoft without any hurt to their pride; but accept Southwold as equal to Dunwich in every way, and likely soon to become superior, that they could not do. The wording of the original Southwold charter did not help to soothe their feelings. It stressed the 'many great variances and debates' which had 'long tyme beyn had and contynued' between the two towns, the 'hurt and inconvenience that had fallen', and declared that the main reason for granting the charter was 'for rest and amyte to be had and contynued for ever-more betweene them.' What hope was there of 'amity', when Dunwich was never again to be allowed to collect one penny of tolls and customs from Southwold?

Of course they had to accept the situation, just as they had to accept the fact that their town was not merely declining, but disappearing. Their acceptance of that fact, and their continued presence there nevertheless, causes me to marvel at the pertinacity of these rugged men, which puts them in the same category as crofters in remote highland areas and dwellers in bleak inhospitable places everywhere. Why did they stay? Was it the magic of 'home', the soil in which their lives were rooted? Did they believe, despite the bitter experience of centuries, that each succeeding 'tumult of the sea' would be the last, that storms would one day cease and leave their stricken town in peace? Something made them cling with grim determination to the acres that remained, as long as any did remain. Was it because their 'acres' now were mostly acres of the sea, and no one could take those acres away? Dunwich was no longer a port; it was a fishing-village; a 'haven' in the figurative sense, a place of safety to which the fishermen returned.

I think the fishermen and their families accepted that. I think they accepted the fact that Walberswick and Southwold men were no longer rivals to be hated, but rather comrades sharing their own dangers and hardships; that all the charters and 'liberties' of Dunwich counted for nothing in terms of real life, and death. Not so the 'rulers' of the town, however, nor the rulers of the country. They were set in attitudes of hide-bound tradition which tidal waves could not dissolve. It was not that they did not *know* the truth; they simply made up their minds not to *see* it; persisted for another two centuries and more in making believe that Dunwich was still a place of some importance when in fact it was of no importance at all except to those simple fishermen. The war-games and the law-games were over; now began the game of make-believe. This is the theme of my last chapter. Slightly depressing, perhaps – I would have preferred to recount amusing anecdotes or finish on a note of stoic heroism – but not without a touch of sardonic humour or a philosophical reflection here and there; and I, too, would be guilty of make-believe if I failed to record faithfully what seems to me the dominant aspect of the story of Dunwich from the year 1490 on.

King Henry VII set the tone when he appointed Clement Plumstede, one of the grooms of the king's chamber, as 'keeper of the passage of the port of Dunwich and waterbailiff of the same, rendering for the said offices as much as others have done before'. Whatever Clement paid for the 'offices', by the time he had bought himself a uniform and worn it out by sitting on the alehouse bench waiting in vain for something to supervise he would be very much out of pocket. At least the Dunwich bailiffs would derive some amusement from his august presence; that is, assuming he stayed for more than a few weeks.

King Henry VIII in 1523 confirmed the famous charter, granting to his honest burgesses of Dunwich everything that King John, King Richard, the Edwards and the other Henries had granted them, complete with 'Sok and Sak, Toll, Thein and Infanthef' and liberties without end. In 1540 he obliterated Black Friars, Grey Friars and the other religious houses in one of the greatest make-believe moves of all time, converting faith into cash more effectively than they had ever done, but benefitting Dunwich not at all. In 1547 the charter was confirmed yet again, benefitting the king to the extent of sixty shillings just in time to help pay his funeral expenses. Edward VI, or his uncle, went through the whole rigmarole again in 1550. Queen Elizabeth outdid them all. Her charter of 1559 was the best sixty shillings worth the burgesses of Dunwich had ever had. To quote but one small part of it:

'We by the humble information of our well beloved the Burgesses of the Towne aforesaid, understanding that Towne one of the auncientest of our Kingdom of England upon the Sea-Side, for the resistings of our Enemies intendinge to invade our aforeseyd Realme, and for the Defence of the Partes theere neare, and by the violence and Force of the Sea much weakened and impoverished, and considering the manifold Costs, Expence and Charge which the aforeseyd Burgesses about the Defence of the same Town, and of the Countrie adjoyninge, and also for the Withstandinge of our Enemies before these Tymes, have laid out, etc. etc. etc.

In addition to all the other 'liberties', they were to have a 'Cleark of the Markett' and an 'Admirall'. That was really something – if only they had had a market of more than a couple of fish-stalls; and if they had had a fleet of anything but fishing-boats. According to official records Dunwich did have a fleet, but the records omitted to state that it was in fact based on Walberswick; and even so the number of ships and men shows a steady decline throughout the reign of Elizabeth. The Dunwich burgesses got sixty shillings worth of high-sounding words without any real meaning. One sympathises with the lawyers who perpetrated that farrago of nonsense; they were paid to do it. One can understand that archbishops, bishops and earls should have signed it; they were too busy to read what they signed. But had any of them, I wonder, ever *seen* Dunwich?

Several Londoners of note did see Dunwich at about this time, and realised that here was a possible subject for one of those 'histories' which were so popular at a time when England's greatness needed to be established by reference to her past. The very word 'ancient' was a commendation in it-self. Any legend, however improbable, was eagerly sought after and used as part of the foundation of an edifice of fame and glory. The idea of writing a 'history' of Dunwich certainly emanated from one 'Master Deye'. John Daye was a native of Dunwich, born there in 1516. As he is the one and only man of Dunwich to have qualified for a modest niche in the Hall of Fame, I feel justified in departing from my theme for a mo-ment to say a little about him. Having emigrated to London, he set up as a printer there, being the first English printer to use a 'Saxon' type. He printed Fox's *Book of Martyrs* and lost money on it; then made money, whether by printing or by an advantageous – and fruitful – marriage is not clear. There is a superb monumental brass to his memory in the lovely Saxon church of Little Bradley, which is just about as far as one can get from Dunwich and still be in Suffolk, and where he died on July 23rd 1584. Here is his epitaph:

Heere lies the Daye that darkness could not blynd.
When popish fogges had overcast the sunne,
This Daye the cruell night did leave behynde.
To view and shew what bloudi Actes weare donne
He set a Fox to wright how Martyrs runne
By death to lyfe. Fox ventured paynes & health.
To give them light Daye spent in print his wealth,
But God with gayn retorned his wealth agayne
And gave to him, as he gave to the poore.
Both wives he had partakers of his payne,
Each wife twelve babies, and each of them one more.
Als twas the last encreaser of his stoore
Who mourning long for being left alone
Set upp this tombe, her self turned to a stone.

'Master Deye' commissioned someone, generally thought to
have been John Stowe, to write a description of Dunwich for
him in 1573. The result is still extant in the form of the
Harleian MSS No. 532,f.54 in the British Museum. Stowe, if
it was he, wrote of:

> —the curiosity of visiting this place where I beheld the re-
> mains of the rampart, some tokens of Middlegate – foundations
> of down-fallen edifices – remains of dead exposed – naked wells
> divested of the ground about them by the waves of the sea –
> divers coins, several mill-hills and part of the old key – seven
> or eight great high hills there standing—

He estimated the area of the town as 200 acres, which seems
excessive; and the population as 'not above 750, including
strangers', about a third of whom seem to have been living
outside the limits of the medieval town. He was clearly more
concerned with 'antiquities' and 'curiosities' – 'bullwarks,
walls, towers and castelles' – than with facts, especially facts
about people. Though he does confirm a lot of things; that
only St Peter's and All Saints churches were standing, for
instance. St John's had been demolished about forty years
earlier. The 'history' was never written, which is probably no
great loss, but the manuscript remains of considerable interest.

Intended to accompany it was a map, which has not survived but was fortunately seen by Gardner and copied for him by Joshua Kirby in 1750 or thereabouts. The original was drawn by Ralph Agas in 1587, and is of such interest that it is reproduced in this book as an end paper. There are several features on it which call for notice as raising some doubt about its absolute accuracy: (a) a street lined with houses along the very edge of the cliff, (b) a cluster of build-ings – they could be huts – on the shingle by the Old Key, (c) a group of seven houses between the Leper Hospital and Leet Hill – they must have been *very* small indeed, (d) the absence of the market-place, which the sea is said not to have reached until 1677, when the Cross was dismantled, (e) fishing-boats beached on the edge of the cliff, (f) three-masted ships moored at the Old Key. Let us be grateful to Ralph Agas and Joshua Kirby, bearing in mind that they both probably used a certain amount of imagination. Agas went even further in his written account of the town in 1589, making the ridiculous suggestion that a sluice built where the old haven used to be would 'pre-serve the town from danger of the sea and might bring the town *near to her former estate and condition*'. That was surely carrying make-believe too far. I wonder if it was prompted by the hopeful talk of some of the Dunwich burgesses.

I said earlier that the law-game was over. Actually there was one last glorious and costly round to come. Those burgesses had continued to assert their rights over Walberswick for forty years after the settlement of 1410, even though the men of Walberswick and Blythburgh had blandly ignored them. Now the burgesses – would they *never* learn? – were playing the same game of make-believe with Southwold, one hundred years after the Southwold settlement. When the new South-wold haven was cut in 1590, 'Dounwyche Men would not agree unto it'. They said it ought to be cut nearer to Dun-wich than to Southwold, that their port ought to be repaired – at Southwold's expense – and got themselves entangled in a law-suit which dragged on for ten years, at their expense.

The sea did not change its habits. In 1570 it again inflicted 'incredible damage' on the town, an injury which eventually touched the hearts of those in high places. In 1578 Queen Elizabeth

> Being credibly informed that her town of Dunwytche is by Rage and Surges of the Sea daylie wasted and devoured, And the Haven of her Highness said Towne, by diverse Rages of Wyndes continually landed and barred, so as no Shippes or Boats can either enter in or oughte—

kindly decided to *lend* the men of Dunwich £62 18s. 4d., which money was to be raised by the sale of the bells, lead, iron, glass and stone from the decayed and disused church of Ingate.

The farm rent remained at the figure of £12 6s. 8d. throughout the sixteenth century and most of the seventeenth, two of the burgesses being answerable for its payment. In 1673 King Charles II reduced it to £5, and magnanimously remitted all arrears 'in consideration of the poverty and low estate of the town'. A year later he granted the £5 per annum as part of a settlement on Queen Catherine. When she died in 1705 the burgesses owed her £1260, being the arrears of 21 years at £60 a year! How about that for make-believe? Or a joke in very bad taste. In 1718 the burgesses were sued by the Crown for non-payment, and ten of them were put in prison at Beccles, others having absconded. At the trial, 'in consideration of their poverty', it was adjudged that 'where it could not be had, the king must lose his right', and the prisoners were discharged. A touch of realism at last! Then Sir George Downing obtained the grant of the fee-farm at £5 a year for *ninety-nine years*. So much for realism.

The famous naval battles with the Dutch – those 'Flemings' were back again – of 1665 and 1672 belong more properly to the history of Southwold. Dunwich would have seen little of the first one, though it would have lost nothing in the telling. The action of the second, on May 28th 1672, was wholly obscured from watchers ashore by fog and then by smoke. Dunwich men knew that officers and men were offering them large sums of money for boats to rejoin their ships in desperate haste, and that, having insufficient boats, many of the naval men had to be content to stay ashore to listen to the 'great concussion' shaking the houses of Dunwich, Southwold and Walberswick. They knew that it was a 'great victory', and probably guessed that that was yet another case of make-believe, especially when the wounded were brought ashore.

St Peter's church, stripped of its lead, timber and bells in 1702, toppled over the cliff a few years later. The gaol was transferred to Grey Friars. For whom? The charters were exemplified in 1700 by William and Mary. For what? For £10 'paid into the hamper'.

In 1671 a knight makes his first appearance on the list of bailiffs. Knights, baronets and 'gentlemen' monopolise the office from 1696 on, and by virtue of holding it were justices of the peace. Worthy gentlemen, all of them, no doubt; but that is one of the most blatant bits of make-believe of all. The electorate consisted of *seventeen freemen residing in the town* and sixty-three freemen residing elsewhere. It was matched by the parliamentary representation of this 'borough'. None of the members had any connections with Dunwich; they represented nothing but themselves, and yet the farce continued until a third of the way through the nineteenth century.

The sea had had enough of this pretence. It had never once in two and a half centuries relaxed its efforts, but between the years 1739 and 1749 decided to end the matter for all time. December 1740 saw the most devastating attack:

> The wind blowing very hard about North-East with a Continuance for several Days, occasioned great Seas, doing much Damage on the Coast during that Time by Inundations breaking down the Banks, and overflowing many Marshes, etc.

That was virtually the end. All Saints still stood, unused, dismantled but defiant on the cliff-top for another hundred and fifty years. About a hundred souls remained, and some of the bodies which had contained them were actually buried in All Saints graveyard. The stone which marks the site of one grave stands there still. Be careful, if you go to look at it. Do not go too near the edge. The sea has not finished yet.

A good many people do go there every summer; not perhaps to mourn the premature death of John Brinkley Easey who died in 1826 at the age of twenty-three, but rather to admire the view and speculate as to how much longer that solitary gravestone will be part of it. Some, like me, may find in the stone and its situation a symbolic statement about life in general and about the men of Dunwich in particular.

John Easey was the last of them; or as near to the last as we are likely to get; his grandfather was living in Dunwich during those great storms of the 1740s, and John himself was certainly one of the last to be buried in the shrinking churchyard of All Saints. There were men of Dunwich after him. There are men of Dunwich now, but the Dunwich that is now is not the Dunwich of my story, and few of them claim to be Dunwich men – in fact I could discover only two whose link with the place goes back more than two generations. There must be many families all over the country – all over the world – whose remote forbears were among my men of Dunwich, those who were forced to abandon the town and settle elsewhere. One of them, John Donwych, turned up here in Foxton in 1550, and his descendants (with the name changed to Dunage or Dunnidge) lived here until 1725. That was just one of the chance details which directed my thoughts towards the writing of this story. It would be extremely difficult to trace any of those men back through the generations, for many of the names have changed – for instance, most of the FitzJohns, FitzRogers, FitzRichards became Johnsons, Rogersons, Richardsons, and so on – many more were names common to all localities, and the modern bearers of some of those names might not much care to claim ancestry among my men of Dunwich. I might not, but I have a sneaking hope that somewhere there still survives at least one Gonomanaway, and that he will get in touch with me.

Meanwhile, for just a little longer, I cling to the name of John Easey as the last link with the vanished town. Only for a little while. The cliff-edge crumbles year by year, assisted by the morbid curiosity of those hoping perhaps to catch a glimpse of poor John Easey's bones before they roll down the sandy slope as a last propitiatory offering to the implacable sea.

Fig 12 John Easey's Tombstone

Bibliography

Calendar of Close Rolls.
Calendar of Charter Rolls.
Calendar of Patent Rolls.
Calendar of Fine Rolls.
Calendar of Inquisitions.
Calendar of Inquisitions Post Mortem.
Curia Regis Rolls.
Diplomatic Documents.
Chancery Warrants.
Liberate Rolls.
Memoranda Rolls.
Pipe Rolls.
Feet of Fines.
Placita de Quo Warranto.
Rotuli Hundredorum.
Rotuli Parliamentorum.
Domesday Book.
Anglo-Saxon Chronicle.
Letters of Reign of Henry III.   (Rolls Series.)
De Naturis Rerum – Neckham.   ,,
Matthew Paris – Historia Anglorum   ,,
Memoranda de Parliamento.   ,,
Memorials of St Edmund.   ,,
Red Book of the Exchequer.   ,,
Bede – Historia Anglorum.
Chronique de Jordan Fantosme.   ,,

Dugdale, Sir W.   *Monasticon.*
Dutt, A.   *Highways and Byways in East Anglia.* Macmillan. 1914.
Gardner, T.   Historical Notes on Dunwich, Blythburgh and Southwold.
                   1754.
Jolliffe, J.   *Froissart's Chronicles.* History Book Club 1967.
McKisack, M.   *The Fourteenth Century.* Oxford. 1959.
Poole, A. L.   *From Domesday Book to Magna Carta.* Oxford. 1951.
Powick, Sir M.   *The Thirteenth Century.* Oxford. 1953.
                   Proceedings of the Suffolk Institute of Archaeology.
Steers, J. A.   *The Coastline of England and Wales.* Cambridge. 1946.
Scarfe, N.   *The Suffolk Landscape.* Hodder & Stoughton. 1972.
Suckling, Rev. A. *History and Antiquities of Suffolk.* 1846.
                   Victoria County History of Suffolk.
West, J. F.   *Faroe.* Hurst. 1972.

Index

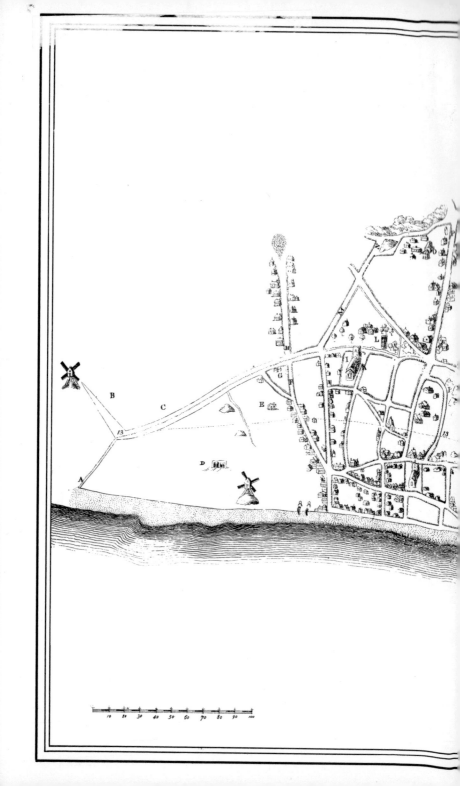